Ending Global Poverty

Praise for book
Ending Global Poverty

'What a fantastic story and a fantastic book. This is the behind-the-scenes story about how four women, ministers from four different countries, teamed up, defeated the cynics and changed the politics of aid to make a real difference. Their efforts led to debt relief for poor countries, expanded education for girls, a serious shift to a poverty focus in the World Bank and the IMF and in 2000 to the Millennium Development Goals -all delivered in partnership with recipient countries. In a world too often ruled by vested interests and horrible conspiracies, it's uplifting and truly inspiring to read of an open political partnership with noble aims and such positive results. One is left amazed at the boldness of these four women and seriously doubting whether four male ministers would ever have the courage and commitment to do the same.'

Sir Richard Jolly, Institute of Development Studies, Sussex.

'Discover how four great women improved the lives of millions around the world, how they succeeded by persistence, by winning allies in politics and international institutions and most of all: by joining their four voices to a shared mission – ending poverty. Today, on an ever hotter and crowded planet, it is more urgent than ever to eradicate poverty without eradicating our natural livelihood. There is a lot of work to be finished to reach the UN Sustainable Development Goals by 2030 – like empowering women, combating corruption, shifting to sustainable technology or balancing trade policies. This book gives hope in hard times. Let it inspire young people to take action!'

Horst Köhler, former President of Germany, former Managing Director of the IMF.

'This incredible book will immortalize the golden age of development co-operation and provide a living memory of what it could be again, considering where we are now. There is no better way of sustaining that memory than getting an insightful account of what it was from the champions of the approach and an exemplary case of how effective partnership in development can deliver strong results and hugely reduce transactions costs of development assistance. This is a must read for all development practitioners aspiring to be effective.'

Benno Ndulu, Mwalimu Nyerere Professorial Chair, University of Dar es Salaam; Chair of the Board UNU WIDER; former Governor of the Central Bank of Tanzania.

'The U4's unparalleled passion for development is brilliantly captured in this compelling volume. From improvements in aid effectiveness, marshaling of support for debt relief, to emphasis on true partnership between collaborating countries, the U4 sought to move developing countries beyond aid to sustainability. This will always be remembered as their enduring legacy.'

Ngozi Okonjo-Iweala, Chair of the Board of GAVI, former Managing Director World Bank, former Minister of Finance and of Foreign Affairs, Nigeria.

'On the eve of the new Millennium the landscape of international development was radically transformed. Many were involved: The G-8, the Jubilee Movement on debt relief and the campaigns against global pandemics. In this fight four women led from the front: Clare Short, Heidemarie Wieczorek-Zeul, Hilde Johnson and Eveline Herfkens. This book tells their transformational story, which is of great relevance to today's continuing challenges to end poverty on a sustainable basis.'

Donald Kaberuka, Chair of the Board, Global Fund; Former Finance Minister Rwanda Former President African Development Bank.

'Michalopoulos has written a brilliant book about four heroic female politicians who changed development policy at a critical point in history. He provides an astute analysis of development cooperation from the 1990s to the present and the way four ministers from Europe withstood the dominant economic paradigm on debt and trade and chose unambiguously for the poorest. Their legacy is of utmost relevance in times of rising inequality and exclusive and deficient multilateralism. This splendid book also forms an invaluable contribution to the debate about what ails development and inclusivity and what can be done about it by courageous women-politicians. It details all their steps in winning over their own governments and how they marched inside the multilateral institutions. Everyone worried about the state of the world should read this book and learn from it.'

Bert Koenders, Special Envoy Fragility World Bank and Professor at Leiden University, former Minister of Foreign Affairs and for Development Cooperation, the Netherlands and Undersecretary General of the United Nations.

Ending Global Poverty

Four Women's Noble Conspiracy

CONSTANTINE MICHALOPOULOS

OXFORD
UNIVERSITY PRESS

OXFORD
UNIVERSITY PRESS

Great Clarendon Street, Oxford, OX2 6DP,
United Kingdom

Oxford University Press is a department of the University of Oxford.
It furthers the University's objective of excellence in research, scholarship,
and education by publishing worldwide. Oxford is a registered trade mark of
Oxford University Press in the UK and in certain other countries

First Edition published in 2020

Impression: 1

Published in the United States of America by Oxford University Press
198 Madison Avenue, New York, NY 10016, United States of America

British Library Cataloguing in Publication Data
Data available

Library of Congress Control Number: 2019957204

ISBN 978–0–19–885017–5

Printed and bound by
CPI Group (UK) Ltd, Croydon, CR0 4YY

To: Greta, Malala, Nadia and the new generation of young leaders,

*humanity's best hope to eradicate poverty
and achieve sustainable development*

Preface

The four women in the title of this book are Eveline Herfkens from the Netherlands, Hilde F. Johnson from Norway, Clare Short from the United Kingdom, and Heidemarie Wieczorek-Zeul from Germany. They became ministers in charge of their governments' policies of development cooperation in 1997–8. They were passionate in their commitment to end global poverty and thought that the best way to achieve their objective was to join forces and collaborate in the implementation of their programmes and in the global institutions where decisions are made affecting the poor all over the world. They became known as the Utstein Four, after the Norwegian Utstein Abbey where they formalized their collaboration in 1999.

Their active collaboration lasted only a few years, until 2002–3 as first Herfkens and then Short left their government positions. Johnson stayed on until 2005 and Wiezcorek-Zeul until 2009. Over the next decade, Eveline Herfkens, my long-time partner in life and work, introduced me to her three colleagues and we had the pleasure of hosting them individually at our home in the United States.

Following the end of their tenure as ministers, the Utstein Four kept in touch and from time to time talked about the idea of having a reunion in Norway. They also thought that their story may have relevance to the challenges currently faced by the international community and the continuing struggles for the empowerment of women. But they were too busy to either get together or write a book.

In early 2018 I had just finished writing my own story about economic development and globalization in the last fifty years in the course of which I recognized their contributions. The few pages I devoted to their collaboration did not do justice to their work and it occurred to me that it deserved treatment in a separate volume. In this era of increased awareness about gender issues, I was hesitant to suggest that I author a book about four formidable women. Still, I suggested to Herfkens that she explore the possibility with her three friends that they all help me write this volume. They quickly agreed and Johnson offered to host the long-delayed reunion at her summer home in Stavern in late June 2018. The substance of the book took shape in the discussions we had over the next few days. And there was a subsequent reunion hosted by Wieczorek-Zeul in Berlin in February 2019 to review progress, at which it was decided to add a separate chapter that addressed their efforts to empower women.

Needless to say, this book could not have been written without the support of the Utstein Four. They provided me with information from their personal files, they contacted the archives of their former ministries to obtain official records, and they reviewed and commented on drafts of all individual chapters and the volume as a whole. In addition, Wieczorek-Zeul helped me obtain access to the IMF archives; and Herfkens was invaluable in securing and conducting interviews on my behalf, as well as assisting me in translating and obtaining research material and the photographs included in the volume. I am very grateful to all of them. While I am completely responsible for all judgements and remaining errors and omissions, in many ways this is their volume which I helped them write.

The historical dimensions of this volume benefitted from two types of sources: archival material in various ministries and international organizations and inputs from contemporaries. On the archival side I am especially grateful to Bert van der Zwan, the historian of the Netherlands Ministry of Foreign Affairs, as he provided support for this project by employing for six months a research assistant, Inger Wesseling, who did a great job in retrieving and providing me with Utstein-relevant documents. I would also like to thank the archives of Germany's Federal Ministry of Economic Cooperation and Development, Norway's Royal Ministry of Foreign Affairs, Sweden's Ministry of Foreign Affairs, and the UK's Department for International Development for providing me with access to various official documents for this volume; similar thanks are extended to the IMF's archives and in particular to Steffen Meyer, Germany's Executive Director at the IMF and Sevda Karimova, IMF's archivist for expediting access to letters and documents.

In part, because of the very extensive documentation provided by the Netherlands archives, Herfkens' equally extensive files and comprehensive coverage by the Dutch press, Netherlands' participation in the Utstein collaboration is more fully documented than for the other three countries. As a result on occasion it may appear that it provided disproportionate leadership to the group. In fact, it was a collaborative effort which involved an equal partnership.

A very large number of individuals contributed knowledge, documents, and commentary for this book. I single out first Ruth Jacoby, who in her various positions in Sweden's Ministry of Foreign Affairs collaborated with and ultimately became part of the Utstein group, and who helped me both by reviewing and commenting on several chapters as well as securing Utstein-related documents from her ministry's archives. Next there is a group of individuals who helped through interviews and in some cases through both interviews and commentary on one or more chapters about the work of the Utstein Four. These include James Adams, Masood Ahmed, KY Amoako, Jan Berteling, Koen Davidse, Paul Isenman, Ron Keller, Bert Koenders, Horst Köhler, Benno Ndulu, Marina Ponti, Koos Richelle, Alexander Shakow, and Gerrit Zalm. Finally, there is a group who reviewed one or more chapters, and provided comments and/or materials. They are: Michael Crosswall, Sally Fegan-Wyles, Otto Genee, Barbara Herz, Danny Leipziger, Richard Manning, and Henk van den Dool. I thank them all. I should also add thanks to the many other development professionals all over the world, in ministries, in international institutions, and in partner countries, labouring anonymously, who helped the Utstein Four address the challenge of ending world poverty.

I am grateful to Gordon Bodnar and Kelley Kornell of the International Economics and Finance Program at Johns Hopkins, SAIS who provided me with the support of a research assistant, Yanqi Xie, during the academic year 2018–19. She did an excellent job in developing statistical material and references for the volume. I would also like to thank Sergius Seebohm for his research assistance regarding Germany's policies and programmes. I appreciate also that Roeland Stekelenburg, Marco Urban, and Photothek let me use their photographs of the Utstein Four at no charge.

Finally, I would like to thank Springer Nature for their permission to use material from my book *Aid, Trade and Development: Fifty Years of Globalization*, Palgrave MacMillan, 2017.

Contents

List of Plates

1. Johnson, Short, Herfkens and Wieczorek-Zeul during the World Bank/IMF Spring meetings, April 28, 1999. Photo by Photothek.

2. Johnson, Short, Herfkens and Wieczorek-Zeul in front of the Utstein Abbey, July 25, 1999.

3. Short, Herfkens and Wieczorek-Zeul, Utstein Ministerial II in The Hague, May 12–13, 2000.

4. Herfkens, Short and Johnson on the river Congo, February 12, 2002.

5. Short, Johnson and Herfkens with President Kagame of Rwanda, February 13, 2002, photo by Roeland Stekelenburg

6. Herfkens, Wieczorek-Zeul and Johnson, Development Committee Meeting, April 9, 2002

7. Herfkens and Johnson with Nancy Birdsall (Center for Global Development) and Moises Naim (Editor Foreign Policy magazine), receiving on behalf of the Utstein Group, the first annual Commitment to Development Award, April 28, 2003.

8. Johnson, Short, Herfkens and Wieczorek-Zeul during their reunion in Berlin, February 21, 2019, photo by Marco Urban.

Chronology of Events Relevant to the Utstein Four

1997

2 May	Clare Short appointed Secretary of State for International Development.
17 Oct.	Hilde F. Johnson appointed Minister for International Development.

1998

3 Aug.	Eveline Herfkens appointed Minister for Development Cooperation.
27 Oct.	Heidemarie Wieczorek-Zeul appointed Federal Minister of Economic Cooperation and Development.

1999

28 Apr.	Development Committee Meeting provides first occasion for the four ministers to coordinate their strategy and priorities focusing on HIPC debt.
11–12 May	DAC High Level meeting—the four ministers coordinate on untying towards LDCs.
18–20 June	G8 meeting (with Wieczorek-Zeul) in Cologne, Germany, results in major improvements in debt relief for HIPC.
25–6 July	Utstein Ministerial I, Stavanger: Germany (Wieczorek-Zeul), Netherlands (Herfkens), Norway (Johnson), UK (Short)—formal establishment of U4.
10 Aug.	U4 op-ed in *International Herald Tribune*: 'If we are serious, we do something about poverty'.
26 Sept.	First ever joint meeting of IMF's Interim and World Bank/IMF Development Committee on PRSP and HIPC chaired by Gordon Brown; U4 discussions with IMF Managing Director Camdessus and World Bank President Wolfensohn.
30 Nov.–2 Dec.	WTO ministerial in Seattle.

2000

18 Mar.	Ann Sydnes, appointed Norway's Minister for International Development.
10–14 Apr.	Herfkens, Short, Sydnes, Wieczorek-Zeul visit Tanzania.
26–8 Apr.	World Education Forum, Dakar (Herfkens, Short).
1 May	Horst Köhler appointed Managing Director of IMF.
12–13 May	Utstein Ministerial II, The Hague: Herfkens, Short, Sydnes, Wiezcorek-Zeul.
June	IMF, OECD, UN, and World Bank jointly launch *2000 A Better World for All*.
8 Sept.	Millennium Declaration on the Millennium Development Goals.
19–20 Nov.	UN ECA 'Big Table I', Addis Ababa.

2001

25 Apr.	DAC High Level agreement to untie aid to LDCs.
10–14 May	EU announces proposal for quota-free and duty-free entry of LDC exports to EU markets for 'Everything but Arms' at UNCTAD conference in Brussels.
14–16 Oct.	UN ECA 'Big Table II', Amsterdam.
19 Oct.	Johnson returns as Minister for International Development of Norway.
5–6 Nov.	Utstein Ministerial-III, Birmingham: Germany (Wieczorek-Zeul), Netherlands (Herfkens), Norway (Johnson), UK (Short).
9–13 Nov.	WTO ministerial, Doha.

2002

11–14 Feb.	Herfkens, Johnson, and Short visit the DRC, Burundi, Uganda, and Rwanda.
18–21 Mar.	Monterrey Conference on Finance for Development.
10 Apr.	Education-for-All, Fast Track Initiative launch in Washington DC (Wolfensohn, Brown, Herfkens, Johnson).
17–18 July	Utstein Ministerial-IV, Wiesbaden: Germany (Wieczorek-Zeul), Netherlands (Herfkens), Norway (Johnson), Sweden (Karlsson), UK (Short).
22 July	Herfkens last day in office.
26 Aug.–4 Sept.	World Summit on Sustainable Development in Johannesburg (Johnson, Short, Wieczorek-Zeul).

2003

17 Jan.	UN ECA 'Big Table III', Addis Ababa.
24–5 Feb.	First High Level Forum on Aid Effectiveness, Rome.
29 Apr.	CGD 'Commitment to Development Award' to the Utstein Four.
12 May	Short's last day in office.
20 Sept.	Utstein Ministerial-V, Doha (Dinner): Canada (Whelan), Germany (Wieczorek- Zeul), Netherlands (van Ardenne), Norway (Johnson), Sweden (Jacoby), UK (Amos, Brown).

2004

30 Mar.	Utstein Ministerial-VI, Berlin (Dinner): Germany (Wieczorek-Zeul), Netherlands (van Ardenne), Norway (Johnson), Sweden (Carin Jamtin), UK (Hilary Benn).

2005

25–7 Feb.	Second High Level Forum on Development Effectiveness, Paris (Johnson, Wiezcorek-Zeul).
17 Oct.	Johnson's last day in office.

2008

2–4 Sept.	Third High Level Forum on Aid Effectiveness, Accra (Koenders, Wieczorek-Zeul).
14 Sept.	Lehman Brothers' collapse.
29 Nov.–2 Dec.	Doha conference on Financing for Development (Wiezcorek-Zeul).

2009

27 Oct.   Wiezcorek-Zeul's last day in office.

2011

29 Nov.–1 Dec.   Fourth High Level Forum on Aid Effectiveness, Busan.

2015

25–7 Sept.   UN Sustainable Development Goals Summit.

List of Acronyms

ACP	Africa, Caribbean, and Pacific
ACWL	Advisory Centre on WTO Law
AfDB	African Development Bank
AFRITAC	African Regional Technical Assistance Center
AID	Agency for International Development
ALA	Asia and Latin America
BMZ	Federal Ministry for Economic Cooperation and Development [Germany] (Bundeministerium fur wirtschaftliche Zusammenarbeit unt Entwicklung)
CAP	Common Agricultural Policy
CBTF	Capacity Building Trust Fund
CDU	Christian Democratic Union
CEB	Chief Executives Board for Coordination
CGD	Center for Global Development
CSO	civil society organization
DAC	Development Assistance Committee
DDR	disarmament, demobilization, and reintegration
DfID	Department for International Development
DFQF	duty free, quota free
DG	Director General
DRC	Democratic Republic of Congo
DSM	Dispute Settlement Mechanism
DTI	Department of Trade and Industry
EbA	Everything but Arms
EBRD	European Bank for Reconstruction and Development
ECA	Economic Commission for Africa
ECOSOC	United Nations Economic and Social Council
EfA	Education for All
EIF	Enhanced Integrated Framework
EITI	Extractive Industries Transparency Initiative
ESAF	Enhanced Structural Adjustment Facility
EU	European Union
FAO	Food and Agriculture Organization
FCO	Foreign and Commonwealth Office
FCV	fragility, conflict, and violence
FDI	foreign direct investment
FfD	Finance for Development
FTI	Fast Track Initiative
GAERC	General Affairs and External Relations Council
GAVI	Global Alliance for Vaccines and Immunization

GDP	gross domestic product
GNI	gross national income
GNP	gross national product
GTZ	German Technical Cooperation Agency (Gesellschaft fur Technische Zusammenarbeit)
HIPC	Highly Indebted Poor Country
HLPF	High Level Policy Forum
IDA	International Development Association
IDG	International Development Goal
IDT	International Development Target
IFI	international financial institution
IHT	*International Herald Tribune*
ILO	International Labor Organization
IMF	International Monetary Fund
IPM	International Partnership for Microbicides
JDO	Joint Donors Office
KFW	German Development Bank (Kreditanstalt fur Wiederaufbrau)
LDC	Least Developed Country
MDB	Multilateral Development Bank
MDG	Millennium Development Goal
MDTF	Multi-Donor Trust Fund
MOPAN	Multilateral Organisation Performance Assessment Network
MP	Member of Parliament
MTN	multilateral trade negotiations
NEPAD	New Partnership for Africa's Development
NGO	non-governmental organization
NRC	*NRC Handelsblad*
ODA	Official Development Assistance
ODI	Overseas Development Institute
OECD	Organisation for Economic Cooperation and Development
OED	Operations Evaluation Department
OOF	other official flows
PCD	policy coherence for development
PCSD	policy coherence for sustainable development
PEPFAR	President's Emergency Plan for AIDS Relief
PFP	policy framework paper
PGBS	Partnership General Budget Support
PIU	project implementation unit
PREM	Poverty Reduction and Economic Management
PRGF	Poverty Reduction and Growth Facility
PRIO	Peace Research Institute
PRSP	Poverty Reduction Strategy Paper
PSIA	Poverty and Social Impact Analysis
RBF	results-based financing
RBM	results-based management

SDG	Sustainable Development Goal
SDSN	Sustainable Development Solutions Network
TRIPS	Trade-Related Aspects of Intellectual Property Rights
UNCTAD	United Nations Conference on Trade and Development
UNDG	United Nations Development Group
UNDP	United Nations Development Programme
UNESCO	United Nations Educational, Scientific and Cultural Organization
UNFPA	United Nations Population Fund
UNICEF	United Nations Children's Emergency Fund
USAID	United States Agency for International Development
VNR	Voluntary National Review
WDR	World Development Report
WFP	World Food Programme
WHO	World Health Organization
WSSD	World Summit on Sustainable Development
WTO	World Trade Organization

Constantine Michalopoulos has worked on and written about economic development and poverty eradication for more than half a century. In 1982-2001 he was a senior official at the World Bank where he served as Director for Economic Policy and Coordination and Senior Economic Advisor for Europe and Central Asia. Before that he was Chief Economist of the US Agency for International Development. In 1997-1999 he served as Special Advisor at the WTO. Following his retirement from the World Bank he was a development consultant to governments and international organizations such as the World Bank, the IMF, UNCTAD, the EU Commission, and DfID. He also taught economics at several US universities, including American University and Johns Hopkins University in Washington DC. Most recently he was appointed Senior Policy Advisor at ELIAMEP a think tank in his native Athens. He is the author of *Aid, Trade, and Development* (Palgrave Macmillan, 2017) and *Emerging Powers in the WTO* (Palgrave Macmillan, 2014) amongst others.

Also by Constantine Michalopoulos

Aid, Trade and Development
Emerging Powers in the WTO
Migration Chronicles
Developing Countries in the WTO
Trade in the New Independent States (with David G. Tarr)
Aid and Development (with Anne O. Krueger and Vernon W. Ruttan)

1

Introduction

'If you want to go fast, go alone; if you want to go far, go together'
African Proverb

At a time when global institutions are under attack from the triple scourge of nationalism, protectionism, and xenophobia, it is salutary to step back and assess the possibilities for global renewal by looking to the recent past, a scant twenty years ago when the world was on a different path. It was around the turn of the last century when there was a flurry of international action to promote and solidify cooperation in many fields: trade, economic assistance, debt, the environment. It was a time when the world could join hands in the United Nations to launch the Millennium Development Goals (MDGs). It was not the end of history, but it certainly seemed the beginning of a new era of international cooperation, integration of the developing countries in the world economy, and collaboration to put an end to poverty and destitution. And this effort benefitted greatly from the strong leadership provided by four women Ministers for International Development working together: Eveline Herfkens of the Netherlands, Hilde F. Johnson of Norway, Clare Short of the United Kingdom, and Heidemarie Wieczorek-Zeul of Germany, the so-called Utstein Four.[1] This volume is their story.

It is a tale of women's empowerment. It is also a story about the power of collaborative leadership, which is the kind of leadership needed to address the complex challenges of the twenty-first century. It is told today in the hope that it will inspire new generations working together, to take on the continuing global challenge of ending poverty on a sustainable basis.

By the mid-1990s eradicating world poverty had become an important objective of the global community. Several UN-sponsored conferences resulted in agreements on specific targets for improving various dimensions of poverty as well as what the international community should be doing to help developing countries achieve them. The World Bank and other international development institutions had started to make poverty-focused programmes operational.

But the reality on the ground was different: enormous debts stifled progress in poor countries especially in sub-Saharan Africa. Old-style aid projects proliferated stretching developing country capacity while promoting developed country political and economic interests rather than partner country objectives.

The four ministers' main goal was to help eradicate poverty by bridging the gap between rhetoric and reality. Their motto was 'A Conspiracy of Implementation'.

The implementation involved a new approach to international development, addressing major impediments to development in the poorest countries in trade and a heavy debt burden, making IMF and World Bank policies more pro-poor, as well as reforming development cooperation to be a true partnership. The reforms highlighted four elements: first, a rebalancing of donor and partner country responsibilities so that development cooperation was a genuine partnership positioning the partner in the 'driver's seat' rather than donors hectoring and imposing their views; second, a coherent plan to reduce poverty developed in collaboration with multilateral and bilateral donors; third, ensuring that all development programmes were coordinated under this framework; and fourth, making greater use of budget support as an instrument of development assistance instead of the traditional project-based interventions.

Germany, the Netherlands, Norway, and the UK, all had substantial aid programmes in the 1990s. When they acted together in international forums, others had to listen, especially because what they had to say made sense. The four ministers realized that and joined forces to introduce changes in their own assistance programmes and to promote their 'conspiracy' in international forums. Because they were together, they went far.

Their first focus in late 1998 and early 1999 was ending the debt problem of the Heavily Indebted Poor Countries (HIPC) in a way that also helped reduce poverty. In the summer of 1999, they formalized their alliance and programme thrusts at a meeting in Norway's Utstein Abbey. Following the meeting, the Utstein Four (U4), announced their views to the world through an 'op-ed' in the *International Herald Tribune* (*IHT*) which concluded: 'We call for genuine partnership, first and foremost with developing countries but also with action-oriented groups in civil society, the private sector and the best minds in the academic community. There is no need more urgent, no cause more noble; no responsibility weighs more on us.'

Also at the outset, the U4 helped forge a link between the UN pronouncements of what became the Millennium Development Goals and implementation through coherent pro-poor strategies developed in collaboration with the international financial institutions, especially the World Bank and the IMF. They raised the profile of women's empowerment issues globally and increased the resources devoted to such programmes in their own aid and in the multilateral institutions. Their key focus was on girls' education in the belief that 'if you educate a man, you educate an individual; but if you educate a woman you educate a nation'. Still later, their proposed approach to make aid more effective in addressing poverty was codified in international agreements with the participation of both developed and developing countries. The U4 did not succeed in everything they tried: their efforts to increase coherence between developed countries' aid policies and trade policies towards developing countries received mostly lip-service, having foundered on the rocks of national commercial interests.

The four original ministers were together only for about four years, 1998–2002 (with a year's break for Johnson in between); but the Utstein Group lasted longer until roughly 2005 and expanded to include Canada and Sweden. Johnson continued as minister until 2005 and Wieczorek-Zeul until 2009 (see Chronology of Events in the front matter). But collaboration between the countries continued and there were still reports of an 'Utstein' group meeting at the staff level more than a decade later. Their global impact diminished over time, but institutions they founded, such as the Utstein Anticorruption Resource Centre, are still functioning today.

Following the 2008 financial crisis, the pattern of international collaboration for development that characterized the previous decade changed. There were changes in donor political priorities and in the mode of assistance delivery. There was an increased emphasis on so called 'results-based management' and a phasing out of budget support programmes and the stress on delivering aid through enhanced local systems. There was also more focus on 'vertical' funds such as GAVI and the Global Fund and an increase in the priority given to 'fragile' states. Countries like India and China have emerged as aid donors as opposed to aid recipients. The world celebrated the achievement of most of the MDGs in 2015 and launched an ambitious set of new Sustainable Development Goals (SDGs) to be achieved by 2030. But earlier donor commitments regarding aid effectiveness which had been strongly advocated by the U4 have not been honoured. And many donors have reverted to aid practices that were proven ineffective in the 1990s.

This volume is organized as follows: Chapter 2 discusses issues of aid and development in the 1990s. This was a period of growth for most developing countries, with sub-Saharan Africa lagging; it was a period of increased international collaboration for development; but also continued divergence between the lofty pronouncements of UN conferences and the development realities on the ground. Chapter 3 discusses the beginnings of the U4 collaboration and their contribution to the establishment of a debt relief mechanism which could rid the HIPC of their debt burden and ensure that the resources released would go to poverty eradication programmes. Chapter 4 describes U4's formal organization at their first ministerial meeting at Utstein Abbey in July 1999, outlines their agenda and strategy of networking with like-minded countries and leaders of global institutions to deliver on poverty eradication, and of promoting reforms in both multilateral and bilateral aid.

Chapters 5 and 6 are devoted to a discussion of their work to increase the effectiveness of the multilateral institutions in which they participated and their own bilateral aid programmes. Chapter 5 discusses especially their efforts to increase the poverty focus of World Bank and IMF programmes as well as to strengthen the collaboration between them and the United Nations. Chapter 6 highlights their focus on sub-Saharan Africa, including joint programme visits and interventions in the DRC, Sierra Leone, Sudan, and Tanzania; their contribution to the setting-up of regional bodies like the 'Big Tables' for Africa where donors and partners could address pro-poor policies, good governance, and aid effectiveness issues; as well as their efforts to spread their aid effectiveness 'conspiracy' to formal donor institutions such as the OECD's Development Assistance Committee.

Chapter 7 outlines their role in support of the establishment and implementation of the MDGs and other international initiatives that changed the international landscape for development in the early 2000s. Their advocacy for increased aid levels, improved aid effectiveness and coherence between aid interventions and trade policy contributed greatly to the success of the UN Conference on Finance and Development in Monterrey in 2002. They also played an important role in the establishment of the 'Education for All' initiative that addressed the second Millennium Development Goal of achieving universal primary education.

Chapter 8, 'Poverty has a Woman's Face', focuses on their programmes to promote women's empowerment in poor countries. The four ministers had been active on women's issues much before they rose to their lofty positions. Their collective presence in global forums had an important demonstration effect on women everywhere. But they also undertook a number of initiatives in their own assistance programmes and through multilateral institutions which are summarized in this chapter.

Coherence, especially between aid policy and developed country trade policies vis-à-vis the developing world is the topic of Chapter 9. This is an important issue as development objectives pursued through aid, such as strengthening small farmer—usually women—production in poor countries, can be undermined by developed country policies that subsidize their own exports. Moreover, export interests in developed countries have often demanded that aid funds be spent on goods and services in the donor country, irrespective of their cost, a practice known as 'tied aid', thus diminishing the value of the assistance provided. The chapter discusses the U4's valiant efforts to stop these practices which met only with limited success, for example through liberalizing access to developed country markets for products from the Least Developed Countries (LDCs).

The Utstein collaboration continued, although not at the same level, after the departure of Herfkens and Short in 2002 and 2003, respectively. Chapter 10 describes the long transition period until 2009, Wieczorek-Zeul's last year, which witnessed the culmination of a number of earlier efforts in which the U4 were especially active. This included the Rome/Paris/Accra conferences on aid effectiveness which codified internationally U4 collaboration practices that had emerged through discussions in the Development Assistance Committee (DAC) and with African ministers on the so-called 'Big Tables'; and UN reform to which several of them contributed.

The roughly two decades from the emergence of the U4 in 1998 to the present can be divided into two halves: the first decade or so until the financial crisis of 2008 and the period from the crisis to the present. The first decade was full of collaboration and promise; the second was characterized by an early upheaval, a lull, and then starting in 2016, further upheaval. Chapter 11 traces the impact of these events on practices in international development over the last decade. It starts with a review of aid practices in the U4 programmes over the whole twenty-year period and asks the questions: did the U4 practices match their rhetoric? And how did these practices evolve over time? How much of the U4 legacy is intact? And what were the reasons for the changes that did occur?

Destructive changes in international cooperation have accelerated in recent periods. On the current path it will be very difficult to achieve the Sustainable Development Goals that were agreed in 2015 with disastrous effects on poverty and climate change. Does the U4 experience have any lessons for addressing the global concerns of today and tomorrow? This is the question that the last chapter of this volume will try to address.

Note

1. Their formal titles were: Herfkens: Minister for Development Cooperation; Johnson: Minister for International Development; Short: State Secretary for International Development; Wieczorek-Zeul: Federal Minister of Cooperation and Development.

2

Aid and Development in the 1990s

Introduction

Momentous political and economic events shook the established world order during the early 1990s and shaped the future course of aid and development. In 1990, the world rejoiced for the freeing of Nelson Mandela and the end of apartheid soon thereafter. In 1991, the peaceful demise of the Soviet Union and the abandonment of central planning ushered a period of international cooperation on global issues and a somewhat exaggerated emphasis on the role of the private sector in development. The parallel rise of China and the spread of globalization created new challenges and opportunities for the developing world which had just started to recover from the 'lost decade' of the 1980s. While developing country experience with growth and poverty reduction was overall significantly better than during the debt-ridden 1980s, performance was extremely varied: China and East Asia were moving rapidly ahead leaving sub-Saharan Africa far behind.

Reducing global poverty became the clarion call of aid institutions all over the world. In 1990, the United Nations Development Programme (UNDP) launched its first annual Human Development Report highlighting different dimensions of poverty and human deprivation. The World Bank's 1990 World Development Report (WDR) on poverty with its striking black cover was symbolic of the growing emphasis placed on poverty reduction by both multilateral and bilateral aid agencies. A new theme was emerging from these declarations: developing countries had to take charge of their own destiny. They should be in the driver's seat in shaping plans and programmes to reduce poverty. Aid should be used to address partner country objectives, not to promote developed country political and economic interests.

But by the middle of the decade, on the ground reality still differed greatly from these lofty pronouncements. The burden of debt had not been fully lifted from poor countries—aid allocation had not adapted significantly to reflect changing developing country needs, and old-style aid continued to suffocate developing country governments and impede progress. It was in this generally benign and supportive international political context when international goodwill was forthcoming, but implementation was lagging, that four development ministers coincidentally came to office in the UK, Norway, the Netherlands, and Germany, all important donors, and instigated major improvements in aid effectiveness and development policy globally.

This chapter will first summarize the development progress and the varying needs for external assistance of different groups of developing countries in the 1990s. Next, the emerging consensus on how to best utilize economic assistance to reduce poverty will be discussed including the various pronouncements coming out of the global UN conferences and their links to the establishment of the International Development Goals (IDGs) in the OECD. The last section will review the main shortcomings of development cooperation implementation, requiring policy reforms to increase aid effectiveness in reducing poverty.

Progress in Reducing Poverty

Riding a wave of globalization with expanding international trade and investment, global incomes rose substantially in both developed and developing countries in the 1990s.[1] Developing country growth and poverty reduction improved significantly relative to the debt-ridden 1980s. But it was extremely varied. And globalization raised the spectre that poor people in poor countries would be left behind unable to cope with external forces beyond their control.

The East Asian countries used export-led growth to move rapidly ahead and were able to halve the number of poor living in absolute poverty between 1990 and 1999. The results in terms of both growth and poverty reduction were so spectacular in both China and the rest of the region that by the mid-1990s the whole world was talking about the 'East Asian Miracle'. Although expectations were tempered by the financial crisis that gripped several of these countries late in the decade, the region achieved roughly double the growth rates of those in the rest of the developing world. And it was labour intensive growth with widespread benefits.

Sub-Saharan Africa was at the other extreme and appeared to be left behind. Gross domestic product (GDP) growth in the 1990s recovered from the low 1980s level and the percentage of people living in absolute poverty decreased slightly. Yet, because of high rates of population growth, the number of very poor (those earning less than $1 a day) grew by 25 per cent. The absolute number of poor people grew five times more than the figure for Latin America and twice that for South Asia in the period 1980–97. Social indicators improved but much more slowly than in other regions.

Economic stagnation in many countries caused much poverty. A handful of small countries such as Botswana and Cape Verde achieved growth rates close to 5 per cent per annum. In Ghana and Uganda, earlier reforms also started to yield results. But overall per capita growth was negative. At the same time, the continent had high levels of inequality which worsened in the 1990s. Gender inequality was especially grave with limited access for women to physical, social, and human capital.

Next to East Asia, South Asia was the region that showed the greatest progress in reducing poverty. In the 1990s, this region, which had traditionally been plagued with massive poverty, achieved substantial GDP growth, and was able to reduce the absolute number of very poor people. But at the end of the twentieth century the region was still home to half a billion very poor. A great number of them were in rural areas, largely illiterate and depending on low wage employment or subsistence farming for their livelihood.

In Latin America, the reforms undertaken in the 1980s also yielded results in the 1990s. Strong economic performance in countries like Chile and Peru contributed to robust growth throughout the region with positive results on poverty. Although the absolute number of the very poor did not change very much over the decade, their share in the population fell to 15 per cent. The poverty problem was exacerbated by income inequality. Latin America had and, despite recent progress, still has the worse income distribution among all the developing regions.

Finally, the 1990s witnessed the emergence of a new group of countries whose development drew the attention of aid donors: the countries in transition from central planning to market. Except for the developed countries, this region had the smallest amount of poverty in the world in 1990. But the sharp and protracted declines in incomes following the transition from plan to market combined with increases in income inequality resulted in the incidence of poverty more than doubling in the decade. In most countries in the region poverty was shallow with many households around the poverty line. However, there were some deep pockets of poverty in countries like the Kyrgyz Republic and Tajikistan. The new poor were largely working families with children, typically with low education levels which reduced their ability to find jobs.

Capital Flows and Assistance Needs

Over the years, external finance, both from the private sector and foreign aid, have made important contributions to development. On the other hand, a variety of ill-advised policies in both developed and developing countries resulted in unsupportable debt burdens that constrained development in the 1980s.

In the 1990s, strong growth performance in East Asia as well as the Latin American rebound were supported by a massive increase in private capital flows. Initially, these flows went to a small group of countries primarily in these two regions. In the following decade they were to spread also to other Asian countries and sub-Saharan Africa. The increased private capital flows in the 1990s were of two kinds: foreign direct investment (FDI) and portfolio and bank lending.

FDI flows grew for three reasons. First, there was a general improvement in the global attitude towards the role of private capital in growth and development deriving in part from the demise of the system of central planning and the dissolution of the former Soviet Union, which carried over to attitudes in developing countries. Second, there was a genuine belief that FDI could be beneficial to developing countries by combining their cheap but productive labour with the superior technology brought in by multinationals to produce both for the domestic and export markets as part of the emerging global value chains. Third, multinationals started to exploit significant advantages in offshore production resulting from differential taxation of corporate profits in both the developed and developing world.

The increased flow of loans and portfolio investment resulted from two major developments: first, starting in 1989, the international community helped address the debt problems of the middle income developing countries and restore their creditworthiness through the so-called 'Brady' schemes that reduced their debt burden to private creditors in exchange for increasing the security of being repaid.[2] Through the 1990s, seventeen developing countries, many from Latin America, managed to reduce their debt burden by 30–50 per cent through these schemes and return to borrowing from the international capital markets. Second, developing countries liberalized their own controls of capital flows and the financial sector. This was not without dangers as the 1998 East Asian financial crisis demonstrated. But overall, the net effect was to increase the capacity of middle income developing countries (with per capita income more than $825 in 2004) to rely on external finance from private sources as well as borrowing from the World Bank and Regional Development Banks and reduce their needs for aid in the form of grants and loans on soft terms which are formally classified as Official Development Assistance (ODA, see Box 1.1).

At the same time there were increased needs for assistance to a number of poor transition economies. However, the bulk of the latter's financing needs could be addressed through financing from the World Bank, bilateral export credit agencies, and the newly established European Bank for Reconstruction and Development (EBRD), all of which provide assistance through loans on harder terms.

This meant that by the middle of the decade, the main needs for concessional resources (ODA) were in sub-Saharan Africa and to a lesser extent South Asia, which continued to have many poor but where substantial GDP growth was moving countries like India to lower middle income class status. These changing needs should have been reflected in ODA becoming more focused on poor countries, particularly in sub-Saharan Africa. They were not. In fact, ODA to sub-Saharan Africa declined between 1990 and 2000 both in absolute terms and as a proportion of total ODA.

Total ODA flows also declined over the decade and bilateral ODA declined even further. In particular, US aid fell by 30 per cent from $18.5 billion in 1990 to $13.2 billion in 2000. Bilateral aid from other donors increased somewhat, but not enough to make up for the US decline. The changes in aid levels did not appear to be the result of changing developing country needs but rather the result of other

---

Box 1.1. A primer on foreign aid and other official finance for development

---

Developed countries provide economic assistance for different reasons, in different forms and on different terms. Official Development Assistance (ODA) includes assistance given as grants or loans from the donor's public sector for developmental purposes, net of repayments of previous aid. Only concessional loans, on soft terms with a grant element of at least 45 per cent for low income countries and Least Developed Countries (LDCs) are included (10 per cent for other countries). The grant 'element', i.e. the extent to which a loan is like a grant, is calculated by reference to how different the interest rate and maturity of the 'aid' loan is relative to a benchmark interest rate (5 per cent) and maturity for loans given by commercial banks. It includes flows from the World Bank's International Development Association (IDA—the World Bank's 'soft' loan window) and other Multilateral Development Banks (MDBs) 'soft' windows which are provided on ODA terms. Other official flows (OOF) from these institutions which are on harder terms than ODA but softer than what can be obtained in the private capital markets from banks or through the issuance of bonds, as well as other official flows from bilateral donors, which do not qualify as ODA, are measured separately. Most International Monetary Fund (IMF) financing is excluded because it is too short-term to qualify, as is all military assistance. ODA is extended in the form of expert services (technical assistance) which for bilateral donors are usually provided as grants, direct shipments of goods, financing for the purchase of goods and services, or as cash for budget support.

---

factors: the easing of the cold war tensions reduced the amounts of aid channelled to countries primarily for geopolitical 'security' objectives. At the same time there was increasing donor aid fatigue and decreasing public support for aid, for example to sub-Saharan Africa, as it did not appear to yield results. Therefore, increased attention started to be directed to aid effectiveness and especially on its impact in reducing poverty.

Poverty Focus

In the early 1990s, World Bank management under pressure from its board, in particular the executive directors of the Nordic countries and the Netherlands, started to operationalize the WDR findings on poverty by developing a Poverty Handbook and initiating a series of country poverty assessments. That same year it introduced a programme of targeted interventions which included projects that either had a specific mechanism for targeting the poor or involved a higher proportion of poor people among the beneficiaries than in the whole population. Over the next several years these projects were to rise to about a third of total World Bank lending, but around 50 per cent of its soft IDA loans to poor countries and even more in sub-Saharan Africa.

The assistance programmes also had a different slant: recipient government ownership was being emphasized. The World Bank was encouraged to persuade governments to undertake reforms rather than prescribe conditions. There was the beginning of understanding the fundamental fact that if policymakers in developing countries themselves want the reforms or are persuaded of their usefulness, conditionality is not needed; and if they are not, it will not work. Therefore, there was a shift of emphasis in giving assistance on the basis of *reforms already completed.*

All too often in the past the World Bank and the IMF would persuade Ministries of Finance, who needed the external financing, to commit to reforms which did not have the support of the sector Ministries that were supposed to implement them (Box 1.2). In order to ensure that reforms were based on full government ownership, the World Bank started to develop so-called policy framework papers (PFPs), supposedly with the country's government, which attempted to provide a comprehensive perspective on needed reforms.

In the 1980's the IMF was the main target of people concerned about poverty as demonstrated by the publication of the volume *Adjustment with a Human Face.*[3] The main concern was that IMF stabilization programmes ignored their effects on poverty. And as the World Bank was perceived, sometimes unfairly, to be in step with its sister organization, it also became the target of widespread criticism. It was hoped that things would change with the elaboration of the PFPs in which the IMF would have an input. Things did start to change, at least in principle on paper, as some of the IMF documents in the early 1990s demonstrate.

The increased poverty focus was also reflected in pronouncements of bilateral donors articulated in the Development Assistance Committee (DAC) of the OECD, which since the early 1960s had been the main forum for articulating aid policies of developed country members of the OECD. Bilateral donors, concerned about weakening constituencies for aid, needed ways to improve its effectiveness, explain its purpose, and showcase its results. In 1991 the DAC launched its first Development Assistance Manual and in 1992 it produced Principles of Aid Effectiveness aimed at disseminating 'best practices' for aid effectiveness. In 1995 the DAC High Level Meeting Communique stressed that the principal responsibility for development rests with each developing country and emphasized the importance of integrated strategies for development addressing economic, social, and environmental objectives.

Box 1.2. Global governance and coordination on aid

Bilateral economic assistance policy and programmes are frequently housed in sub-cabinet-level agencies under the general supervision of Foreign or Finance Ministries. A few countries (Germany, the Netherlands, and the Nordics) traditionally had Development Ministers at cabinet level, as had the UK since 1997. Bilateral assistance programmes of members of the OECD are coordinated by its Development Assistance Committee (DAC). Policy in the IMF and the Multilateral Development Banks (MDBs: World Bank and the Regional Development Banks) is made by their boards of Executive Directors, which represent constituencies of one or more members. Government representatives at the IMF are appointed by Ministries of Finance and/or Central Banks and meet twice a year in the so-called 'International Monetary and Finance Committee' (previously called 'Interim Committee'). Representation at the MDBs is mostly by the Ministry of Finance, and in a few cases by cabinet-level Ministries for Development Cooperation. Coordination between the IMF and the World Bank is done at ministerial level in the 'Development Committee' where representation is either by Ministries of Finance or cabinet-level Ministers of Development Cooperation. UN representation is either by Ministries of Foreign Affairs or in the case of specialized agencies by the appropriate sector ministry, for example health in the World Health Organization (WHO), agriculture in the Food and Agriculture Organization (FAO).

Finally, the World Summit for Social Development held in Copenhagen in 1995 reached a new consensus on the need to put people at the centre of development: it pledged to make the conquest of poverty, the goal of full employment and the fostering of social integration the overriding development objectives.

Global Initiatives 1990–1996

The early 1990s witnessed a significant increase in global initiatives with major implications for development. Two of these initiatives on debt and trade reflected the culmination of a long process of negotiations started in the 1980s.

On debt, while the 'Brady' schemes had helped middle income countries, many poor countries were still facing an unsustainable debt burden. Most of the forty so-called Highly Indebted Poor Countries (HIPCs) were in sub-Saharan Africa. Their debt burden had been reduced somewhat by unilateral initiatives by a number of bilateral donors, such as the UK, who cancelled debt owed by low income developing countries, especially LDCs. But HIPCs were also saddled by large debts to multilateral donors such as the World Bank and the IMF.

After considerable pressure from NGOs, especially Oxfam and the Jubilee Coalition, the international community finally established the HIPC programme to reduce the debt burden of poor developing countries in 1996. Eligibility was limited to low income countries which met the per capita income criteria for soft loans from the World Bank's IDA and the IMF's Enhanced Structural Adjustment Facility (ESAF) that provide grants and interest free or heavily subsidized loans. The countries also had to meet several requirements besides an unsustainable debt burden: a good track record of reforms under IMF/World Bank programmes and a PFP, the World Bank's new vehicle for defining the strategy of collaboration and lending with its developing country members. The most important breakthrough of this initiative was the opportunity for eligible countries to reduce debt not only for commercial creditors—of which they had little, but also official creditors as well as multilateral institutions such as the World Bank, the IMF, and the African Development Bank.

On trade, the 1994 Marrakesh conference resulted in the conclusion of the Uruguay Round of multilateral trade negotiations, which had started a decade earlier, and the establishment of the new World Trade Organization (WTO). The latter introduced many global rules that were designed to provide special and more favourable treatment for developing countries' trade and even greater benefits for the LDCs. It also created new challenges in requiring developing country commitments to safeguard intellectual property as well as establish sanitary and phytosanitary standards which, for lack of institutional capacity, these countries were ill-equipped to implement. To address these weaknesses the WTO charter contains many developed countries' promises to provide developing countries with additional technical and financial assistance.

The reduction in global political tensions following the break-up of the Soviet Union contributed to the convening of several UN-sponsored conferences that resulted in recommendations on specific targets for improving various dimensions of poverty as well as what the international community should be doing to help developing countries achieve them. In addition to the Copenhagen Summit of Social Development mentioned earlier, there were conferences on children (New York, 1990), Education for All (Jomtien, 1990), the environment (Rio, 1992), population (Cairo, 1994), and the status of women (Beijing, 1995).

In 1996, the DAC picked up and consolidated the conclusions and recommendations from the various conferences and prepared a report whose first part presented a set of International Development Goals (IDGs) that were intended to guide bilateral donors in the provision of economic assistance, which by that time all had agreed—at least in principle—should be focusing on poverty reduction (see Box 1.3). The second part recommended a partnership approach to development cooperation that was to form the basis of future donor–recipient relations.

Box 1.3. The original OECD International Development Goals

- a reduction by one half in the proportion of people living in extreme poverty by 2015
- universal primary education in all countries by 2015
- demonstrated progress towards gender equality and empowerment of women by eliminating gender disparity in primary and secondary education by 2005
- a reduction by two thirds in the mortality rates for infants and children under age 5 between 1990 and 2015
- a reduction by three quarters in maternal mortality rates between 1990 and 2015
- access through the primary care system to reproductive health services to all individual of appropriate ages as soon as possible and no later than 2015
- implementation of national strategies for sustainable development in all countries by 2005 so as to ensure that current trends in the loss of environmental resources are effectively reversed at both global national levels by 2015

We commit ourselves to do the utmost to help:

- by a willingness to make mutual commitments with our development partners supported by adequate resources
- by improving the coordination of assistance in support of locally owned development strategies
- by a determined effort to achieve coherence between aid policies and other policies which impact on developing countries[4]

A key objective of the initiative was to generate support for reversing the downward trend in bilateral ODA: the idea was that aid fatigue could be battled by effective communication of its purposes to the public and ensuring that aid could contribute to achieving the IDGs. It could be argued that 'there is no such thing as aid fatigue. There is, however, fatigue among northern taxpayers and parliaments when it comes to bailing out local elites who fail to deal with poverty in their own country, and who prefer to continue rent seeking instead of pushing for reform in order to achieve real and sustainable poverty reduction.'[5]

While the IDGs were essentially agreed by the global community in UN conferences which were dominated by the very large number of developing country members—as UN conferences typically are—the adoption of the IDGs by the DAC gave them an unwelcome imprimatur. It appeared that they were being pushed by the donor community at a time when there was a strong consensus that development priorities should be determined by the recipients— not the donors.

Initiatives and Realities

As the second half of the 1990s began to unfold, it became apparent that on the ground realities in developing countries had not materially changed to reflect the lofty objectives of the global initiatives. This was not unexpected: ministers are often content with signing an uplifting resolution in New York or Geneva and then returning home without an intention to translate these into national policies. Similarly, it takes time for sclerotic bureaucracies to implement the dictates of their far away leadership in Washington or London.

First, there was a long-standing commitment of developed countries to provide ODA amounting to 0.7 per cent of their GDP. This commitment was made back in the 1970s. It had been reiterated in a very large number of UN and other international conferences for more than two decades and had been supported in principle by all developed countries except the USA. In 1993, it had been modified conceptually to relate ODA to gross national income (GNI). But in practice by the mid-1990s only four countries met or surpassed it: Denmark, the Netherlands, Norway, and Sweden, all of whom had done so for two decades. And the averages were declining for the OECD as a group.

On trade, it became obvious very quickly that the aid commitments made by developed country trade ministers had not been made in consultation with their colleagues who actually decided aid policy and budget. As a result, there was little increase of aid for trade for more than a decade. This lack of policy coherence was to bedevil international cooperation efforts for many years to come.

It turned out that the HIPC initiative also suffered from significant shortcomings: in country after country the savings obtained from debt relief did not result in more resources being invested in health, education, and other social needs critical to addressing poverty issues. Moreover, the criteria used for providing debt relief were too stringent—thus few countries were able to qualify, and the relief obtained early on was quite limited.

Old-style aid continued to dominate practices. Project-oriented World Bank staff tended to view 'poverty projects' as a separate sector, rather than try help to develop coherent poverty reduction programmes. Recipient governments did not have the institutional capacity to draft the new World Bank PFPs and had to rely on the staff of the Bretton Woods institutions for their preparation. PFPs written in Washington did little to improve developing country government ownership.

In Tanzania, the original draft of the 1994 PFP was done in Washington. Although it appeared that significant give and take between the government and the staff of the World Bank and the IMF, the government found itself negotiating amendments to a document prepared by others, thus producing an outcome which doubtless differed substantially from that which would have resulted from a more genuinely consensus building document. Moreover, the World Bank then effectively reneged...by introducing additional conditionalities during the negotiation of a new structural adjustment loan.[6]

According to a local bilateral aid official, 'there is no way the World Bank can be influenced in what it has made up its mind to do'.[7] Such arrogance, reported in contacts between World Bank officials and African policymakers in early 1980s, was thought to have stopped.[8]

Despite lip service to the principles of aid effectiveness as articulated by the OECD, bilateral donors were also guilty. An evaluation of the Dutch aid programme stated that country policy documents are prepared by the Dutch aid bureaucracy without recipient government involvement in their preparation:

> Each donor has its own aid policies and 'agenda' and is anxious to pursue its own objectives even when these are not shared by the government. Constitutional, parliamentary and accounting requirements aimed at ensuring proper accountability for the use of taxpayer's money may also increase donor intrusiveness, a tendency that can only be enhanced by the perception already noted that corruption is a large and growing problem in Tanzania.[9]

The situation in Tanzania was reflected in the technical assistance programmes elsewhere in sub-Saharan Africa:

> In almost all African countries...aid donors orchestrate the technical cooperation show. They conceive most project ideas, arrange their design, hire most of the experts, and oversee implementation...The most significant (cost and inconvenience) is that African authorities have little ownership of activities with which they have been so little involved, making commitment problematic...[10]

Traditional technical assistance tended to supplant local capacity, undermine local knowledge and institutions and render recipient countries more vulnerable and dependent on aid. There were many reasons for these shortcomings.

In general, donor-driven projects were not derived from aid recipients' development priorities and reflected donor attitudes that 'they know better', 'they lecture, and recipients listen', 'they give, and poor countries receive', 'they take care of things, because poor countries cannot'. Such attitudes perpetuated aid dependence and destroyed people's motivation to take charge of their own futures.

Donors continued to demand ways to make their projects visible: ministers wanted to have a photo opportunity and hoist their national flag in front of the little school that their taxpayers' money had built—without considering how recurrent costs such as teacher salaries would be paid. 'Cooperation is about giving serious priority to the interests of developing countries, instead of using aid money to serve the interests of some sub-group or for marketing the donor's own products.'[11] The problem was exacerbated in the mid-1990s as the number of small bilateral donors grew (e.g. the new EU member states, for whom this was one of the conditions for EU membership).

There was also uncoordinated proliferation of projects. There were apparently 2,000 ongoing projects by forty donors in Tanzania in the early 1990s. This reflected both weaknesses on the part of the government to define and insist on priorities as well as donor commitment to their vested interests for identifiable 'monuments'.[12]

EU aid programmes during this period were characterized by fragmentation and incoherence: there were programs for the ACP countries (former colonies in Africa, Caribbean and the Pacific); and there were also programmes for Latin America. There were others for the countries of the former Soviet Union and more still for the Mediterranean area. All these without a consistent policy focus or approaches to address poverty problems in recipients.

The UN also contributed greatly to project proliferation and fragmentation:

At the country level, operational incoherence between UN funds, program and agencies is most evident. More than one-third of UN country teams include 10 or more UN agencies on the ground at any one time. Several teams include 20 or more. The cost of doing business with the UN is thus too high for both recipient countries and donors.[13]

Project fragmentation and proliferation burden the capacity of developing countries to deal with multiple agencies. At one point it led the Tanzanian government to call a 'holiday' during which no aid agency would be permitted to visit their government counterparts, so they could focus on defining and governing their own priorities.

Partner institutions continued to suffer from serious weaknesses, including corruption—sometimes abetted by multinationals, especially in extractive industries. Until the mid-1990s this was the 'elephant in the room' that nobody wanted to talk about or face up to, despite its huge economic and social costs (see Box 1.4). Instead, several donors, including the World Bank, introduced their own management teams to implement projects in so-called project implementation units (PIU) to ensure 'their' dollars and deutschmarks would be well spent. Such practices naturally did nothing to strengthen institutional capacity development in partner countries: on the contrary, as most often the most capable civil servants

---

Box 1.4. Corruption: the elephant in the room

Corruption is a serious problem which afflicts all societies in varying degrees. For a long time, it was not talked about either in developed or in developing countries. The following is a summary of a very complex and important issue which started to receive attention in the mid-1990s, but on which detailed information has been developed only recently.

'*Corruption impacts societies in a multitude of ways. In the worst cases, it costs lives. Short of this, it undermines moral standards and can cost people their freedom and their wealth. The cost of corruption can be divided into three main categories: political, social and economic.*

Corruption is **a major obstacle to democracy and the rule of law.** *In a democratic system, offices and institutions lose their legitimacy when they are misused for private advantage. This is harmful in established democracies, but even more so in newly emerging ones. It is extremely challenging to develop accountable political leadership in a corrupt climate.*

Corruption **corrodes the social fabric.** *It undermines people's trust in the political system, in its institutions and its leadership. A distrustful or apathetic public can become yet another hurdle to challenging corruption.*

Corruption **depletes national wealth.** *Corrupt politicians invest scarce public resources in projects that will line their pockets rather than benefit communities, and prioritize high-profile projects such as dams, power plants, pipelines and refineries over less spectacular but more urgent infrastructure such as schools, hospitals and roads. Corruption also hinders the development of fair market structures and distorts competition, thus reducing efficiency.*

Corruption **increases inequality.** *The poor lack access to decision makers, which is necessary in corrupt societies to obtain certain goods and services. Resources and benefits are thus exchanged among the rich and well connected, excluding the less privileged. They might also be completely excluded from basic services like health care or education, if they cannot afford to pay bribes requested illegally. Recent estimates show that the cost of corruption amounts to anywhere between $1.5 and $3.6 trillion or up to 5 per cent of global GDP.*'[14]

---

were poached for this purpose. Neither did it help to deal with the problem of corruption.

In donor countries corruption was downplayed by pro-aid actors as it had been used by aid opponents to advocate reductions in ODA. In 1992 the topic was mentioned for the first time in the DAC High Level Meeting Communique, and in 1993 two former World Bank staff, Peter Eigen and Michael Wiehen, founded Transparency International, an international NGO to take action to combat global corruption.

The basic remedy for these problems is to transfer much greater responsibility for management of cooperation to local hands. In addition, efforts were obviously needed to strengthen local institutions, improve public expenditure management, particularly its transparency, and fight corruption.

Moreover, development assistance has traditionally involved tied procurement to the donor. This means that assistance funds had to be spent to purchase goods and services in the donor country. The practice resulted both in reducing the real value of aid by supporting higher cost, uncompetitive firms or organizations in the donor country, as well as tilting the products or services to those produced by the donor rather than those needed by the recipient. The practice had created vested interests in donor countries which were very difficult to overcome. Frequently, these interests are vocal supporters of aid programmes, provided these programmes continue to offer employment opportunities or export financing to their members. In agriculture, for example, US programmes of food assistance for a long period consisted of high-cost rice, produced in the state of Louisiana. High-cost rice consumption was thereby introduced to sub-Saharan Africa, undermining the incentives for local cereal production. In the health sector simple supplies for basic health centres are often not produced in donor countries. Tied aid thus reinforced the already existing bias for shiny hospitals with the latest equipment, dominantly accessible to the elites, at the expense of investment in basic health in rural areas.

The cost of tying aid procurement by source has been variously estimated at upwards of 30 per cent. Moreover, by radically limiting the number of potential suppliers it is also very prone to corruption. Despite several efforts within the DAC to untie bilateral assistance on a multilateral basis, tied aid still accounted for about 30 per cent of all bilateral aid in the mid-1990s, while the rest was mostly 'partially untied', that is, developing countries' suppliers could participate in tenders—but as they were not informed of these opportunities, it was very much a dead letter.

Finally, aid practices in 1990s were bedeviled by an old problem: there was an obvious lack of coherence between what governments were attempting to do through economic assistance and their policies on trade. Despite a lot of lip service, developing countries faced significant problems in accessing developed country markets in such sectors as agriculture. What was the point of development ministers offering assistance to raise agricultural production, if the resulting product increase could not be exported, or could not compete against subsidized produce exported to their markets? Similarly, while development agencies insisted that developing countries reduced public expenditure on armaments or other 'white elephants', many such projects were being promoted by their colleagues in defence or export agencies.

Again, on paper, the lack of coherence was acknowledged. For example, the European 1992 Maastricht Treaty (Article 130v) states that 'The Community shall take account of the objectives referred to in Article 130u [containing the many lofty objectives of the Community's Development Policies] in the policies that it implements which are likely to affect developing countries.' This, however, rarely resulted in concrete action.

Conclusion: Narrow the Gap between Rhetoric and Reality

Development prospects improved significantly in the early 1990s. The global economy rebounded from the lost decade of the 1980s based on increased trade and investment. The end of the Cold War ushered in a period of international cooperation that resulted in lofty pronouncements, the conclusion of new agreements alleviating debt problems in middle income countries and the launch of a new international trade organization; and foreign aid programmes started to focus on the main problem: alleviating poverty.

But the recovery was uneven, with sub-Saharan Africa falling behind; globalization was raising concerns about its impact, not on industrial countries, but on the poor in developing countries. Most importantly, the reality on the ground regarding the provision of coherent economic assistance did not reflect the high rhetoric contained in the international agreements. Action was needed to bridge the gap between rhetoric and reality. Steps had to be taken to implement the policy pronouncements. This was the international stage onto which four actors appeared almost simultaneously and started to engage the development establishment in order to design a more effective war on poverty.

Notes

1. This section is based on Chapter 7 of C. Michalopoulos, *Aid, Trade and Development* (Basingstoke: Palgrave Macmillan, 2017).
2. After US Treasury Secretary Nicholas Brady. The basic elements of the scheme involved asking creditors in the private sector to take a loss either by reducing the outstanding value of the debt or the cost of servicing it in exchange for increasing the security of being repaid.
3. See G. A. Cornia, R. Jolly, and F. Stewart, *Adjustment with a Human Face*, 2 vols (Oxford: Clarendon Press, 1987).
4. OECD, *Shaping the 21st Century* (Paris: OECD, 1996).
5. E. Herfkens, Speech at Finance for Development Conference, Monterrey, 22 March 2002.
6. Gerry K. Helleiner et al., *Development Co-operation Issues Between Tanzania and Its Aid Donors*, Report of the Group of Independent Advisors, 1995, available at http://www.tzdpg.or.tz, pp. 9–10.

7. Ibid., p. 11.
8. See K. Y. Amoako, *Know the Beginning Well* (Trenton, NJ: Africa World Press, 2020 forthcoming); C. Lancaster, 'The World Bank in Africa', in D. Kapur et al., *The World Bank: Its First Half Century*, vol. II (Washington, DC: Brookings Institution Press, 1997).
9. Helleiner et al., *Development Co-operation Issues*, p. 11.
10. Elliot J. Berg (coordinator), *Rethinking Technical Cooperation*, New York: UNDP and Development Alternatives Inc., 1993), pp. 249–50, cited in Helleiner et al., *Development Co-operation Issues*, p. 9.
11. Hilde F. Johnson in J. A. Nekkers and P. A. M. Malcontent (eds), *Fifty Years of Dutch Development Co-operation, 1949–1999* (The Hague: Jdu Publishers, 1999), p. 14.
12. Helleiner et al., *Development Co-operation Issues*, p. 13.
13. UN, 'Delivering as One', Report of the Secretary General's High Level Panel, 9 November (UN: New York, 2006).
14. See IMF, 'Corruption: Costs and Mitigation Strategies', Staff Discussion Note (Washington, DC: IMF, 2016); 'Corruption is costing the global economy $3.6 trillion every year', available at http://www.weform.org.

3

Organizing Collaboration

Introduction

Leadership, or its absence, undoubtedly plays a role in explaining many historical developments. But collaboration among several leaders in the pursuit of common objectives, other than their narrowly defined national interests, is a rare phenomenon that depends very much on their personalities as well as the institutional and political environment in which they functioned.

The story of Eveline Herfkens, Hilde F. Johnson, Clare Short, and Heidemarie Wieczorek-Zeul, all of whom, with different titles became ministers in charge of development cooperation in the Netherlands, Norway, the UK, and Germany in 1997–8, and what they did together to bridge the gap between rhetoric and reality in the war against global poverty, will start with a short discussion of their background. This will be followed by a discussion of the political situation and the different government arrangements that determined development policy in their countries at the time. The last part of the chapter will review the beginnings of their collaboration until the formal establishment of their coordination in Norway's Utstein Abbey in July 1999. 'It would be exaggerated to speak of a conscious timing of the initiative: it started out as an initiative of female Ministers for Development cooperation who wanted to make the difference by becoming concrete, moving from abstract policies into actual implementation and up-scaling.'[1]

The Four Protagonists

Germany, the Netherlands, Norway and the UK, all had substantial aid programmes in the 1990s. Together, the four countries accounted for more than a quarter of ODA provided by the OECD. When they acted together in international forums, others had to listen. And since the positions proclaimed by their ministers were both sensible and well-articulated, people and organizations did.

As can be expected in parliamentary systems, all four ministers had a parliamentary background. Johnson, the youngest of the lot, had served in Parliament only for four years when she became minister in 1997. The others had at least a decade as Members of Parliament (MPs), while Wieczorek-Zeul had also served in the European Parliament for almost a decade. This meant that they were well-versed in the political give and take needed to accomplish anything—when to compromise and when to stick to your guns. They were all early bloomers, having been elected in their twenties and thirties.

All four were members of centre/left parties (Labour/Social Democrat in the case of the UK, the Netherlands and Germany, Christian Democrat in Norway). Except for Herfkens, the other three were perceived to be on the left of their parties. Both Short and Wieczorek-Zeul were political heavyweights, powerful within their parties and governments, unusual as the development portfolio is often held by less prominent politicians. As they represented the parties' left in their governments, they provided cover for the efforts of their respective leaders (Blair and Schröder) to move to the political centre.

Herfkens and Johnson shared an interesting background in that they both spent a significant portion of their childhood in a developing country, Venezuela and Tanzania, respectively, where the contrast between the lives of expatriate children and those of poverty-stricken locals made an indelible impression. Short was born in Birmingham from Irish parents and easily identified with developing country problems. In 1997, in a famous exchange with Kumbirai Kangai, Zimbabwe Minister of Agriculture, she said: 'My origins are Irish and as you know we were colonized not colonizers.' Johnson frequently referred to Norway's recent independence in 1905 from 400 years of Danish and Swedish colonial rule.

Wieczorek-Zeul, often called 'Rote [red] Heidi', spent many years both in the European Parliament and the Bundestag on foreign affairs, and as vice chair of her party. Both she and Short spent a good deal of their time in Parliament on women's issues. As representatives of countries in the G8 group they were able to use their positions to move what was then—and is somewhat less now—an important group on issues of aid volume, debt, and aid effectiveness in ways that Netherlands and Norway, though with long traditions in development cooperation, could not. Moreover, they were the only ones in charge of development cooperation with ministerial rank in the G8 governments.[2]

All four had been involved in development issues in their earlier work. But at the time of their appointments, Herfkens had the longest experience in development cooperation having served as a civil servant in the Dutch Directorate-General for Development Cooperation, spokesperson for her party in Parliament on development, Executive Director at the World Bank and ambassador to UN agencies and the WTO in Geneva.

Their commitment to global sustainable development was so strong that they were willing to stand up against both vested interests in their own countries and other ministries in cases where their definition of national interest may have been narrow, protectionist, or parochial.

All this background contributed in making their views on the substance of development cooperation similar and compatible. But that was not enough. They worked together because they were willing to share the limelight, support each other's strengths, and tolerate each other's weaknesses, and in the process became friends. Some would argue that it happened because they were all women who are intrinsically better able than men to work together for common objectives. Indeed, it is hard to visualize a set of four male ministers of development cooperation submerge their egos for the common objective.

A *Die Zeit* interviewer asked them in 2002, 'Is the women-only composition by accident?' 'In some ways it might be' ... Hilde Johnson brushes the question away, uninterested ... 'but in which way ... ?' she was then asked. Eveline Herfkens thinks women are more impatient and informal. Heidemarie Wieczorek-Zeul says, 'We are not better human beings, but more practical/realistic/down to earth. We better understand how decisions work out for people.' Only Clare Short answers like a feminist: 'It is definitely not by accident', she mocks 'that women are deployed in the charity departments.'[3]

When I asked them the same question in June 2018, they did not deny that there was a special chemistry among them as women who have done well in a—at the time—male-dominated profession. But from early on, they stressed that theirs was not an exclusive or 'ladies only' club. This was part of their 'Utstein' principles. They also pointed to the fact that in 2002, they invited Jan Karlsson, Sweden's male Minister for Development Co-operation to become a full-time member. The group started to disintegrate thereafter, but not because of his presence.

Contacts

Clare Short became minister first, being appointed the first ever Secretary of State (which in the British jargon implies cabinet membership) for International Development in May 1997. She jokes that Prime Minister Tony Blair gave her the appointment to 'shut her up'. She proceeded to make her Department for International Development (DfID) the envy of all by building a highly professional staff, attracting the best including from the EU and the Commonwealth 'without interference from #10'. But she says that soon her prime minister 'wanted to become part of the success story and benefit from DfID's rising reputation'.[4]

Hilde F. Johnson became minister in October 1997 and quickly developed contacts with both Short and Herfkens. Early on she started to work with Short on broader development issues as well as Africa, especially Sudan, where her friendship, partnership, and trust were critical to achieving a peaceful resolution of the conflict.[5] Johnson visited Herfkens in Geneva and was briefed by her regarding the UN agencies and the WTO more candidly than diplomats usually do. She recalls that the 'chemistry was there right away' and she visited Herfkens in The Hague again within a week of Herfkens' appointment as minister in August 1998. Herfkens and Short met on 4 October 1998, just before the 1998 World Bank and IMF meetings.

Heidemarie Wieczorek-Zeul became Federal Minister of Economic Cooperation and Development in late October 1998. She knew Herfkens from the 1980s as they were both members of a group of European parliamentarians that visited the US Congress to protest the Reagan administration policies in Central America. Herfkens phoned Wieczorek-Zeul the day the latter became minister and offered to get in the car to go to Bonn (at the time the German government had not yet moved to Berlin) to brief her on what to do and not to do. In the event, Herfkens did go to Bonn in early November 1998 and introduced Wieczorek-Zeul to Johnson and Short, shortly thereafter.

Programme Priorities

The appointment of Clare Short as UK Development Minister in 1997 'marked the beginning of an era when the UK would become a major player in international development, would focus sharply on poverty reduction, would pursue a strategy of influencing the big players' (World Bank, IMF, UN, US, Japan, and the EU) and would as it were 'punch above its weight'.[6]

The main thrusts of the new UK aid policy were articulated in a White Paper presented by Short to Parliament in late 1997. It outlined many of the points that later would become part of the Utstein agenda.

The first point promises to 'Refocus our international development efforts on the elimination of poverty and encouragement of economic growth which benefits the poor. We will do this through support for international development targets...' The second point commits to 'Work closely with other donors...to build partnerships with developing countries to strengthen the commitment to the elimination of poverty' and 'Pursue these [international development] targets [in partnership with poorer counties...also committed to them'.[7]

The emphasis on the targets was because Short was looking for a device to focus DfID, mobilize support in the UK and drive the international system forward. She found it in the IDTs/IDGs (International Development Targets/Goals, agreed in 1996 at the OECD/DAC). 'It is probably accurate to say that Short did more than any other individual and more than many DAC member governments to promote the IDGs as a central component of the fight against poverty.'[8] The goals, as noted in [C2B3], were a useful device to mobilize public support for development at a time when aid levels were declining for various reasons.

Short writes: 'It was Richard Jolly who pointed me to the report of development committee of the OECD entitled *Shaping the 21st Century*. It drew together the recommendations of the great UN conferences of the 1990s and suggested that great advance was possible if we focused on a systematic reduction of poverty.'[9]

The White Paper committed the UK to achieving the 0.7 per cent ODA/GNI target, but this commitment was in principle only, without any time frame. It did not reflect actual policy as at that point the UK ODA/GNI was only around 0.26 per cent. The Paper went further than the IDGs in several ways, for example by paying special attention to human rights. Perhaps most importantly, it advocated coherence in policies towards developing countries by ensuring 'that the full range of government policies affecting development including environment, trade, investment and agricultural policies takes account of our sustainable development objectives'.[10] This was to prove a major challenge in the years ahead both for the four ministers and the international community as a whole.

Again Short notes that 'The No. 10 and FCO [Foreign and Commonwealth Office] machines expected announcements of donations to be ready for when the Prime Minister and Foreign Secretary travelled. They resented DfID interference on British business interests or arms sales. The trade policy officials in DTI [Department of Trade and Industry] were incensed that we had established a trade policy department; those in charge of environmental policy had little interest in the situation of developing countries.'[11]

In 1998, at the G8 summit in Birmingham, Short's constituency, the group gave strong backing to the IDGs 'despite hesitation in the US Treasury and State Department over whether the goals, accepted by their USAID [United States Agency for International Development] colleagues in the DAC should be formally accepted by the US government as a whole....' Short's advocacy in Washington helped resolve this problem and the summit concluded: 'We commit ourselves to a real and effective partnership in support of developing countries efforts to reform, to develop and to reach the internationally agreed goals for economic and social development, as set out in the OECD's 21st Century Strategy.'[12]

Norway's policy thrust was very similar to that of the UK's. Johnson wanted to focus aid programmes even more on countries whose governments were committed to poverty eradication. She wanted to get away from 'old-style' aid and put the recipient in the 'driver's seat' to implement programmes based on comprehensive approaches and plans as articulated through the cooperation of governments. And she wanted to do this collaboration with other similarly oriented donors. In a speech at the Overseas Development Institute (ODI) eerily suggesting the subsequent collaboration, she welcomed the new UK White Paper saying: 'This gives me hope that we may be able to work more closely in the years ahead both in concrete on-the-ground development assistance as well as in efforts to bring a larger measure of coordination and consistency in international development assistance. Through joint efforts we may achieve so much more than we could otherwise hope for.'[13]

She resented aid priorities focusing on national interest and instructed NORAD (the Norwegian aid agency) and aid staff to get rid of the Norwegian flag in all aid projects. In a statement to the Norwegian Parliament she said:

> We cannot continue to quarrel about whose flag will be raised over the various projects...We cannot take up all the available time of the recipient countries' authorities for separate consultations and meetings...We must make it easier for

them to govern their country, not more difficult! If the donors cannot disregard their own interests, ignore their need to improve their own profile, and coordinate their efforts more efficiently, the practical effect of our efforts will be considerably reduced.[14]

Shocked officials were used to getting opposite instructions. The Prime Minister and Foreign Minister were also refused donations and ribbon cutting ceremonies when on travel. As to aid volume, Norway for a long time had met the 0.7 ODA/ GNI target, for years close to 1 per cent. The coalition agreement of her new government had a clear target of reaching 1 per cent of GNI.

All this was music to Herfkens' ears. At the time, she was familiar with Johnson's views but was not aware of Short's White Paper. Yet, its thrust was completely in keeping with the directions in which Herfkens wanted to move her programme from the outset. The Dutch as well as the German positions on development cooperation were articulated in the 'coalition' agreements of the parties that formed their new governments in 1998. Both coalition agreements stated the purpose of development cooperation to be social, environmental, and economic sustainability with the Dutch being more specific on the poverty focus, such as the provision of clean water, basic education, and health and economic empowerment of the poor. Both coalition agreements mentioned empowerment of women with the German agreement elaborating on the importance of economic independence for women and the need to strengthen basic health and education for women and girls. In addition, the Dutch showed a strong emphasis on partner government ownership: 'the objectives of development policy should be decided and implemented by countries concerned. Aid cannot replace good policies by recipients.'[15] All this was very close to the IDGs, although not explicitly mentioned.

From her position on the Board of the World Bank, and in alliance with the Nordics, Herfkens had been pushing the Bank to give priority to poverty reduction in the context of well-articulated plans put together and 'owned' by developing country governments. She wanted the Bank's country-specific policy framework papers (PFPs) to become more focused on poverty and the centrepiece of a truly cooperative effort, designed by the developing country government and supported with appropriate and coordinated assistance from bilateral and multilateral donors. The German coalition agreement was also moving the programme in similar directions: it stated that the government would make efforts to change the World Bank and IMF structural adjustment policies to make these better meet environmental and development criteria.

Like Short and Johnson, Herfkens was also determined to concentrate government-to-government support on poor, decently governed countries committed to poverty reduction objectives. Given staff constraints, she intended to reduce the number of focus countries for Dutch assistance. She also wanted to get away from the old-style aid, where the 'donors know best' (see Box 3.1). Helpfully, the coalition agreement stated that bilateral aid would focus on countries with good governance and give budgetary priority to social rather than military expenditures.

On debt relief there were differences: the German position simply stated that international debt relief initiatives for poor and highly indebted countries would be supported—and in that respect was very similar to the UK statement. The Dutch had advocated debt relief for a long time, and as we will see later, were far more committed to providing resources for this purpose. The same was the case for Norway. In 1996, before taking office, Johnson had championed a debt relief plan in Parliament together with her parliamentary leader, Kjell Magne Bondevik who subsequently became prime minister. This plan was included in the coalition agreement of the government which took office in October 1997 and was presented in Johnson's first statement to Parliament in May 1998. The Norwegian

---

Box 3.1. Country ownership of development programmes

'As Development Cooperation Minister in the Netherlands, the first African country I went to was Mozambique. The Netherlands had been spending some 60-odd million Guilders every year in Mozambique. So, I met with the officials of the Finance Ministry—by then Luísa Dias Diogo was not the Minister yet, maybe the number two or three—and nobody in the Finance Ministry had a clue where that 60 million was being spent on. We were just spending it left and right, in regions, for the University, with some sector Ministry but we never even informed the Finance Ministry. How could the schools or whatever we were building be sustainable? I found this just incredible, how a fairly decent and functioning government would not have any oversight on how the huge amounts of aid money at stake were actually used.

'Part of what we had done was in the environmental sector; conserving the environment has been a staying political priority of the Netherlands. So, we had actually built the environmental Ministry (in Mozambique), staffed it, provided equipment, which included fax machines and computers. When I met the Environment Minister, I asked: "you have got this wonderful building and all your staff, what are your priorities now?" To this he responded: "what do you think they should be?" This effectively made the point: "was it not you who wanted this, so now tell us what we should be doing?" At the root of what is wrong with traditional aid is the perception by donors that they, or their aid, develop developing countries. Wrong. Developing countries develop themselves: they are responsible for and take charge of their development. Without developing country "ownership" no aid yields lasting results.'[16]

Debt Relief Strategy, the very first internationally, was passed in Parliament in the subsequent national budget for 1999.

Similarly, there were important differences in the ODA/GNI target. The Dutch and Norwegians had for almost 25 years met or surpassed the 0.7 ODA/GNI target. In the Netherlands this had become 0.8 as they implemented the principle agreed at the 1992 Rio Conference on Environment and Development that aid for environmental purposes should be additional to traditional ODA. Compared to the UK in principle commitment, the German coalition agreement only was able to state in a very convoluted way that, 'in order to get closer to the internationally agreed 0.7 objective, the coalition will turn around the down-ward trend of the development budget and especially increase commitments continuously moderately'.[17]

Finally, both coalition agreements, just like the UK White Paper, sought to improve policy coherence. The Dutch stated that in order to enable good devel-opment policies, policies in other sectors (e.g. trade, agriculture, and arms exports) needed to be brought in line with these. In the German case the German coalition agreement intended to promote consistency with development objectives on two issues: arms exports and export guarantees. Heidemarie Wieczorek-Zeul became a member of the Federal Security Council where she would be able to limit German arms sales to developing countries. At the same time the export promotion and granting of export guarantees were to be reformed to meet environmental, social, and developmental standards.

Institutions, Politics, Allies, and Vested Interests

The ability of the U4 to engineer concerted policy change depended in part on the government institutions which they led. And it was shaped by their relationships with their parliaments and other ministers, as well as civil society and vested interests in the four countries. They were ministers representing their countries and as such tried to maintain the values they agreed to in all their work. Waging war on poverty required waging war on the development establishment, both domestic and international.

In the case of DfID, I noted earlier its creation and expansion under Short's leadership. In Germany the ministry had a large staff, perhaps 600, located in the Bonn headquarters and a very large staff, perhaps 10,000, in the field offices of GTZ (the German Technical Assistance agency) and somewhat less in KfW (the German Development Bank) all of whom reported to the ministry. The problem was that in the period before the new red/green government came to power in 1998, the staff was stuck in its old ways and difficult to move in new directions, including the need to cooperate with other bilateral aid agencies. German bur-eaucracy resisted reform. As the Christian Democratic Union (CDU) had run the place since 1982, it had been a while since Germany belonged to the progressive 'like-minded' donors. For example, the German staff did not think that the IDGs were something that the ministry should be interested in.[18]

By contrast, in Norway, Johnson found only limited resistance to introducing new approaches beyond traditional projects. It was apparent that the new-style aid programmes would be less beneficial to Norwegian interests. As a result, there was some resistance against lowering the Norwegian flag, and untying aid in the business community and in the trade ministry. However, untying aid was also included in the coalition agreement, and she was able to push reforms forward without much difficulty.

In the Netherlands, Herfkens had practically no staff of her own except for a small Directorate-General and had to rely on the regional staff of the Ministry of Foreign Affairs for implementing bilateral programmes. Even counting these, she was chronically understaffed with the fewest staff per amount of aid disbursed of all OECD members. Her Director General (DG) and a substantial part of her staff were fully on board and committed to the reforms she intended. 'At the same time, they had to overcome a lot of resistance from large segments of the staff who were raised and "educated" in a project-based policy environment, where ownership from the recipient country hardly played a role'[19] (see Chapter 4).

Obviously, ministers are accountable to their Parliaments, which can constrain their policy actions. In the British system, where at that time ministers had automatic parliamentary majorities for their policies, this was not an issue. In Norway, though a multi-party coalition government, Parliament was generally progressive and did not care to micromanage development policy. In Germany, however, the Budget Committee of the Bundestag had to be convinced of the wisdom of specific aid policies, such as the provision of budget support. In addition, each party's spokesperson for development in the Budget Committee is an *ex officio* member of the Supervisory Board of the German Technical Cooperation Agency (GTZ), making it extremely difficult to change policy or country priorities. The Netherlands was somewhere in between the two extremes. As in coalition governments, ministers needed to spend time to build parliamentary consensus. Herfkens spent many hours convincing Dutch MPs of the rationale of her reforms, including moving from projects to programmatic approaches as well as budget support to governments with decent policies, committed to poverty reduction. At the end of the day she usually got her way, except on occasion with some delay as in the case of Rwanda.[20]

Relationships with other ministers pose a second constraint. For development cooperation, Foreign Affairs is important and must be managed carefully. In the Netherlands, the Development Minister, while a Cabinet Member, is formally a minister 'without portfolio', making use of the staff of the Foreign Ministry while being responsible for development cooperation and its budget.[21] This often leads to tensions. However, Herfkens had a very good relationship with her Foreign

Affairs colleague Josias van Aartsen and succeeded early on in convincing him that global poverty reduction should be an overarching Dutch foreign policy objective, thus minimizing potential tension.

In the UK, Short is on record as saying that 'building the new department meant taking on a series of battles with Whitehall. This hostility to DfID was institutional rather than political... The institutional arrangements and world view of most of those who occupy dominant positions in government were framed to run the Cold War world... Africa came low down the Foreign Office priorities, but they certainly did not want DfID poking its nose in.'[22]

In Germany, Wieczorek-Zeul as a minister had enough political space and weight to disagree with Foreign Affairs, which she did for example in the case of Namibia and Cuba. In Norway's case Johnson was also Minister for Human Rights during her first tenure. Although this could create tensions at times, she was of the same party as the Prime Minister and the Foreign Minister and all three were similarly committed to the development and human rights agenda. Relations became more challenging in her second term when the new coalition included a conservative Foreign Minister. While her party had ensured development-oriented commitments in the coalition agreement, the influence of foreign policy interests in relation to specific countries, such as Iraq and Afghanistan, increased tensions, which only abated when her Prime Minister resisted US pressure to participate in the Iraq War.

Finance Ministers were also important, particularly for Short and Wieczorek-Zeul, battling for budget increases and stronger commitments towards the 0.7 per cent ODA target. Short got along well with the Chancellor of the Exchequer, Gordon Brown, and was happy to share credit and positive publicity regarding British development policies with him, hoping to convince him to raise the budget. But, she wrote, 'Treasury officials had written off unpayable debt before and did not need new conditions which would link debt relief to the establishment of poverty reduction strategies.'[23]

Wieczorek-Zeul had an excellent rapport with her first Finance colleague, Oscar Lafontaine, even though he tried (in vain) to take the World Bank governorship from her. But he left, half a year into the government's term, and was succeeded by Hans Eichel, with whom the relation was frostier, for example regarding increases of ODA towards the 0.7 per cent target. In all cases she relied more on her connections with the Chancellor for results.

In the Netherlands, with its twenty-five-year standing commitment to spend at least 0.7 per cent of its GNI on ODA, there was little controversy about the aggregate budget level. The Finance Minister, Gerrit Zalm, often supported Herfkens by wholeheartedly and loudly voicing development-friendly positions in both the IMF (e.g. on HIPC funding) and the European Economic and Financial Affairs Council (Ecofin) where he advocated the need for other governments to achieve the 0.7 per cent target.

In Norway, despite agreement on the target of 1 per cent of GNI, there were regular battles with the Ministers of Finance over the aid budget, for example on the funding of debt relief or whether to include funding of refugee costs as aid. Nevertheless, support from the prime minister made it possible to steadily increase aid and overcome these challenges.[24]

Relationships on trade issues were important in promoting policy coherence towards development. Herfkens was good friends with her Trade Minister colleague and as a former WTO ambassador helped to actively influence Dutch positions on trade in the EU. Also, her colleague for agriculture was willing to advocate development-friendly reform of the European Common Agriculture policy—a lonely voice in the European Council. Short strengthened DfID's analytical capacity in trade to the chagrin of her Trade Ministry colleague. But in the end for the three countries that were EU members, this presented very difficult challenges. Trade policy is an EU competence, predominantly designed and implemented by the EU Commission in Brussels, and overseen by the Council of Trade Ministers, in which a few pro-development voices would not make much of a difference. At first, they tried to get the EU Development Council more effectively involved. When this failed, Short and Herfkens created a 'coherence network', where knowledgeable British and Dutch staff shared information and suggested positions to be taken by other EU countries who might be interested.

Norway has been a major contributor to international funds, including those of the WTO, aimed at increasing LDC capacity to trade while maintaining considerable protection in agriculture. But given the small size of its market, its impact on developing country exports especially LDCs—which have traditionally been the focus of its assistance—has not been significant.

In all four countries there were many NGOs focusing on development; civil society in general was supportive of aid programmes. As opposition MPs, the four ministers had worked closely with NGOs and were appreciative that civil society campaigns and lobbying in their countries gave a voice to the poor and helped extract promises from often reluctant governments at the various UN summits in the 1990s. But after they became ministers not everything was smooth.

In Norway, NGOs blamed Johnson for embracing the MDGs: their focus was anti-globalization.

The Jubilee 2000 campaign and other NGOs had a profound impact in keeping the debt issues faced by poor countries alive. Jubilee 2000 was an international coalition movement in over forty countries that called for cancellation of poor countries' debt by the year 2000.[25] But both Short and Herfkens clashed with their NGO's on the specifics of debt relief. Contrary to the NGOs, which were pushing for generalized unconditional debt forgiveness, they felt that relief should be provided on a case by case basis and linked to policies to reduce poverty (see next section). On the other hand, in Germany, NGOs supported the Wiezcorek-Zeul position against unconditional debt relief. As the decade wore on, Short and

Herfkens clashed with NGOs on globalization, which they regarded as potentially helpful in reducing poverty, while many NGOs questioned its benefits to the poor—at least in developing countries: in those years no one questioned the impact on low-income groups in rich countries.

The four ministers' radical commitment to promote development clashed with vested interests in their own countries. In the Netherlands, the development cooperation programme started in the late 1940s, partly as an employment programme for tropical experts returning home after Indonesia's independence. This created a long history of vested interests in technical assistance programmes linked to sectors such as health and agriculture. When Herfkens decided to terminate the provision of expensive health services provided by Dutch doctors in Ghana and instead give budget support to the health sector, the leader of the Dutch opposition claimed 'Herfkens Kills Babies'. Dutch parliamentarians also complained bitterly when she decided to give Norway the lead in aid efforts to Sudan; and they wanted her to create a Dutch demining agency instead of simply funding the existing Norwegian one.

Vested interests had to be fought in other countries as well. In both Norway and Germany export industry interests opposed untying aid—which happened de facto if programmes provided for budget support. While most Norwegian aid was untied, there were considerable battles to untie the small remainder. One example was fermented canned fish, a Nordic delicacy, included as mandatory in the country's contribution to the World Food Programme (WFP). Reportedly, no refugees or internally displaced people around the world could stand to eat these fish. They were inedible and ended up rotting in the stores. The fisheries industry and the small fishing communities in Norway's north were furious when an embarrassed Johnson put an end to the practice. In Germany, vested interests did not allow programme changes in technical assistance which as noted earlier was in part controlled by members of the Bundestag Budget Committee.

Whatever the challenges the four ministers faced domestically or internationally, they knew that they had a better chance of success working together than alone. As Short's White Paper (para 1.23) stated: 'We should not over-estimate what we can do by ourselves. We should not under-estimate what we can do with others.' Their main impact started to be felt in the spring of 1999 at the World Bank/IMF Development Committee meetings. The focus was debt relief for the Highly Indebted Poor Countries.

The Heavily Indebted Poor Country (HIPC) Initiative

As discussed in C2P28, the HIPC programme to reduce the debt burden of poor developing countries was established in 1996.[26]

Funding was from three sources: World Bank net income; the IMF's ESAF, which provided concessional financing and was funded by bilateral donors; and a HIPC Trust Fund, similarly funded, set up by the World Bank. Through 1998, the Netherlands was the biggest contributor in paid in and committed funds to the combined HIPC Trust Fund ($60 million) and to the IMF's ESAF-HIPC (about $50 million). By contrast the G8 had made very limited contributions: Japan was the largest contributor to the IMF's ESAF-HIPC with about $100 million committed over five years; Canada, the UK, and France a total of $20 million each; the US, Germany, and Italy none.[27]

It turned out that the HIPC initiative suffered from two significant shortcomings: (a) in country after country the savings obtained from debt relief did not result in more resources being invested in health education and other social needs critical to addressing poverty issues. Moreover, (b) the criteria used for providing debt relief were too stringent—thus few countries were able to qualify, and the relief obtained early on was quite limited.

Herfkens, at the annual World Bank–HIPC Trust Fund meetings in early October 1998, together with her Minister of Finance, met with IMF Managing Director Camdessus in order to encourage him to make the ESAF more poverty oriented. She had argued that as ESAF is paid out of ODA, and ODA's purpose is poverty reduction, the IMF better ensure this, or she would close her purse. Camdessus was non-committal.

Over the 1998–9 winter, the impact of debt relief on poverty and the need to ensure the poor would benefit from debt relief became the first common cause of the four ministers. They felt that until then the poor had paid the price for the adjustment imposed by the international financial institutions (IFIs) to deal with debt crisis and hence they should benefit from any measures to provide debt relief. 'The Ministers played a particularly important role in putting over to the President of the World Bank James Wolfensohn and the Managing Director of the IMF Michel Camdessus the relevance of the IDGs to the area of greatest international development focus at the time: resolving the debt problems of the HIPC.'[28]

On 18 February 1999, Gordon Brown and Clare Short sent a letter to Camdessus and Wolfensohn suggesting a fundamental review of the HIPC initiative. 'We see a need to consider the issues of debt sustainability as well as the link between debt relief, poverty eradication and the International Development Targets.' They went on to say that 'given the costs of the initiative, bilateral contributions are clearly not going to be enough to finance ESAF and HIPC fully. We therefore hope that it will soon be possible to reach agreement on gold sales.'[29]

On 10 March 1999, Camdessus responded positively:

At the moment there is an important opportunity to take advantage of the political momentum given by German proposals in the context of the Cologne

Summit and by your support to strengthen the HIPC initiative to achieve the goals that you put forward—and we share—namely, a comprehensive solution to the unsustainable debt burden of the poorest countries and a contribution to a reduction of poverty world-wide.

But he was not forthcoming on gold sales, and instead talked about interim finance by the bilaterals.[30]

The spring meeting of the Development Committee in 1999 provided the first occasion where the four ministers coordinated their strategy and priorities. They all were members of the Development Committee consisting of Governors of the World Bank. The main focus was to ensure both that poverty reduction would become the overarching objective of all World Bank programmes, and that debt relief should be used for poverty reduction.

Their representatives at the World Bank Board had pushed a proposal to include in the draft Development Committee communique language aiming to ensure that: 'underlying reform programs should have an integral pro-poor growth focus. National policies must be designed to ensure that social sectors can make optimal use of resources freed through debt relief. Programs for HIPCs should fully reflect social concerns, by protecting social expenditure and by ensuring access to markets and to means of production for the poor.'[31] The Netherlands initiated a preparatory meeting with Germany, Norway, and the UK to coordinate their positions for the meeting.

Development Committee meetings traditionally involve a formal morning meeting during which members deliver prepared speeches, without engaging with or even commenting on what other speakers have said. Alex Shakow, who then served as Executive Secretary of the Committee remembers that 'under World Bank President James Wolfensohn, the pattern was changed. An effort was made to get rid of the prepared speeches and identify specific agenda topics on which Ministers were asked to comment. Of course, some read prepared texts focused on the specific agenda item.'[32]

A communique is normally agreed without discussion. The meeting is followed by a lunch, for principals only. The four ministers broke the pattern: in the morning they orchestrated and coordinated their interventions to follow and comment on specific speakers emphasizing different points on the same theme. Shakow recalls that the main effect was that they 'all spoke with one voice on the importance of addressing poverty through the resources freed from debt relief in the context of the PRSPs [Poverty Reduction Strategy Papers]'.[33]

The four were the only Development Ministers in the Development Committee: all other countries were represented by Ministers of Finance and Central Bank Governors, and those from rich countries were clearly not as engaged with the poverty agenda.[34] 'The Australian Finance Minister was not amused and announced he would not attend these meetings anymore as long as these women were around...'[35] Indeed, 'We were so effective that the Brazilian Finance Minister, while walking out of the meeting, sighed: "I am all for gender equality, but this is too much..." Well—we were four out of twenty-four.'[36] And Johnson recalls that Larry Summers, then US Deputy Treasury Secretary, was so upset that walking out of the meeting he told Hilde Johnson that we were mistaken if we thought the Development Committee was going to become the Socialist International. At which point Johnson clarified that she was actually a Christian Democrat.[37]

At the lunch that followed the morning, they continued to make a nuisance of themselves by daring to question the precooked communique and reiterating the amendments tabled before by their Board Members, much to the chagrin of the other participants. While their proposed language did not make it into the communique on that occasion, ministers were agreed of 'the importance of ensuring a clear link between debt relief and the goals of sustainable development and poverty reduction and looked forward to the results of ongoing consultations in this area. From the outset, the underlying reform programs should have an integral pro-poor growth focus. Programs for HIPC should fully reflect social concerns by protecting social expenditures.'[38]

> How often did Clare end up in conflict with the then US Treasury Secretary Larry Summers. It was about steps in the debt forgiveness: not all countries received that at the same time. In the end, a process with clearly defined conditions was negotiated. In the disagreement over specific points in the Communique, Clare wanted to see her and our position, anchored, which Larry Summers had contradicted often enough. Since the Communiques need to be accepted by consensus, some stubbornness can go a long way. And Clare could be stubborn. Normally the Communiques would be adopted in the morning sessions at the end of the World Bank Meeting, after which there was a luncheon hosted by the Chairman of the Development Committee and was attended by the Governors, the President of the World Bank, the Managing Director of the IMF and the Executive Secretary of the Committee. Clare sometimes extended the disagreement so long that the point in question could only be decided upon at the luncheon. That was the point at which Larry Summers finally gave up.[39]

The four ministers could not agree on a formal common position regarding the funding of debt relief. As until then much of the funding of HIPC was coughed up by the Netherlands, the Nordics and Switzerland, which together had shouldered two thirds of the burden of funding HIPC in 1996–8, Herfkens and Johnson felt it was high time for the G8 to put up money: 'burden sharing' became their rallying cry. If the G8 paid up, HIPC would be fully funded, and result in freeing resources for poverty reduction in several poor countries. Hence they continued to call on the G8 to 'put their money where their mouth was' and that it was time to stop 'rounding up the usual suspects' for funding. But, of course, at that point, while Short and Wieczorek-Zeul shared their perspective, they could not sign up for language their Ministers of Finance colleagues would not agree to.

The NGO debt coalition continued to exert pressure on Organisation for Economic Cooperation and Development (OECD) governments to unconditionally cancel HIPC debt. The Jubilee campaign produced millions of signatures. The Vatican was proposing that debt repayments be put into a fund that would be used address poverty issues. Massive campaigns were mounted throughout the G8 and some other European countries focused on influencing the G8 meeting in Cologne, Germany, in June 1999. Herfkens handed over many boxes containing the signed petitions of tens of thousands of Dutch citizens supporting debt relief, shipped over the Rhine, to a representative of Wieczorek-Zeul at the Rhine crossing on the border of the two countries.

The German government had pursued its traditional sceptical approach on debt. However, in the first six months of 1999 leading up to the meeting, Wieczorek-Zeul took the initiative and was instrumental in forging a change in the German position to endorse debt relief. And as is common to G8 meetings, the host government always feels pressure to come up with a new initiative to highlight the success of the meeting. With the German NGOs, including church groups mounting pressure and prodded by Wieczorek-Zeul, the German Prime Minister Schroeder decided to make strengthening of HIPC the main 'deliverable' of the G8 meeting on 18–20 June 1999.[40] According to Short, 'Cologne was used to unblock German opposition to HIPC.'[41] On the day of the G8 meeting, Cologne was witness to massive manifestations, involving civil society, church groups and politicians. A chain was built with Wieczorek-Zeul standing hand in hand with church group representatives celebrating an important joint success.[42]

The G8 Cologne agreement proposed to improve the HIPC programme in several ways: first, to permit countries to obtain debt relief easier and faster; second, to design mechanisms that would ensure that countries receiving debt relief would increase their spending in social programmes; and third, to permit the IMF to participate more fully.

However, the new programme required much more funding. This was supposed to be achieved in part through increasing the value of the IMF's gold reserves, but also through additional contributions from bilateral donors to the HIPC Trust Fund. When for the umpteenth time the G8 discussed funding but failed to pledge any, Gerrit Zalm, the Dutch Finance Minister, reacted: 'Can the emperor pay for his own clothes, please?'[43]

The Utstein group (which by that time had had its first formal ministerial meeting in July, and thus their name) continued to push the link with poverty reduction and the need for 'fair burden sharing': in August they published an op-ed in the *International Herald Tribune* (*IHT*) stating:

> We need to address the debt crisis in the poor countries with urgency. The Group of Eight's debt relief initiative presented at the recent Cologne summit is very good news. By implementing the G8 proposal, we will enable poor debtor countries to allocate more funds for poverty reduction.
>
> However, the initiative's success depends on two critical factors. First is the collective ability of all bilateral and multilateral creditors to secure sufficient financing, based on transparent and fair burden-sharing. Second is the ability to transform debt relief into real poverty reduction and sustainable development.
>
> Strengthening the social dimension of the IMF's structural adjustment facility for the poorest countries would be a key contribution.[44]

They also sent a letter along to IMF Managing Director Camdessus elaborating this last line.

By the time of the annual meetings of the IMF and World Bank, at the end of September 1999, Camdessus clearly got the message: the IMF changed the name of ESAF to Poverty Reduction and Growth Facility (PRGF); and Camdessus was actively handing out little cards with the seven pledges (IDGs) to everyone.

The Utstein Four, now formally declared as a group, met with Camdessus to discuss the challenges needed to concretize the poverty focus, including awareness building among IMF staff. Camdessus had indeed changed his tune: 'The funds had to be spent better; we need to demand better results in favor of vulnerable low income population.'[45] Wieczorek-Zeul remembers that when Herfkens asked Camdessus why he had not acted on this earlier, as she had raised these issues with him the year before, he answered that the political winds had changed.[46] The Utstein group remained sceptical to what degree a name change could lead to real change in content on the ground and the Netherlands announced that it would monitor implementation not just through progress reports at headquarters level, but in the field.[47] But *ex post* it would appear that this meeting marked the start of a strategic shift in the IMF to include assessments of the poverty impact of its programmes.

Still, the financing of HIPC was not solved. HIPC was discussed in the first ever joint meeting of the Development Committee and the IMF's Interim Committee initiated by the UK's Gordon Brown, the new Interim Committee Chair. The Development Committee consisted of the G8 plus seventeen other members, who had agreed in the spring meeting's communique, 'for increased contributions—with fair burden sharing' to the HIPC Trust Fund.[48] Thus, when, during the meetings at the end of September, the G8 wanted to use even more of the World Bank's net income to pay for multilateral debt relief they ran into opposition from the Netherlands, Norway, and ten other 'like-minded' countries as well as the World Bank President Wolfensohn.[49] Since the net income was usually transferred to the World Bank's International Development Association (IDA) to provide credits to the poorest countries, such a use would in fact imply that these countries, many of which dutifully did repay debts, ended up paying for the debt relief provided to other poor countries. Moreover, the HIPC Trust Fund received money from bilateral donors who had committed to provide ODA in amounts linked to their GNI: 0.7 per cent in the Netherlands and close to 1 per cent in Norway. Since debt relief counted as ODA, HIPC would have de facto resulted in diverting funds that would otherwise have been spent on other poor countries/issues. At some point, the G8 also suggested increasing the fees charged by the World Bank for credits to higher income borrowing countries. The Netherlands, Norway, and obviously all borrowing members, refused to accept such an interpretation of the concept of 'burden sharing'.

Herfkens and Johnson had been prepared to foot some of the HIPC additional bill at the outset to prompt others to join, but their generosity had reached its limit. Still, the G8 counted on getting its way, as usual, and quelling opposition. The two had mobilized a non-G8 majority on the World Bank Board ahead of the meeting. This had reached the ears of the British Treasury, raising alarm. Johnson was requested to meet with Treasury Secretary Gordon Brown late at night, before the meeting. The two had a good rapport, but this time she recalls meeting a dishevelled and agitated Secretary with his notepad and a pencil trying to add the numbers, showing her that using IDA funds was necessary, with his ever present chief economic advisor Ed Balls adding to the pressure: 'Gordon Brown counted on us to cave as publicity would be on his side, resulting in a shouting match with Ed Balls behind the scenes...'[50]

At the meeting, the Netherlands and Norway threatened not to proceed with HIPC until the funding issue was resolved; and as that did not happen during the meeting, it was referred to the official Development Committee lunch. Here, Herfkens stated, supporting the earlier developing country speakers: 'We, the non-G8 donors, flatly refuse to let other developing countries pay for debt relief' and added 'while my country is a G8 size donor—we will not join the G8 in this Bank robbery: it is time to go Dutch!'[51]

The lunch did not reach an agreement either. But, in the end, the Netherlands and Norway and the other 'like-minded' got their way. The Development Committee communique stated that debt relief would be additional to IDA and not at the expense of the World Bank's financial integrity. 'Financing of debt relief should not compromise the financing made available through concessional windows such as IDA.'[52] Later in the year at the suggestion of the U4, it was agreed to use the two billion Euro unspent money of the European Development Fund (an EU Fund designed to assist developing countries, primarily previous colonies) to pay off HIPC debts to European creditors. At the time the quality of EU aid was dubious (see Chapter 6) and was years behind in its disbursement. As the contributions to this fund are related to EU members' GDP, this ensured improved burden sharing, resulting in a significant increase for the UK, German, and other Europeans contributions to the HIPC Trust Fund. Eventually, the USA also contributed substantial amounts.[53]

Unfortunately, the HIPC funding story did not end there. There were continuous difficulties in implementing a 'pay as you go' fund for poor countries linked to IDA and IMF financing, a topic that would occupy the U4 and their successors in later years and which we will revisit in Chapter 10. It would continue to be a topic of discussion among the U4 in their formal annual gatherings at ministerial level, the first of which occurred at Norway's Utstein Abbey.

Notes

1. Koos Richelle, email, 25 March 2018.
2. The Group of 7 (G7) consisted of Canada, France, Germany, Italy, Japan, the UK and the US. It was formed in 1975 (Canada was added in 1976) to promote global economic cooperation among the major OECD countries. Russia was added in 1996 to make it the G8 and dropped in 2015.
3. Die Zeit, 17 April 2002.
4. Johnson organized a meeting of the four former ministers at her home in Stavern, Norway, 21–2 June 2018 to discuss the substance of this volume. Their discussions were taped and transcribed and are referred to as Stavern, 21-2 June, 2018, transcript'.
5. H. F Johnson, Waging Peace in Sudan (Eastbourne: Sussex Academic Press, 2011), p. 26.
6. See D. Hulme, 'The Millennium Development Goals (MDGs): A Short History of the World's Biggest Promise', Brook World Poverty Institute, BWPI Working Paper 100, University of Manchester, 2009, p. 21.
7. UK DFID, Eliminating World Poverty: A Challenge for the 21st Century. White Paper on International Development, 1997, p. 6, available at https://webarchive.nationalarchives.gov.uk/search/.
8. Hulme, 'The Millennium Development Goals', pp. 23–4.
9. C. Short, An Honourable Deception? (London: Free Press, 2004), pp. 53–4.
10. UK DFID, Eliminating World Poverty, p. 7.
11. Short, An Honourable Deception?, p. 79.
12. See R. Manning, Using Indicators to Encourage Development, DIIS Report 2009–11 (Copenhagen: Danish Institute of International Studies, 2009), pp. 87–8.
13. H. Johnson, Speech at ODI, 19 February 1998.
14. Statement to the Parliament, the Storting, on development cooperation policy, 5 May 1998.
15. Dutch Government Coalition Agreement (1998), The Hague: Tweede Kamer de Staten-General Kabinetsformatie 1998, Tweede Kamer vergaderjaar 1997–1998, 26024 nr.10.

16. E. Herfkens, *Africa and Development Cooperation* (Zimbabwe: ACBF Development Memoirs Series, 2004), p. 19.

17. German Government Coalition Agreement (1998), Koalitionsvereinbarung zwischen der Socialdemocratischen Partei Deutschlands und Budnis/90 Die Grunen Bonn, October, available at http://www.spd.de/fileadmin/documente.

18. H. Wieczorek-Zeul, Stavern , 21-2 June , 2018 transcript.

19. R. Keller, email, 30 March 2019.

20. Herfkens, Stavern, 21-2 June, 2018, transcript.

21. The same arrangement, i.e. sharing the Foreign Ministry staff, was apparently in place in Norway as well.

22. Short, An Honourable Deception?, pp. 78–9.

23. Short, An Honourable Deception?, p. 79.

24. H. Johnson, Stavern, 21-2 June, 2018, transcript.

25. The concept derived from the biblical idea of the year of Jubilee, every 50th year, in which, as quoted in Leviticus, those enslaved because of debts are freed, lands lost because of debt are returned, and community torn by inequality is restored.

26. The World Bank originally objected to having its debt forgiven because of the potential impact on its own capacity to borrow from the capital markets.

27. Development Committee, "The Initiative for Heavily Indebted Poor Countries" September 1998, p.13.

28. Manning, *Using Indicators to Encourage Development*, p. 88.

29. Letter from Brown and Short to J. Wolfensohn and M. Camdessus, 18 February 1999. Note that the IDGs were frequently referred to as the International Development Targets. They are the same—but IDG is a more appropriate designation (R. Manning, email, 21 April, 2019).

30. M. Camdessus (1999), Letter to G. Brown and C. Short, 10 March 1999: IMF Archives.

31. Helmut Schaffer (Executive Director for Germany at the World Bank), email, 27 April 1999.

32. Alex Shakow, comment, 5 May 2019.

33. Alex Shakow, interview, 12 March 2018.

34. When Johnson became minister in 1998, Norway happened to be in the chair of the annually rotating Nordic representation on the World Bank/IMF Development Committee; she kept the chair even after her rotation was over because the other Nordic countries were represented by Ministers of Finance.

35. Alex Shakow, interview, 12 March 2018. Henk van den Dool, who was at that time Herfkens' personal assistant, recalls that 'U4 performances would be perceived as quite direct, overwhelming and forceful. No doubt you recall that the four of you were—especially when not around—also regularly referred to as 'The Spice Girls' or, less benevolently, as 'The Witches of Eastwick': H. van den Dool, email, 1 May 2019.

36. E. Herfkens, Stavern, 21-2 June, 2018, transcript.

37. H. Johnson, Stavern, 21-2 June, 2018, transcript.

38. Development Committee communique, 28 April 1999.

39. H. Wieczorek-Zeul, *Welt Bewegen* (Berlin: Vorwärts Buch, 2007), p. 38.

40. H. Wieczorek-Zeul, Stavern, 21-2 June, 2018, transcript.

41. C. Short, Stavern 21-2 June, 2018, transcript.

42. H. Wieczorek-Zeul, email, 27 February 2019.
43. *Haagse Courant*, 28 September 1999; confirmed in Zalm interview, 28 August 2018.
44. *IHT*, 10 August 1999.
45. *Haagse Courant*, 28 September 1999.
46. E. Herfkens, Stavern, 21-2 June, 2018 transcript.
47. E. Herfkens, letter to Parliament, 27 October 1999.
48. Development Committee communique, 28 April 1999.
49. The other ten were Austria, Belgium, Denmark, Finland, Iceland, Luxemburg, Portugal, Spain, Sweden, and Switzerland; E. Herfkens letter to Parliament, 27 October 1999.
50. H. Johnson, Stavern, 21-2 June 2018, transcript.
51. E. Herfkens, interview, 17 February 2019.
52. Development Committee communique, 27 September 1999.
53. IMF (2017), *Debt Relief Trust Fund Accounts*, p. 26.

4

Utstein

Introduction

Following several months of extensive informal collaboration over the winter of 1998–9 culminating in the spring 1999 Development Committee meetings and the May OECD/DAC High Level Meeting, the four ministers decided to intensify their collaboration by organizing a formal ministerial meeting. Johnson offered to host the meeting at the Utstein Abbey on 25–6 July 1999. Subsequent ministerial meetings were organized by the other members of the group on an annual basis. This chapter discusses the key principles guiding the Utstein group and the main topics addressed in their first ministerial meeting. Subsequent chapters focus on the specific actions implemented on the various issues over the next several years.

The Utstein Abbey Meeting

The Abbey, built in 1265 by Irish and Augustinian monks, is located on Mosterøy, a small island, near the shore off the southern coast of Norway, about thirty minutes from Stavanger. It has a chapel and a small conference centre. 'The cloister lies behind thick walls in a dreamy garden. The sea laps softly against the shore. In the summer the sun hardly goes down and the nights are mild.'[1] Johnson chose it as the meeting place for the first ministerial meeting as it was located near her own home and within her parliamentary district.[2]

The small meeting room contained a large square table with a minister seated at each side, each with two men behind them, their personal secretaries and their Directors General (DGs), that is, the top bureaucrats in their ministries. Koos Richelle, the Netherlands DG at the time, recalls that

> The meeting started without any agenda. The Ministers were talking all the time, only occasionally checking figures and such with the men behind them. Sometimes they were talking through each other, as most of them were used to dominate the floor and push their positions. It was quite chaotic at times: let us do this, let us do that, with the men behind them having a hard time keeping up taking notes. But it became clear early on that opinions very much converged on many important issues, such as on finance for development, ownership, limiting the number of 'focus' countries, identifying countries in which we would work

together, women's issues. In the end it was quite clear what was discussed and what was the outcome: some 35 points of action—even if details were not hammered out and clarified. A lot of the consensus was elaborated later on.[3]

The meetings lasted the whole day. The congenial atmosphere contributed to the development of friendships among both the ministers and their staff. I am told that in the evening they moved from the conference centre to the adjoining chapel, where Henk van den Dool, Herfkens' personal secretary at the time, started to play the piano. He was soon joined by Johnson who sang—she does not remember what—and Herfkens who danced.[4] Koos Richelle recalls the song was 'Swing Low Sweet Chariot', soon followed by the more exotic rhythms of her youth;[5] van den Dool remembers also 'Summertime', with the forward-looking lyrics: 'one of these mornings / you're gonna rise up singing / you'll spread your wings / and you'll take to the sky'.[6]

There were four main themes: first, a passionate desire to focus aid on eradicating poverty. There was too much old-style aid: 'Donor land is Disneyland. Donors have the money to spend on their fads—to make irresistible offers recipients cannot refuse.'[7] This meant that it was necessary first and foremost to respect country 'ownership' (see Box 4.1); 'Donors do not develop countries; they develop themselves.'[8] Developing countries themselves had to get their act together by mobilizing domestic resources, fighting corruption, and establishing coherent policies to address poverty. Thus, assistance needed to focus on well-governed countries for aid to help reduce poverty.

Second, a commitment to implementation; there were too many glorious international resolutions about doing great things, contrasting sharply with poor implementation and continuing to do business as usual. Theirs was a conspiracy of implementation 'a conspiracy to make it happen'.[9]

Third, a recognition that aid alone was not enough, and not even that relevant: there were many other developed country policies affecting developing country prospects, particularly international trade, which had to be congruent with aid if poverty was to be seriously affected.

Box 4.1. The meaning of 'ownership'

Ownership consists of two elements: first, control and second, internalized responsibility. The first implies the existence of independent stakeholders who together give direction and meaning to national development. The second implies the acceptance of responsibility, not because it is imposed from outside, but because it is motivated from within.

Finally, an understanding that these common perspectives on what needed to be done had a much greater chance of success if the four worked together. This meant collaboration among the four countries' bilateral assistance programmes and collaboration among the four ministers and their bureaucracies in influencing decisions made in international organizations and forums. 'We can make a bigger fist at international meetings'.[10] It also involved agreement on which country would take the lead in pursuing which issue; and that not all needed to be involved in all cases.

They articulated their views in a communique issued at the conclusion of the two-day meeting, highlighting eleven key issues that needed to be addressed jointly (with other countries and international organizations) whose main points are reproduced in Box 4.2. The issues included better coordination of economic assistance, debt relief and increased aid flows, coherence of aid with trade policies, as well as actions by developing countries to improve governance, reduce corruption, and implement better poverty reducing policies. And they agreed to meet again the following year in The Hague.

Box 4.2. Press statement—Utstein Abbey, Norway, 26 July 1999 (excerpts)

Four Development Ministers on a Common Course

Donors must coordinate better, put more resources into development assistance and strengthen the multilateral system in order to help developing countries eradicate poverty and support global sustainable development. This was the message of the four development ministers, Ms Clare Short (United Kingdom), Ms Eveline Herfkens (the Netherlands), Ms Heidemarie Wieczorek-Zeul (Germany) and Ms Hilde F. Johnson (Norway) gathered at the Utstein Abbey in Western Norway. On the 25-6 July they met to discuss future strategies for cooperation on a number of development issues. Making a difference in development is the ambition of the network of these four ministers. They identified eleven key issues that need to be addressed jointly with other countries and international organizations. In four important areas the donors in particular need to get their act together:

Increased coordination: All donors must be prepared to adjust their programmes to achieve better coordination and thereby more effective assistance. The recipient country must be in the driver's seat.

Untying of aid: Further untying of development assistance will imply increased efficiency, improved quality, and more development.

Institutional and Financial gap: Closing the gap between humanitarian assistance and long-term development cooperation is vital.

(continued)

Box 4.2. *Continued*

Greater coherence of all policies affecting developing countries: Better aid practices are not enough. Donor countries need to be equally concerned to put in place coherent policies on matters such as trade, investment, and environment which support sustainable development.

We need to see provision of more resources and the setting of new priorities

- *The debt initiative:* Implementing the debt relief measures by the recent Cologne Summit will enable poor countries to allocate more funds for poverty reduction.
- *The multilateral system:* It is vital to support the United Nations and the development banks both through fulfilment of the financial obligations, international coordination effort, and through policy priorities.
- *Financing Development:* Fighting the global poverty menace requires imaginative thinking and action to reinvigorate development financing... We will work together to reverse the decline in ODA. We call for a renewed commitment by all partners concerned to the international development targets, including halving the proportion of people living in absolute poverty by 2015.

The developing countries need to put their act together

- *Combating corruption:* Corruption is stealing from the poor; it is a major obstacle to development...
- *Strengthening democracy and good governance:* Democracy and competent and strong public authorities are the best guarantees for sustainable development.
- *Preventing conflicts:* Peace is a fundamental prerequisite for development.
- *Implementing poverty reducing policies:* Developing countries themselves have to create an enabling environment to stimulate private sector investment, ensure an equitable distribution, and make public expenditure more efficient and transparent.

The Utstein Meeting is only the beginning

The four ministers will continue their collaboration on these eleven key development issues. Ms Eveline Herfkens, Development Minister from the Netherlands, will host the next meeting in the summer of 2000. In the meantime the four ministers will work jointly and separately to carry the Utstein agenda forward.

They communicated their views more widely by publishing the op-ed in the *International Herald Tribune* mentioned in Chapter 3. The *IHT* article summarized the proposals contained in the communique, provided detail on the debt issue, decried OECD countries falling short of the ODA/GNI target for assistance, and identified the World Bank's 'Comprehensive Development Framework', a country planning instrument, as having the potential to become 'an important catalyst for change' in developing countries that decided to adopt it. The article appeared sometime after the actual meeting: in order to ensure ownership of their bureaucracies and thus actual implementation by their own ministries, the proposals and specific language used were cleared by all four bureaucracies. It concludes with the statement quoted in Chapter 1 that there is 'no need more urgent, no cause more noble; no responsibility weighs more on us' than genuine partnership.[11]

From Projects to Budget Support

The sweeping reforms of the U4 bilateral programmes were based on lessons learned from independent evaluations of aid programmes by the DAC, the World Bank, their own evaluation units, or other sources such the Helleiner Report regarding Tanzania, mentioned in Chapter 2. The basic lesson was that without developing country 'ownership', no aid yields lasting results. Moreover, individual donor-designed and -managed projects often ignored the overall policies and responsibilities of the developing country government. For example, many schools and health centres had been built without consideration of whether the poor country could afford to pay for salaries and maintenance after the donor left. The real bottleneck for improving health care and education in poor countries was the chronic shortage of health workers and teachers for which poor countries lacked the resources to train and pay. Instead of thinking about 'our' German or Dutch projects, and imposing our agendas and priorities, the U4 felt that donors needed to focus on 'their'—the developing country priorities and processes.

This perspective led them away from the traditional project-oriented approach to focus on broader budget support for whole sectors. Budget support could not be a blank cheque: it required a minimum level of confidence in the country's development plans, its financial management, and its commitment to improving these. And it would have to go hand in hand with a serious donor–recipient policy dialogue (see Box 4.3). This entailed reaching an understanding regarding the overall development strategy and the quality of the recipient's financial managements systems and providing support for their improvement. Not all developing countries could meet all these requirements to warrant budget support programmes.

Box 4.3. The mosquito-net case

Finance Ministers take policy concerns of donors that provide budget support quite seriously; and they do not have to be part of explicit conditionality: In a 1999 meeting with Ghana's Minister of Finance, to discuss budget support to the Ghanaian health sector, Herfkens wondered casually why mosquito-nets carried the highest VAT rate making their cost prohibitive to most of the needy population. Soon after the discussion, the VAT on mosquito-nets was terminated making nets affordable and spreading their use throughout the country, thus accomplishing far more than any Dutch project that would have provided nets to a few villages.[12]

The U4 also felt that the traditional old-style project aid entailed huge and wasteful transaction costs. Partner governments needed to follow different procedures of dozens of different donors, often operating in the same sector, have meetings with them, and prepare scores of written reports requiring the same information. They felt that the already scarce capacity in poor countries should be focused on managing their development—not satisfying donor procedural requirements. In their view donors should transfer aid management to the partner government, allowing recipients to use their own procedures, and ensure that the use of aid funds is subject to scrutiny by their citizens and parliaments.

Explaining this new approach to their constituents and parliaments was not easy—particularly in the case of the German Bundestag, given concerns about corruption and demands that taxpayers' money should be properly accounted for. Public opinion of donors typically held the view that projects would allow for more donor government control, as if by keeping funding in off-budget projects ensured that it went to the 'right' kinds of expenditures, for example primary education, rather than military spending. But, the U4 felt that by providing funding for the 'right' kinds of expenditures, donors typically released partner governments from the responsibility of providing those same services, freeing up resources within their budgets which could be spent on other things. Money is fungible and trying to ring fence aid by keeping it off-budget in a project simply provided donors with a false sense of security. No external intervention could be isolated from the overall context. Thus, donors might get an illusion of control, but in fact they undermined development effectiveness.

Misappropriation of funds could not be prevented in projects. And, there was no evidence that budget support funds, in practice, had been more affected by corruption than project aid. On the contrary, there was evidence that budget support was ultimately more effective in reducing corruption, as it would lead to strengthening of public finance management. Indeed, the U4 felt that using the recipient's financial systems was key to improving them.

Finally, perhaps the most important argument was that development partners' governance would improve only if government accountability was strengthened: only by using partner country systems could their governments move from accountability to donors (paymasters) to accountability to their own parliaments and people (see Box 4.4).

Box 4.4. The Utstein approach to development cooperation*

Let me explain the division of labour between North and South, by making a comparison with the division of labour between the driver and the passengers in a car:

- The *developing country* should be in the driver's seat;
- We, *the donors*, should be like the passengers; we may check whether the driver has a clean licence, i.e. whether the developing country government has a decent poverty reduction strategy;
- But, we must keep our hands *off* the steering wheel by respecting local ownership of the development process, and by aligning ourselves to local policies and procedures;
- We must not distract the driver with conflicting advice. In a real car we would not force the driver to switch from the left side to the right side of the road. So we must not provide conflicting advice on development. Instead we must harmonize and coordinate, and refrain from imposing irrelevant conditionalities;
- We, the passengers, should also pay our fair share for the fuel, i.e. by keeping our commitment to the 0.7 per cent ODA/GNI target; *but*, when paying for the fuel, we must not demand a particular brand, i.e. Shell or Chevron. That is, we must stop tying our aid, and stop forcing the developing country to buy goods and services from own country.

Having said that, the passengers cannot just 'sit back, relax and enjoy the view'.

- The passengers should care about the car's suspension system and take measures to lighten the load. We need to lift countries' *debt burden*;
- Donors must also help the driver by clearing the road of boulders and fallen trees; particularly those boulders the passengers put there in the first place. This means getting rid of outdated *aid modalities and procedures*, which stand in the way of enabling developing countries really being

(continued)

Box 4.4. *Continued*

in the driving seat and really taking responsibility for their own development;
- It also means donors must break down the walls they have built in the *global trading system*, which prevent products made by poor people in poor countries from reaching our rich consumer markets. Particularly, we, Europeans must change our *agricultural policies*, which destroy rural livelihoods in poor countries.

* Herfkens standard speech to parliamentarians 2002–8

The reduction in project assistance and the focus on countries with poverty reduction programmes resulted in significant reductions in the number of country programmes. Germany reduced the number of cooperating countries from 119 to seventy-five; the Netherlands from more than eighty countries to less than thirty 'focus countries' (concentratielanden);[13] Norway, from thirty-four to twenty-six cooperating countries. Later, Norway reduced the main partner countries even further from twelve to seven, all LDCs. In the UK there was no conscious policy decision to reduce the number of partner countries. However, the emphasis on poverty reduction and ownership probably did reduce the number somewhat, by the termination of programmes in several high-income countries in South America and the Caribbean. Naturally, all reductions took time to implement as the four donors had to design appropriate phase-out strategies with their partners.

The internal reforms also focused on creating awareness of the interconnectedness of other government policy areas with the assistance efforts. Notably, developments in international finance and trade had a direct and indirect impact on development potential. As discussed earlier, what is the point of aid supporting increases in farm production, if these products cannot compete with imports from rich countries which subsidize their exports? Thus, the U4 ministers focused increasingly on creating domestic political awareness of their policy responsibilities with those of other cabinet ministers.

The Bureaucracies

The U4 cared deeply about bringing along their bureaucrats: after all, the lack of implementation that characterized a lot of the international agreements was due to ministers and bureaucracies reverting to business as usual after the ministers returned home. 'In the case of the Dutch and English civil servants, they were happy to be empowered by the U4 to act. The effort was regarded as very helpful as the issues were relevant and reflected what civil servants—be it not in Germany initially—felt should be done.'[14] In order to promote understanding of the linkages between aid and other policies, the Netherlands and the UK established internal 'coherence units'. But, as we will discuss below, not all bureaucrats were happy!

All the above-mentioned internal reforms were executed under the guidance and responsibilities of the U4 DGs. Ron Keller, Herfkens' DG from 2000 on, recalls that

U4 DGs also met on a regular basis without the presence of Ministers. They met at least four times a year on a rotating basis in one of our four countries; sometimes in the margins of U4 ministers' meetings, sometimes free standing, sometimes at headquarters, sometimes at airport lounges or other convenient locations. The Utstein coordination process touched almost all corners of our bureaucracies. Each of my Directors and their staffs had their own U4 coordination meetings. It is fair to say that the intensity and effectiveness of these meetings varied widely, depending on political pressure and actual relevance.[15]

The Networks

The U4 did not have a formal organization or secretariat. However, they prepared agreed 'minutes' for their formal ministerial meetings and follow-up reports on the actions they had agreed to take in them.[16] To achieve their objectives in the international arena, the U4 worked through both official and unofficial networks.

There were several formal networks which provided the main forums for launching and pursuing development initiatives: the first two, the Development Assistance Committee of the OECD and the European Union's Development Council involved only aid donors to developed countries; the third, the World Bank/IMF Development Committee involved both developed and developing countries. Of course, they were all also members of the UN, which on several occasions was the forum for global initiatives affecting development. And they also became actively involved in trying to bring the international financial institutions (IFIs), mainly the World Bank and the IMF, to work together with the UN; and to get donors and recipients to agree on a set of actions that would enhance aid effectiveness and reduce poverty. They did not always agree. But, when they did not, they did not oppose each other publicly. And, given their different national priorities, they found that in different country or policy settings, two or more would act together—and, on occasion, they had to act alone.

Their typical mode of operations was, first, to organize collaboration among the four countries. Once established, there was an effort to expand its applicability by bringing together other 'like-minded' countries such as Sweden and ultimately to involve the rest of the donors for which the OECD's Development Assistance Committee (DAC) was the obvious forum. The purpose was not just to increase involvement and 'ownership' of others—but to ensure sustainability. The OECD had another forum as well: this was the so called 'Tidewater Meetings' which involved annual informal meetings of principals only, that is, ministers and heads of international aid agencies, including the IFIs. On many occasions they tried to get the Development Committee and the World Bank involved because the World Bank is a large donor with headache-causing procedures, and also because it had qualified staff in many areas—though often they had to create and fund a special 'Trust Fund' in the World Bank or the IMF to enable this participation.

Multilateral institutions, such as the Multilateral Development Banks and the UN sometimes did not appreciate the 'ganging-up' by some of their shareholders/ members. However, at the same time, the political pressure exercised by the U4 in governing bodies and international meetings liberated staff in relevant international organizations who shared their agenda to speak out and push for that agenda within their organizations.[17]

The two most important of the non-institutional groups were the G8 and the Nordic Group. Both Short and Wieczorek-Zeul felt that the U4 coalition and its views were useful in influencing positions of the G8, a group whose support was needed for major global initiatives such as debt relief. Short was somewhat concerned, however, that the G8 tended to pick up a different subject each year accompanied with a wordy declaration and no funding commitment. The Netherlands—which had felt slighted when the original G7 was formed as it had not been included although it was a larger donor than Canada or Italy (see Chapter 3, note 2)—was also irritated by the fact it was expected, nevertheless, to foot the bill for such initiatives.

Norway's membership in the Nordic group offered both challenges and opportunities. Of the other Nordics, Denmark and Sweden shared a great number of the U4 priorities. Indeed, Sweden's membership in the EU made it an obvious partner on trade issues, and in 2002 it formally joined the group. On the other hand, there was some concern among the Nordics that the U4 would undermine Nordic cooperation and made them appear as excluded and (wrongly in their eyes) not as 'progressive'. Johnson's bureaucracy was also sceptical for the same reason: was she betraying the long-standing Nordic cooperation? But Johnson was focusing on influence and results, where the U4 had much more potential, while continuing to work with Nordic colleagues, including through their regular ministerial meetings.

The Netherlands was also a part of the Benelux group. Both Belgium and Luxemburg during this period had progressive Development Ministers whose interventions were usually very helpful in the context of the EU Development Council (see Chapter 7) and the OECD/DAC where the quality of the interventions is more important than country size.

The U4 also contributed to the establishment of networks with developing countries in sub-Saharan Africa, for example the 'Big Tables' organized by the ECA providing a forum for dialogue of Development Ministers with Finance Ministers from the region (see Chapter 6); and through that to broader networks of sub-Saharan African countries.[18]

Collaboration is not glamorous. Networking is time consuming and not at all easy. Effective collaboration means that egos have to be put aside, headlines shared and processes established with other bureaucracies in other countries and other cultures.[19] What the U4 achieved in that respect in a short time was due in part to hard work and in part to the strength of their message.

The Utstein Principles

Johnson's participation in the group was interrupted for about a year and a half because of government changes in Norway, and during that time she was replaced by Anne Kristin Sydnes who was invited to join and participated in the Utstein ministerial meeting in The Hague in May 2000. Possibly in response to criticism by the Nordics and others that the group was closed, possibly as a basis of 'enlightening' new members or new ministers, the group decided in 2000 to articulate a set of 'Utstein Principles'. The Netherlands and the UK were tasked to prepare a draft for 'internal use' which emphasized that the Utstein initiative was an 'open and inviting one' and 'different coalitions' would be appropriate for different issues. A copy of these 'Principles' dated 20 October 2000 has survived and is reproduced in Box 4.5. Its substance is very similar to the 'Utstein Communique' of the previous year with the addition of the 'non-exclusivity' principle—which was also explicitly extended to the question of gender.

Concrete Actions from Utstein

While there were no formal minutes of the Utstein meeting, there was explicit written agreement on steps to be taken and which country would take the lead. As Short remembers it, 'The development world was good at conferences. What we did was implement.'[20] This involved an extraordinary number of thirty-five specific actions ranging from debt and 'untying' aid, to development assistance in conflict situations, and identifying one country and one sector in which to showcase a coordinated bilateral assistance approach. In the run-up to the meeting in The Hague, Norway prepared a document called 'A Conspiracy of Implementation' which reviews the progress made on the concrete steps the four ministers had agreed to take almost a year earlier.[21] The responsibility for

Box 4.5. Utstein Principles

The 'Utstein-Group' is a group of ministers responsible for Development Cooperation, working in a concerted way to drive the development agenda forward, focusing on implementing the international consensus. At this point in time, the 'core group' consists of the respective ministers of Germany, the Netherlands, Norway, and the United Kingdom, but the Utstein group is by no means intended to be exclusive. The characteristic is rather of an 'impulse group', with issue- or country-specific loose coalitions.

The composition of the Utstein group at working level may therefore vary from situation to situation. At field level, for example, donor countries that are committed to a specific cause may on an ad hoc basis be part of the Utstein group while at the same time on other levels or other issues they are not.

For the sake of clarity: gender is not a criterion for participation.

Participation
Members belonging to the Utstein core group are strongly committed to the reform agenda and are prepared to use their national and international (political) leverage to help implement that agenda effectively with a wide spectrum of actors. On specific issues this means:

Coherence
The Utstein group strongly promotes international policy at large (e.g. conflict management), trade policy, and other relevant areas with development objectives.

Coordination
The Utstein group is prepared to lower the individual flags in order to improve effectiveness through, e.g. harmonizing procedures and indicators and fostering ownership of the recipient country.

Strengthening the Multilateral System
The Utstein group seeks to strengthen the multilateral system, e.g. by using the leverage of Board and Executive Council membership to improve synergy within the international development architecture through interagency cooperation and enhanced focus on the central development goals (seven pledges).

Partnership with the Recipient Countries
The Utstein group demands from recipient countries to put their own house in order by combatting corruption, strengthening democracy and good governance, preventing conflicts and implementing poverty-reducing policies.

Untying of Aid
The Utstein group strives to support actively the process of untying development assistance by all OECD members. In respect of free-standing technical cooperation, it is recognized that our policies may be guided by the importance of maintaining a basic sense of national involvement alongside the objective of calling upon partner countries' expertise.

Debt Relief
The Utstein group pursues speedy implementation of the HIPC initiative and will actively monitor its poverty focus.

ODA
The Utstein group seeks to increase international ODA flows by striving to reach the UN target of 0.7 per cent of GDP, respectively—for those countries already having crossed that threshold—to sustain and enhance the ODA effort working towards 1.0 per cent of GDP.

leadership on the various issues was balanced and evenly spread around the four ministries.

The first set of actions, related to debt relief, were discussed in Chapter 3. They involved continued coordination of positions in advance of the autumn 1999 World Bank/IMF meetings, sensitizing their Finance Ministers on the need for reform of IMF programmes to make them more poverty oriented, and the complex and difficult discussions involved in the funding of the enhanced HIPC.

The next set involved several concrete steps aimed at increasing the effectiveness of the four countries' bilateral assistance programmes. The focus was on reducing the administrative costs of their aid programmes, with their various conditions and requirements for, among others, procurement, reporting, and evaluation per donor, forced on recipients and increasing the use of partner government systems for project and programme implementation. This resulted in proposals to collaborate in three different areas: auditing, evaluation, and common policy development.

As discussed above they preferred to provide budget support rather than project assistance, either to a specific sector through 'basket funding' (i.e. whereby donors combine their funding in one pot and use one set of procedures) or to the general budget, for countries which combined a good overall poverty-oriented strategy with appropriate sectoral policies, and decent and transparent management of their public expenditures. Sectoral budget support had been previously provided only under the World Bank's sectoral adjustment loans which were often co-financed by bilateral donors. The UK, Norway, and the Netherlands had already provided budget support to several countries, but the concept presented difficulties to Germany. World Bank sector adjustment loans had come under a variety of criticisms including the lack of realism and poverty focus of the policy conditions that had to be met by the recipient. The budget support assistance envisaged by the U4 would have to be provided to a sector/country which already had the appropriate policies in place.

That raised two issues: first, to ensure that the overall country strategy and policies would be supportive; and second, to address the nagging concerns that the provision of budget support would avoid the usual checks and supervision done by the aid agencies and be damaged by corruption. This appeared to be one of the concerns which had previously prevented Germany from funding sector budget support programmes.

As noted in many public pronouncements, the U4 believed that economic aid can only be effective in countries where the partner government had elaborated and 'owned' a comprehensive development plan aimed at reducing poverty. Such plans had been most frequently developed in cooperation with the World Bank which in previous years had helped countries put together the policy framework papers (PFPs), whose most recent incarnation were the so-called Comprehensive Development Framework documents to which the Utstein communique and the *IHT* article had referred in the summer of 1999. Recall in this connection that in the spring and summer of 1999 the Bank and the Trust Fund were being criticized by the Utstein group and others who believed that the HIPC initiative should be linked to poverty reduction strategies. The design and implementation of these strategies became a focal point of U4 interventions in meetings with the World Bank and the IMF over the next several years.

Applying the principle of providing assistance only when partner governments were committed to poverty eradication and had effective programmes in place for this purpose, of course required considerable judgement and tradeoffs: some countries may have been exemplary in their government's commitment to development and poverty eradication but failed miserably in their respect for human rights. In other cases, some of the most oppressed and poor people lived under non-reforming governments. How much and what kind of aid is appropriate in such cases? The U4 recognized and encouraged partnerships with reformers wherever possible including interventions that provided some hope for future change but could not ignore the needs for humanitarian assistance to address the plight of poor people.[22]

More broadly, the U4 were keen in strengthening the multilateral system, as announced at Utstein and in the 'Principles'. This presented some problems for Germany where the Development Ministry and the Budget Committee were very much oriented towards bilateral programs. Wieczorek-Zeul recalls that it was a struggle to allocate more than one third of the aid budget to multilateral aid.[23] The ministers agreed on the need to challenge the UNDP in its role of state building and security in conflict situations; and more broadly to review continuously all UN programmes and organizations, with a view to providing 'constructive criticism'. Their efforts to improve the effectiveness of the multilateral system are addressed in Chapter 5.

In the meantime, the ministers realized that all their efforts to increase aid effectiveness had to be tested on the ground and in connection with a real aid programme to a real country. Africa was very much on the ministers' minds.

Tanzania was the country they chose in late 1999 and to which four ministers travelled in April 2000. A discussion of their visit and their broader efforts to raise aid effectiveness in low income countries is the subject of Chapter 6.

The U4 also recognized that post-conflict countries raised special problems that required different priorities and aid interventions. Aid in conflict situations such as Sudan and the Great Lakes area, which was going through a particularly difficult time, and in post-conflict situations such as Sierra Leone became a focal point of U4 attention over the next several years and is also the subject of Chapter 6.

Finally, the ministers committed to further actions in the DAC and elsewhere to promote the untying of bilateral assistance, a topic that will be discussed in Chapter 9. Notably, at the time there was no explicit push to raise the volume of economic assistance, as neither the UK nor Germany at that point were sufficiently committed to credible increases. This would come later.

What is most interesting about the decisions taken at Utstein is the wide range of initiatives discussed and agreed to pursue already at the first meeting, in the first year of formal collaboration. Although, as will be noted in the following chapters, new topics were introduced in subsequent meetings, the bulk of the topics identified at this first meeting were to dominate future discussions.

Notes

1. Heidemarie Wieczorek-Zeul, *Welt Bewegen* (Berlin: Vorwärts Buch, 2007), p. 36.
2. The Abbey had been used for conferences before, including a famous one in 1990 which resulted in the so called 'Utstein Style' guidelines for reporting of data for out-of-hospital cardiac arrest.
3. Koos Richelle, interview by Eveline Herfkens, 28 August 2018.
4. That there was someone 'dancing' at the first meeting was confirmed by the *Die Zeit* interview (see Chapter 3).
5. Koos Richelle, email, 28 March 2019.
6. Henk van den Dool, email, 1 May 2019.
7. Koos Richelle, interview, 28 August 2018.
8. A quote attributed to Burkinabe historian Joseph Ki Zerbo: 'on ne developpe pas, on se developpe': https://www.burkina24.com/2017/03/11/.
9. *NRC* newspaper, 'Conspiracy of dissatisfied quartet', 27 July 1999.

10. Hilde F. Johnson, in *NRC*, 27 July 1999.
11. *New York Times/IHT*, 'If we are serious about poverty, we do something about it', 10 August 1999.
12. Eveline Herfkens, email, 23 August 2019.
13. Ron Keller recalls that when he was appointed DG in 2000 there were in total eighty-four programme countries in three categories; 'in two years we brought each of the three categories down, but the total was still sixty or more. Bringing the programme countries down was difficult both because the developing countries feared that the Netherlands was retracting and because our own staff were involved in projects in these countries': Ron Keller, email, 30 March 2019.
14. Ron Keller, email, 3 March 2018.
15. Ron Keller, email, 3 March 2018.
16. The staff of the country that hosted the ministerial meeting would prepare a report on follow-up in advance of the subsequent ministerial meeting.
17. Paul Isenman, interview by C. Michalopoulos and E. Herfkens, 2 May 2018.
18. See Leonardo Martinez Diaz and Ngaire Woods (eds), *Networks of Influence* (New York: Oxford University Press, 2009).
19. Sally Fegan-Wyles, email, 18 April 2019.
20. Stavern, 21–2 June 2018, transcript, p. 10.
21. Norway, Ministry of Foreign Affairs, 'A Conspiracy of Implementation', 8 May 2000, follow-up of the Utstein Meeting.
22. Clare Short, email, 7 February 2019, commenting on draft chapters 5–7.
23. H. Wieczorek-Zeul, Stavern, 21–2 June 2018, transcript, p. 1.

5

Aid Effectiveness

The Multilateral Dimension

Introduction

The collaboration launched by the U4 at Utstein covered a wide variety of development issues handled by different domestic and international institutions. Effectiveness of bilateral and multilateral aid was central to their concerns. This involved collaboration in implementing their individual bilateral aid programmes in some countries, as well as coordination of their positions at the World Bank and the IMF (the international financial institutions—IFIs), the Development Assistance Committee (DAC) of the OECD, the UN and its funds, programmes and agencies, and the EU and regional institutions, especially in Africa. The World Bank/IMF were very important both because of the size and extent of their own programmes but also for helping developing countries manage the overall poverty reduction strategies within which all bilateral aid was supposed to fit.

Coherence in poverty reduction strategies and coherence in the support that the developed world was providing were the hallmarks of the Utstein efforts. Thus, it was not surprising that the first items for action following Utstein had to do with debt relief handled by the World Bank and the IMF, as well as the design of comprehensive poverty reduction strategies in support of debt relief and development more broadly. Increasing the effectiveness of bilateral aid could only succeed if it were part of a consistent overarching multilateral effort.

During the roughly half century between the establishment of the UN and the mid-1990s, the international architecture for development assistance reflected the political realities of the Cold War: the bulk of multilateral development assistance was provided by the World Bank in Washington and, to a lesser extent, the Regional Development Banks, all controlled and funded by the OECD countries. In New York, the UN—whose General Assembly was dominated by developing countries with development their main focus—provided a more limited amount of aid through the UN Development Program (UNDP), the United Nations Children's Emergency Fund (UNICEF), the United Nations Population Fund (UNFPA), and affiliated specialized agencies such as the United Nations Educational, Scientific and Cultural Organization (UNESCO), the World Health Organization (WHO), the Food and Agriculture Organization (FAO), and the International Labor Organization (ILO). Of course, all these agencies were also funded primarily by

OECD countries. The relationships with these institutions were managed by different ministries—the UN by Ministries of Foreign Affairs and Ministries of International Development, the specialized agencies often by sector ministers, and the IFIs usually by Ministries of Finance or the Central Bank. The UN and the IFIs, the two international structures that were supposed to promote development, operated almost completely independently from one another. This reflected at the international level the lack of coherence of national policies both in developed and developing countries.

This chapter starts with a discussion of U4 efforts to promote coherent poverty reduction strategies supported by improved aid effectiveness in the IFIs. It then addresses the challenge of raising the effectiveness of UN assistance programmes. The last part discusses U4 efforts to promote collaboration between the two sets of institutions.

Poverty Reduction Strategy Papers

The headquarters of the IMF and the World Bank (the Bretton Woods institutions) are located very close to each other, across Washington's 19th Street. They have the same membership and governing structure and their staff share a country club in the suburbs.[1] But they have different mandates and traditions. Collaboration between the two had been quite common, but there had also been disagreements over policies and jurisdictions resulting, from time to time, in the drafting of formal agreements on who was going to do what in developing countries and countries in transition.

In the summer and autumn of 1999, pressure by the U4 and others on the importance of developing appropriate poverty reduction strategies both in highly indebted poor countries and in general, resulted in closer coordination between the two institutions. It led in the autumn of 1999 to a first ever joint meeting of their de facto governing bodies, the Interim,[2] and Development Committees. The joint meeting, led by Gordon Brown, then UK Finance Minister and new Chair of the Interim Committee, approved the preparation of a series of documents that were to become central to everybody involved in development for years to come. These were the so-called Poverty Reduction Strategy Papers (PRSPs) which from then until 2013 were supposed to be prepared by all highly indebted poor countries as well as all low-income countries receiving assistance from the two institutions (see Box 5.1).

As discussed in Chapter 2, the World Bank culture in the 1990s evolved into giving greater priority to poverty reduction in Bank programmes. But in some respects, this emphasis was somewhat superficial in that there was a tendency to identify 'poverty' projects as opposed to a comprehensive approach where all policies and programmes focused on poverty reduction. The IMF culture was even

---

Box 5.1. Principles of the New Strategy: Country-Driven and Owned

---

Required broad-based participation of civil society in the adoption and monitoring of a poverty reduction strategy tailored to country circumstances;

Results oriented
Focusing on indicators of outcomes that would benefit the poor;

Comprehensive
Recognizing that sustained poverty reduction will not be possible without rapid economic growth, macroeconomic stability, structural reforms and social stability;

Partnership oriented
Providing a basis for the active coordinated participation, of development partners (the Bank and Fund, regional development banks and other multilaterals, bilateral assistance agencies, NGOs academia, think tanks and private sector organizations);

Long-term perspective
Recognizing that poverty reduction will require institutional changes and capacity building and is therefore a long-term process.[3]

---

more distant as it tended to focus primarily on short- to medium-term macroeconomic and balance of payments adjustment.

The rebranding of the IMF's Enhanced Structural Adjustment Facility (ESAF) into Poverty Reduction and Growth Facility (PRGF) was supposed to have changed all this. Recall from Chapter 3 that in the autumn of 1999, as the political winds had shifted, the IMF at the highest level had changed its tune. Yet, although the Managing Director may have been sincerely convinced of the wisdom of changing the IMF's priorities so that some of its programmes could be more long term and poverty oriented, the culture and the staff were more difficult to change. It was in this context that the Utstein efforts beyond 1999 were critical.

In early 2000, Herfkens wrote to James Wolfensohn about four main concerns the U4 had with the PRSP:

(a) at the conceptual level, the social dimension has not yet been adequately addressed and its translation to the policy level is mostly limited to aggregate expenditures on the social sectors . . . I would like to suggest involving the Social

Development Advisors Network to develop the social dimension of the PRSPs; (b) to promote better coordination among all donors, bilateral donors should participate actively in the process of developing the PRSPs under the leadership of the recipient government; (c) while the most attractive aspect of the PRSP is the country-owned nature of the document... for the first year or two we should not expect confident governments orchestrating a national dialogue on poverty alleviation and taking the lead in developing new policies... This implies that the World Bank and the IMF must allow governments adequate space to develop or expand their sense of ownership... and be flexible in the requirements for interim PRSPs, otherwise governments may not have access to debt relief under HIPC; and (d) in light of the consultative nature of the PRSP process, the local representative offices of donor agencies should be encouraged to play a pro-active role in stimulating the PRSP dialogue at the country level.[4]

At their second meeting in the Hague, 12–13 May 2000, the U4 were happy that the PRSP was confirmed as the basic instrument for the development strategy of individual countries but became concerned that the interim PRSP, which was used by the IFIs to provide debt relief to HIPC eligible countries before a full PRSP was prepared, was used randomly. And they planned to write a letter expressing their concerns and later meet with Horst Köhler, the new IMF Managing Director.[5] The letter was to complain that the new IMF programmes did not focus sufficiently on poverty reduction and that there was a need to undertake poverty 'assessments' in countries receiving IMF assistance.

Köhler started his job at the IMF on 1 May 2000 and picked up the poverty issue very soon. He had meetings with both Kofi Annan who sought his support for the Millennium Summit which was to take place in September 2000 (see Chapter 7) as well as Wolfensohn, who invited him to a retreat at his home in Jackson Hole, Wyoming. There, the two of them put together a two-page document articulating the approach that their two global institutions would take in fighting world poverty. Köhler was convinced that the IMF should not be, in his words, only 'a monetary' institution but should join the World Bank to address world poverty.[6] In that respect he was definitely different from Camdessus who had reportedly characterized the World Bank as a 'Big Truck' compared to the IMF 'Ferrari'.

Köhler's first trip, in June 2000, was to Africa—itself a significant choice— where, meeting with a women's group in rural Mozambique, he got a first-hand glimpse of development challenges at the local level: the problem for them was not the big money that the IMF could offer to the government; the need was for microfinance at the village level.[7]

Short and Gordon Brown did indeed send a five-page (!) letter to Kohler and Wolfensohn on 7 July 2000, articulating precisely the concerns discussed in the

Hague meeting. Though addressed to both the Bank and the Fund, the letter focused primarily on IMF programme issues. After a brief review of the progress made in providing debt relief for seven countries and pending action on thirteen more, the letter focuses extensive attention on the IMF programmes:

> Although structural and microeconomic conditions can also be crucial in poverty reduction, we need to focus on those that are central to the success of the anti-poverty strategy, and take a more flexible approach to those where the link to poverty reduction is not clearly established. Our concern is that many of the conditions in the current programmes predate the development of the PGRF . . . The PGRF needs to become more than just an ESAF programme with a supplemental poverty matrix.[8]

Recall in this connection that this was precisely the concern the Utstein ministers had raised the previous year with Camdessus (see Chapter 3, C3P80).

The 'Tidewater' meeting of heads of agencies was hosted by Wieczorek-Zeul in Bonn, Germany a few days later on 9–11 July 2000. Not surprisingly, a report from the meeting noted that 'The Fund's continued role in supporting poor countries through the PGRF was stressed as a high priority and the press reports coming out of the Managing Director's Africa trip cites as helpful in dispelling any doubts on this front. A smaller subgroup was interested in how the PGRF programs would differ from ESAF.'[9]

The IMF issued guidance on 16 August 2000 on 'Key Features of IMF Poverty Reduction and Growth Facility (PRGF) Supported Programs' which had clearly internalized the shift in emphasis. The document states that 'Greater ownership is the single most cited but also the least tangible change in moving to PRGF-supported programs'; but it goes on to discuss ways in which this would be accomplished including by embedding the PRGF in the strategy for growth and poverty alleviation (presented in the PRSPs) and helping countries develop budgets that are more pro-poor and pro-growth.[10]

The Brown/Short letter also expressed the concerns that the U4 had about the interim PRSPs: 'Interim PRSPs needed to be produced for all countries to reach the Decision Point (the point at which a decision is made to grant debt relief), so the requirements need to be light; it is sufficient for the countries to set out the path to developing their strategy.'[11] Finally, the letter addressed the question of what to do in several HIPC countries affected by conflict—an issue of considerable concern to the UK which had extensive involvement in giving assistance to several of these countries, notably Sierra Leone (see Chapter 6): 'Our aim should be to send a clear signal to those countries engaged in conflict . . . that while we cannot commit to debt relief without some kind of track record, we are prepared to offer positive support to those countries willing to commit to peace and to using their resources to tackle poverty.'[12]

The letter did not directly address the issue of doing poverty assessments in HIPC countries. At the end of the day, the U4 paid for these assessments through the Trust Funds that had been set up for this purpose in both institutions. In Herfkens' view, pressure through letters and meetings was sometimes not enough: 'If you want to be sure to change the way international organizations do business you have to pay for enabling the change . . .'[13]

Reflecting their continued concerns, in early 2001, they sent a joint mission to the IFIs, headed by DfID's chief economist Adrian Wood, with expert membership from all four countries, to assess the institutions' work on the PRSPs. The main conclusions of the mission were:

> The Bank and Fund have made good progress in putting poverty reduction at the center of their operations, in re-focusing their work on the PRSP process and in strengthening their relationships with each other and with their partner countries. In the first phase of the PRSPs, the emphasis was on speed and process, but the focus now needs to shift to quality and content. Moreover, the two institutions need to put pro-poor growth more at the center of their PRSP analyses and strategies, along with such important development issues such as gender and the environment. In further implementation of the PRSP agenda, the Bank and Fund also need to develop close working relationships with bilateral donors and other international organizations.[14]

Wolfensohn and Köhler went together to several sub-Saharan Africa countries in February 2001. This was Köhler's second trip to Africa. It was also the first time ever that the World Bank President and the IMF Managing Director had visited developing countries together, a fact that was highlighted in a letter the two of them sent to Short on 23 March 2001:

> We wish to brief you on the outcome of the discussions we held with African Heads of State during recent summits held in Mali and Tanzania. This was the first joint visit to Africa by the Heads of our two institutions and followed a commitment we made at the Annual Meetings in Prague to put Africa at the center of our activities. The primary purpose of the trip was to listen to African leaders about their vision of how Africa can accelerate growth rates, reduce poverty drastically, and position itself to benefit from globalization, and how the Fund and the World Bank can best assist them in these endeavors.[15]

Over the next several years, the U4 pestered the World Bank and IMF leadership in frequent meetings, letters, and other interventions aimed to ensure that the pro-poor focus of their programmes was being implemented. At their Birmingham meeting in November 2001, they felt that 'The time lag between central policy decisions being made on ESAF/PRGF reform and PRSP in the IFIs and their implementation by local offices was often unacceptable.' They agreed to bring this matter up in the forthcoming Development Committee meeting; but as only two of them were to attend that meeting, they decided to send a letter on 15 November 2001 to the IMF Managing Director and to the World Bank President expressing their concerns.[16]

Köhler and Wolfensohn wrote back on 31 December 2001 responding to these concerns inter alia as follows:

> We share your concern that the Bank and Fund (and other donors) need to place greater emphasis on providing technical assistance and policy advice to countries in developing longer-term strategies for pro-poor growth . . . . We fully agree that country ownership is central to the success of poverty reduction strategies . . . . We are very pleased to be collaborating with you in the area of Poverty and Social Impact Analysis [PSIA]. We believe that good progress has been made this year with the launch of the country case studies. However, more needs to be done for PSIA to be undertaken more systematically. To this end, the Bank is producing guidance material and a learning program for staff, as well as developing new tools for analyzing macroeconomic and structural reforms. We very much hope that other donors will follow your lead on this issue and step up their support. For the Fund, PSIA is being reflected more fully in PRGF staff reports.[17]

Köhler started early on the process of changing IMF conditionality to address poverty issues. This required substantial shifts in the organization's thinking away from strictly monetary policy issues to address problems of poverty reduction and development in general. It also required investing in capacity building, for which the IMF did not have the resources. The Utstein ministers were happy to help with a Trust Fund, enabling the IMF to create regional African Regional Technical Assistance Centers (AFRITACs), starting with one in Dar es Salaam, opened in 2002, to provide technical assistance in core macroeconomic and financial management.[18] In a letter to Wieczorek-Zeul on 16 May 2002 (and similar letters to Short and Herfkens), he wrote:

> I am writing to thank you for the financial contribution that Germany has pledged in support of the IMF's *Africa Capacity-Building Initiative*. I was heartened by your personal support during the recent IMFC meetings and the fact that the IMFC communique explicitly supported the Initiative. I have just returned from a multi-country trip in sub-Saharan Africa—my third since I have taken up my duties at the IMF—during which I had extensive discussions with heads of state, and senior officials, representatives from civil society, and NGOs. The trip further convinced me of the necessity to help countries in sub-Saharan Africa to strengthen much needed capacity to design and implement sustainable poverty reduction strategies. The reaction to our Initiative was enthusiastic, and the

dozen representatives I met from the countries to be covered by the first two regional centers (AFRITACs) are looking forward to the supplementary technical assistance they will provide.[19]

Since then, the programme has expanded to fifteen regional centres across the south of Africa, and in the topics it addresses. Today it is still growing; and it is still supported by, among others, Germany, the Netherlands and the UK.

It had been quite an effort for Köhler in particular to get his organization on board for the new approach. Herfkens recalls that in one of their meetings Köhler said: 'From my office here (on the 12th floor) I might have reached the 6th, but not much further down—let alone our representatives in the field.' In a recent interview he recalls that his staff were originally surprised by the emphasis shift but were willing to provide him with the needed information and while 'not exhibiting too much energy, were always loyal'.[20]

Issues about the IMF's role and its staff continued: At the 2002 'Tidewater' meeting in Norway on 11–13 July, Masood Ahmed reports that concerns were raised about: '(a) the perceived inflexibility of our macroeconomic framework; and (b) while acknowledging progress in our practice . . . in the design and review of programs, there remains a perception that many Fund staff only do this reluctantly and sporadically'.[21] Kohler has scribbled in a handwritten note on the Masood Memorandum, 'Please make a suggestion how we can overcome staff hesitation.'

PRSPs were also discussed at the fourth ministerial U4 meeting that took place in Germany on 17–18 July 2002, where the focus was on what to do about countries that had PRSPs, but which were 'poor performers'. On this occasion as well, they agreed to raise the matter both in the next Development Committee meeting and at another joint World Bank/UN/DAC event.[22]

United Nations Reform

Kofi Annan wrote to the U4 ministers a week after their article appeared in the *IHT* in August 1999, telling them that he shared their view that poverty is above all a 'moral problem' and that 'we must act to wipe out the shame of absolute poverty over the next sixteen years'.[23] The UN's role in development and what can be done to reform of the United Nations system was already on the U4 agenda from their earliest discussions: one of the actions coming out of the Utstein meeting had been a 'Review of all UN programs and organizations as basis for constructive criticism', which was to be followed continuously with the Netherlands and the UK being the 'lead countries'. The follow-up notes a 'comprehensive report that had been received from the Netherlands and will serve as a valuable tool for Norwegian policy formulation'.[24]

In a speech at the Rockefeller Foundation in New York on 26 October 1999, Short said:

> The UN's development impact is well below its potential. It needs to move beyond projects to try to lead and drive forward the IDGs with each agency focusing on its core role and the whole working much more collaboratively. The time of vying between UN agencies is over. The UN has unrivalled authority and legitimacy in developing countries. Its role must be strengthened to help developing countries put in place the strategies needed to meet the targets.[25]

She followed up the speech by negotiating reform programmes with each UN agency, offering increased funding if the programmes were implemented.

There were two distinct dimensions of the reform issue: the first was the question of UN agency reform itself, the topic of this section; the other had to do with its relations with the World Bank, which will be discussed in the section following.

In 1997 Kofi Annan had created the UN Development Group, consisting of all relevant UN agencies to improve the effectiveness of UN development activities at the country level, headed by Mark Malloch Brown who also headed the UNDP and had previously worked at the World Bank. In late 1999, the U4 sent a letter to Kofi Annan proposing a meeting with him and the UN secretariat to discuss ways that they could work together in addressing the problem of poverty in the new millennium. The letter stressed that 'leadership from a strengthened UN system will be critical in achieving the targets for reducing poverty' as 'part of a properly coordinated effort'.[26]

Mark Malloch Brown struggled on two fronts—he recognized the need to change UNDP's culture to enable adequate reform and for the organization to live up to the new responsibilities leading the United Nations Development Group (UNDG). At the same time, specialized agencies like the FAO did not want to be 'coordinated' by the UNDP, and even the UN Funds and Programmes did not welcome stronger coordination. Gro-Harlem Brundtland, Director General of the WHO and Juan Somavia, Director General of the ILO were exceptions who were willing to coordinate activities within the UNDG at the headquarters level. Coordination in the field, however, remained a challenge.

Malloch Brown also had problems convincing the G77, the group of developing countries organized in the 1960s and politically active in all UN bodies, of the need for UNDP reforms, which included focusing on fewer programme areas, and introducing a new programme area, building national capacity for 'good governance'. In early December 1999 he visited Herfkens in The Hague and Johnson in Oslo to enlist their support for such reforms. Herfkens and Johnson committed that the U4 would intervene proactively with the G77 in New York, explaining that generosity for the UNDP, which would translate into UNDP support for their national programmes, would depend on the degree reforms were implemented.

Herfkens also informed Malloch Brown about the evaluation study of the UN agencies that she had commissioned (see Box 5.2). Malloch Brown welcomed the external evaluation but noted that further UNDP ambitions relative to more effective UN coordination would have to wait until UNDP reform had been achieved. He then invited Herfkens to address the meeting of UNDP Global Resident Representatives in New York in late February 2000 to underline the urgency with which relevant donors regarded the need for UNDP to reform.

Box 5.2. The Berteling Report

As noted above, in early 1999 Herfkens had commissioned a study on UN–World Bank relations from Jan Berteling, a long-time UN expert. Beyond the recognition that the UNDP and the World Bank continue to live in separate worlds, the study concluded that:

- the structure and procedures of the World Bank and the various UN bodies are not compatible; the centralized World Bank cannot relate to the decentralized UNDP. Cooperation between organizations depends more on happenstance (familiarity with other organizations, knowing individuals) rather than formal agreements;
- UNDP insists dogmatically on its coordination mandate while the World Bank is bigger, better equipped, more powerful, and richer;
- Many respondents in New York were critical of an 'American slant' in World Bank staff who are seen as arrogant, something that 'the Bank seems to regard as a badge of honor';[27]
- The UNDP was perceived to be more effective on political economy issues;
- The World Bank was finally making the link between macroeconomic issues and poverty, ownership, participation, and good governance. It was embracing targets and strategies agreed on at UN summits and conferences. All this should be welcomed, yet the UNDP saw that as a threat to its mandate.
- In internal communications, Wolfensohn stressed the need for the World Bank to cooperate with UN bodies and his alliance with Kofi Annan is of great importance.

The study recommended Dutch government action to improve coordination among the governing bodies of the various organizations and in particular 'that cooperation within the UN system and between UN bodies and the World Bank merits our constant attention'.[28]

Before she did this, she cleared a letter with her U4 colleagues about the issues she planned to raise in her speech. The letter was hard-hitting: while it recommended that UNDP play a central coordinating role for all UN activities in individual countries it urged the Programme to 'stop trying to do everything and anything' because it resulted in a 'scattered, un-strategic programme' which seriously undermined UNDP's credibility.[29]

Her speech a week later, on 28 February 2000 was even more hard-hitting. She quoted some of the conclusions of Dutch representatives in developing countries regarding their experiences with the UNDP: that its programmes lacked unity and had more people and vehicles than necessary and that the UN had a lot of local staff representing many agencies, each with their own agenda, which impeded the establishment of a coherent programme of support. She recommended that the UNDP build capacity at home, becoming a true centre of excellence for governments that needed help with democratization, peacebuilding and good governance; be able to deploy that capacity fast; and become the lead agency representing all UN agencies in meetings coordinating assistance at the country level.[30]

'The speech by Herfkens came as a shock to the 200+ senior UNDP staff present. Mark had been saying the same, but it had been easy for those opposed to change to attribute his proposed new direction to his World Bank background. Hearing one of our strongest donors say this was a game changer.'[31]

The minutes of the Hague U4 Ministerial on the subject were terse: 'UN people of the U4 countries are requested to compare notes on the assessment of UN programs and on the follow-up of UN conferences and report back.'[32]

The U4 had a long meeting in Bonn at staff level in the summer of 2001 to compare notes on each delegation's appreciation of the various UN programmes. In preparation for the meeting, DfID reported that the Netherlands had organized a staff-level meeting in January 2001 in which the Dutch and UK representatives exchanged assessments of the UN bodies that they had performed; the Dutch reported that they were conducting another wide-ranging survey of Dutch embassies in developing countries on the performance of multilateral agencies; and they all agreed that 'follow-up process to UN conferences contained weaknesses not addressed'.[33]

Not all representatives of multilateral agencies were happy to collaborate with the Dutch review. In one instance an IMF resident representative refused to respond to the Dutch embassy's questions and requested IMF management to inform the Dutch executive director that communications with IMF staff should go through the executive director's office and not directly in the field.[34]

At Birmingham in late 2001, the minutes report that the ministers 'discussed the need to improve their own evaluation processes. They also agreed to develop proposals for a joint meeting in New York as soon as possible, including with representatives from Denmark and Sweden.[35] In 2002, the U4 promoted the establishment within the OECD of the Multilateral Organisation Performance

Assessment Network (MOPAN), designed to monitor and assess the performance of multilateral organizations, including the UN and MDBs at the country level. The Network still exists today, as part of the OECD. It includes most OECD donors and still makes regular assessments of a large number of multilateral organizations (see Chapter 11). Both Herfkens and Johnson believe, however, that over time, the assessments have become less critical as well as less influential.[36]

The issue of the meeting with Kofi Annan continued to be on the agenda for a while including in Wiesbaden in the summer of 2002. But by that time 'the ministers were unclear as to what a visit to New York will achieve'.[37] The meeting with Kofi Annan and the U4 ministers as a group never materialized formally. But individually they met with him frequently, both on a formal and an informal basis at various international meetings, often in New York, but also in Ottawa, in late 2001, so that no formal meeting needed to be arranged.

Kofi Annan did focus on UN reform. In the fall of 2003, he devoted a major part of a retreat of the chief executive board (consisting of the thirty-one executive heads of all UN agencies, the Bretton Woods institutions, and the WTO) to multilateral reform. Johnson was invited to provide the keynote address on global multilateral reform and how the leaders could make the system work better.[38]

In 2005, Annan appointed a high-level commission to propose reforms to the UN development assistance system: Ruth Jacoby, who had served as Executive Director for the Nordic and Baltic countries at the World Bank in 1990s and subsequently was appointed Sweden's ambassador to the United Nations Economic and Social Council (ECOSOC) was one of its members and Koen Davidse, currently the Netherlands executive director at the World Bank, was its research director.

The Commission's report, *Delivering as One*, echoed both the diagnosis (e.g. regarding fragmentation) and the earlier recommendations made by the Utstein group:

> The UN's work on development and environment is often fragmented and weak. Cooperation between organizations has been hindered by competition for funding, mission creep and by outdated business practices. There are many of overlapping functions, failures of coordination and policy inconsistency within the UN system. It also burdens the capacity of developing countries to deal with multiple agencies. Of 60 countries analyzed by the Panel, 17 country teams had an annual budget of less than US$2 million per agency. More than a third of the UN country teams include more than 10 UN entities, some more than 20. The cost of doing business with the UN is thus too high for both recipient countries and donors. Without authoritative leadership by the UN Resident Coordinator, and system wide ownership of the Resident Coordinator system, incentives for better coordination remain limited.[39]

A Tale of Two Cities

In the 1990s the end of the Cold War and the changing world economic order with the ascendance of China and the membership of all fifteen states of the former Soviet Union in the IFIs changed the political realities in New York and Washington. But the traditional suspicions and lack of communication and cooperation between the two sets of organizations in the two cities continued.

In the autumn of 1998, following meetings of the Development Committee in Washington, Herfkens, on her way home from Washington DC, started to visit the UN in New York to address ECOSOC (regarding the subjects discussed in Washington) on their outcome. In October 1998, she said:

> The UN as a world forum with a strong normative function and the World Bank with its powerful resource base are two partners that were made for each other. A marriage made in heaven. But somehow the two have never been properly introduced. The responsibility rests with our countries, which are both members of the UN and shareholders of the World Bank but fail to coordinate in our capitals... At home we use separate bedrooms as well with each Ministry responsible for its own Specialized Agency: the Ministry of Health for WHO; Agriculture for FAO; Trade for WTO; and obviously Finance Ministers and Central Bank Governors run the World Bank and the IMF... We have to learn to speak with a single voice from each capital.[40]

In February 1999, for the first time ever, the World Bank executive board and its President visited officially the United Nations in New York and a programme of New York visits by the World Bank vice Presidents in charge of lending operations for different regions was also organized. So, the introductions were finally made just in time for the cooperation needed for a major UN initiative timed to be launched at the beginning of the new century.[41] But actual collaboration in the field was still a long way off.

Jacoby wrote a few years ago:

> When I came to our mission in New York in 1999, not even two years after having left the Board of the World Bank, I was shocked to find I was in a completely different universe. In the Second Committee of the UN General Assembly we spent weeks negotiating a resolution on 'Debt of Developing Countries' but to my knowledge not a single delegation got instructions or even consulted their respective Ministries of Finance. The same went for trade. The Paris Club, the forum to renegotiate official bilateral debt, was completely unknown in the drafting groups in New York as were the latest WTO negotiations. UN matters were the unique playground of our Ministries of Foreign Affairs; those in our capitals who were responsible for economic issues in the real

world (outside the UN) were at best uninterested, at worse contemptuous. To try and bring the worlds of Washington and New York together, to start a dialogue between them, the Philadelphia (halfway between these two cities) Group was founded by some like-minded countries of the Utstein Group as the core. Eveline Herfkens championed and supported the concept when she still was together with Ruth Jacoby on the Board of the World Bank. The idea was to meet with our own colleagues in the other institutions, to compare notes, exchange information and discuss our differing approaches to a common agenda. It was great fun and extremely useful. In practice, we never actually met in Philadelphia, but were hosted alternatively by colleagues in Washington or New York.[42]

Once a minister, Herfkens used the reports by this group to confront relevant countries when their respective representatives continued to take contradicting positions, which helped improve Bank/IMF–UN collaboration in the run up to the Monterrey Financing for Development Conference in 2002 (see p. 111).

Koen Davidse, a Dutch diplomat, who like Jacoby first served on the World Bank board and subsequently moved to the UN mission in New York, also recalls that it was Herfkens' idea to set up such a group and that he gave its actual name. He believes that the group helped both in promoting policy consistency and in monitoring statements of country representatives in the two cities and alerting the ministers back home of possible inconsistencies. The Netherlands, the UK, and Sweden representing the Nordics were the first three countries that met as the 'Philadelphia Group' for the first time in November 1999 in New York with Germany joining later.[43]

In the next several years, relations between the UN, the World Bank, and the IMF were considerably strengthened in connection with the UN-led Millennium Development Goals initiative (see Chapter 7). Kofi Annan, James Wolfensohn, and Horst Köhler, the leaders of the three institutions during this period, who had developed good personal relations among themselves, were the main architects of these improved relations at the headquarters in New York and Washington.

In May 2000, to promote greater understanding between the two institutions, Jacoby helped organize a Philadelphia Group meeting of some permanent representatives of the UN in New York with the executive directors of the World Bank in Washington. Köhler, in a recent interview, recalled 'a very helpful Swedish Ambassador to ECOSOC at the time (obviously Jacoby!)' and that he invited ECOSOC representatives to meet for the first time with the IMF Board.[44] But problems continued to exist in the field between the Bank and the UN. Johnson reports that, especially in post-conflict situations, there were continuous battles between the World Bank and the UN as to which institution would have the leadership role in coordinating assistance (see Chapter 10).

Delivery as One concluded that 'Over time both the Bank and the UN institutions have gradually expanded their roles so that there is increasing overlap and duplication in their work. There is a balance to be struck between healthy competition and inefficient overlap and unfilled gaps. The Bretton Woods Institutions (BWIs) and the UN need to work more closely together to remove unnecessary duplication, and to build on their respective strengths.'

Conclusion

There is little doubt that the Utstein group played an important role in making the PRSP process more focused on poverty and participatory. According to Masood Ahmed, currently President of the Center for Global Development (CGD), who at the time was a senior World Bank and later IMF official:

> We must credit Utstein for helping ensure that within the Bank poverty became instead of just another sector the overarching objective of all the Bank's programs; and that the PRSP became the overarching framework not just for the Bank but for all external efforts including the IMF. Having four voices in harmony enabled them to set the agenda and push it consistently across all international institutions. The conducive international environment helped but without the U4, it would have been a lot harder to achieve this kind of progress.[45]

As regards the UN, *Delivering as One* generated momentum, championed by the UN Development Group (UNDG), with the four main agencies at the core: UNDP, UNICEF, UNFPA and WFP. Ruth Jacoby wrote in a recent communication: 'one cannot draw a straight line between the U4 and UN reform—only a dotted line. Many of these ideas were also very much part of an intensive multilateral discussion on UN reform, policy coherence and aid effectiveness which had been ongoing in many countries and international fora for several years.'[46] However, the reforms undertaken suggest that in the UN the four Utstein ministers' voices were clearly heard. According to Sally Fegan-Wyles, who served as the secretary to the UN Development Group in New York, 'you have no idea how often I used to refer to you four, when I was trying to get the UN agencies to get serious about reform. You were the only stick/carrot that was strong enough to make them consider change.'[47]

Over time it became apparent that the reform effort continued to face challenges at the country level, not least with the specialized agencies and UNDP's coordination role. The UN undertook a formidable evaluation of *Delivering as One* in eight countries in 2011. This evaluation was championed by Johnson, who at the time was deputy executive director of UNICEF, playing a critical role as a driver of UN reform within the UNDG. The evaluation was intended as a tool for pushing through more forceful reforms of the UN development system at the country level. The results of this evaluation and the role played by Johnson in promoting collaboration between the Bank and the UN in fragile and post-conflict states will be discussed in Chapter 10. Actual collaboration in the field still very much depends on the situation in individual developing countries, the strength or weakness of the partner government, and the attitudes of the local representatives of the international organizations.

Notes

1. Each institution has a resident Board of Executive Directors organized in 'constituencies' of countries based on the shares each country member has contributed to the capitalization of the IMF. Certain constituencies (e.g. Germany, the UK, and the US) are 'one country' constituencies. Norway belongs to the Nordic constituency with Sweden, Denmark, Finland, Iceland, and the Baltics. The Netherlands leads a constituency of twelve countries including Bulgaria, Cyprus, Israel, Macedonia, and Ukraine.
2. Renamed a year later the International Monetary and Financial Committee.
3. Based on an IMF/IDA operational issues paper of December 1999; later versions (see April 2001 PRSP sourcebook), dropped references to the need to 'increase growth' and to 'macroeconomic stability, structural adjustment . . .' in the third principle, and talked vaguely about 'multidimensional aspects of poverty'; also in the fifth principle there was no separate listing of the various 'multilateral' and 'private sector' partners.
4. Eveline Herfkens, letter to James Wolfensohn, 9 February 2000, Netherlands Archives, dossier 2.10.
5. Minutes of the Hague 2000 Ministerial.
6. Horst Köhler, interview by Eveline Herfkens, 20 February 2019.
7. Horst Köhler, interview by Eveline Herfkens, 20 February 2019.
8. Gordon Brown and Clare Short, letter to Horst Köhler and James Wolfensohn, 7 July 2000, UK DFID Archives.
9. Masood Ahmed (2000), Memorandum to the Managing Director, July 17, IMF Archives.
10. See https://www.imf.org/external/np/prgf/2000/eng/key.htm.
11. Brown and Short, letter to Horst Köhler and James Wolfensohn.
12. Brown and Short, letter to Horst Köhler and James Wolfensohn.
13. Stavern, 21–2 June 2018, transcript, p. 5.
14. Adrian Wood, mission report, 7 February 2001, Netherlands Archives, dossier 13.
15. James Wolfensohn and Horst Köhler, letter to Clare Short, 23 March 2001, IMF Archives.
16. Minutes of the Birmingham 2001 Ministerial.
17. Horst Köhler and James Wolfensohn, letter to Gordon Brown and Clare Short, 13 December 2001, IMF Archives.
18. Köhler, interview by Eveline Herfkens.
19. Horst Köhler letter to H. Wieczorek-Zeul, 16 May 2002, IMF Archives.
20. Köhler, interview by Eveline Herfkens.

21. Masood Ahmed, memorandum to IMF Managing Director, 16 July 2002, IMF Archives.
22. Minutes, Wiesbaden Ministerial, 2002.
23. Kofi Annan, letter to Eveline Herfkens, 18 August 1999, Netherlands Archives, dossier 3.12.
24. Norway, Ministry of Foreign Affairs (2000), 'A Conspiracy of Implementation', 8 May, follow-up of the Utstein Meeting. This is apparently a reference to a study of the UN and the World Bank that Herfkens had commissioned to J. Berteling, a Dutch UN expert in early 1999, before the Utstein meeting itself (see below, p. 68).
25. Clare Short, speech, 26 October 1999.
26. Eveline Herfkens, letter to Kofi Annan, 29 November 1999, Netherlands Archives, dossier 3.12.
27. Jan Berteling, *Relations between the World Bank and UN Bodies* (The Hague: Ministerie van Buitenlandse Zaken, 1999), p. 7.
28. Berteling, *Relations between the World Bank and UN Bodies*, p. 8. His report states 'that the "Philadelphia" meeting I proposed in my interim report dated February 24, 1999, has now taken place'. As is common, the successful 'Philadelphia' experiment (see below pp. 71–2) has many parents.
29. Eveline Herfkens, letter to Mark Malloch Brown, 20 February 2000, Netherlands Archives, dossier 3.10.
30. Eveline Herfkens, speech to UNDP, 28 February 2000.
31. Sally Fegan-Wyles, email, 18 April 2019.
32. Minutes, Hague Ministerial, 2000.
33. Bonn meeting, Netherlands Archives, dossier 3.2.
34. Eveline Herfkens, Stavern, 21–2 June 2018, transcript.
35. Minutes, Birmingham Ministerial, 2001.
36. Johnson called it 'another paper tiger': Johnson, email, 3 February 2019.
37. Minutes, Wiesbaden Ministerial, 2002.
38. See https://news.un.org.en/story/2003/10/84092-un-chief-executives-board-begin-its-fall-2003-session-tomorrow.
39. UN, *Delivering as One*, Report of the Secretary General's High Level Panel (New York: United Nations, 2006).
40. Herfkens had tried to bring the world of the UN and the World Bank together earlier on when she brought the head of the ILO to address the World Bank board in 1995 in the aftermath of the Copenhagen summit. She gave a version of this speech first at the Development Committee in September 1998. The version produced here was based on a Tokyo speech a few weeks later on 19 October 1998. She recalls the difficulties of participating at the ECOSOC: if a country was not a member its representatives had to wait until all ECOSOC members had spoken before being able to address the group.
41. See UN, *Progress Report on Cooperation between the UN and the Bretton Woods Institutions*, processed (New York: United Nations, 1999). But cooperation at the local level was a long way off.
42. Ruth Jacoby, letter to C. Michalopoulos, 30 January 2017, quoted in Constantine Michalopoulos, *Aid, Trade and Development* (Cham: Palgrave, 2017), 213–14.

43. Koen Davidse, interview by E. Herfkens and C. Michalopoulos, 5 January 2019.
44. Köhler, interview by Eveline Herfkens.
45. Masood Ahmed, email, 12 June 2019.
46. Ruth Jacoby, email, 7 February 2019.
47. Sally-Fagan-Wyles, email, 9 March 2018. Herfkens was active in promoting UN reform until the very end: in early July 2002, after her party lost the elections but before the new Dutch government was constituted, she participated in a UN-sponsored meeting on UN reform in New York for which she received a thank you letter from Deputy Secretary General Louise Frechette: Louise Frechette, letter to Eveline Herfkens, 10 July 2002.

6

Aid Effectiveness

The Bilateral Dimension

Introduction

This chapter starts with a description of some of the specific steps the Utstein group took to streamline their aid procedures in order to reduce the burdens imposed on partner countries and increase effectiveness in the implementation of their bilateral assistance programmes. This is followed by a similar discussion of U4 efforts to help improve the effectiveness of EU aid in which three of the four ministers were involved. Economic assistance provided by the European Union is not strictly speaking bilateral aid, as it is provided through the European Commission, very much a multilateral entity. However, unlike aid provided by the IFIs, the regional development banks, or the UN, recipients hardly play a role in the governing structure of the institution. Though there are some joint structures, for example the ACP/EU Council of Ministers, these do not get involved in programme financing decisions which are taken by the EU alone.

The chapter then turns to a discussion of the U4 aid to Tanzania which four of them visited in 2000 as a showcase of what they had been advocating. As they delegated decision making to their local representatives, based on the agreed Utstein principles, actual coordination of bilateral programmes took place mostly in the field.

They spread their message about a new approach to development cooperation in which the partner country is in the driver's seat by organizing so called 'Big Tables' with African leaders (including Ministers of Finance) that permitted a frank exchange of views on ways to make aid more effective in achieving poverty reduction. The final part of the chapter reviews U4's support to fragile states, focusing on their joint efforts in several countries, including the Democratic Republic of Congo, Sierra Leone, and Sudan.

The First Steps

Recall from Chapter 4 that a key component of increasing aid effectiveness was to reduce aid recipients' administrative burdens. In pursuit of this objective, the U4, as a first step, requested their four Auditor Generals to cooperate in developing common accepted standards of auditing and reporting. The standards were to be made flexible and responsive to the standards already adopted by recipients. Norway organized a meeting in Oslo in June 2000 which was also attended by other Nordic Auditor Generals. The meeting was instructed to also consider standards for aid provided in the form of budget support. The Auditor Generals met several times subsequently and eventually this work was integrated in the DAC work on harmonization of donor practices.

In early 2000, the evaluation units of the U4 countries prepared a joint paper with proposals for intensified cooperation on several issues which the ministers endorsed strongly at their second meeting in The Hague. They emphasized the importance of strengthening the developing countries' own institutional capacity in this area. Over time, the U4 undertook many joint evaluations with Utstein partners and others, with different countries taking the lead on various issues: for example, on basic education (the Netherlands), the UNFPA (Germany), decentralization (Germany), peacebuilding (Norway—examined later in this chapter), and budget support (multi-donor—see Chapter 11).

An important dimension of the new approach was to focus on the results of programme interventions. To do this it was necessary to develop information on outcome indicators, which in turn required the strengthening of developing country statistical capacity. After considerable deliberation involving U4 statisticians and the OECD, it was decided to hold a meeting hosted by the DAC on 18–19 November 1999. Short, who had been working on this issue for some time, campaigned in the European Council meeting the week before for as broad and as high a level attendance as possible. The DAC meeting decided to establish Paris21, a 'Partnership in statistics for development in the 21st century'. This was, and still is, an international consortium in support of statistics capacity building in developing countries with the participation of the UN, the EU Commission, OECD, the IMF, and the World Bank. The consortium, which is housed in the OECD headquarters in Paris, continues its work in developing countries and has also been asked to develop several indicators that measure progress in achieving the Sustainable Development Goals. Its motto on its website's first page is a quote from Short's speech at its establishment:

We are a disparate group but hope united by a common belief in the value of good statistics and a commitment to do better.

In addition, the UK and the Netherlands committed substantial funds to a World Bank Trust Fund providing support to developing countries in this area. The UK and the Netherlands were also collaborating with the DAC in the development of so-called 'Key-sheets' which summarized 'state of the art' perspectives on development policies in various sectors. In order to ensure that all four countries were on the same wavelength regarding the policies they would be recommending in countries, the two countries shared their perspectives with Norway and Germany.

These initiatives were important only in part because of what the U4 were able to accomplish with their programmes. Perhaps even more important was that their efforts resulted in the establishment in 2000 of a DAC Task Force on harmonization of donor procedures, chaired by Richard Manning, Director General of DfID, which, as we will discuss below, led to proposals which were ultimately adopted by the DAC and the World Bank and still later by the whole donor community.[1]

From the very beginning of their collaboration the U4 also placed high priority in addressing the corruption issue in a balanced way: Johnson launched a new strategy to combat corruption in her first policy paper to the Norwegian Parliament in May 1999, stating that: 'Corruption is stealing from the poor.... It is not only politically, socially and economically unacceptable. It is morally reprehensible.'[2] Herfkens, in a speech at an anti-corruption conference in The Hague stressed that 'In the North, the perception is that the South is the problem. The developing countries point the finger at the North for provoking the phenomenon... The truth is: we have met the enemy and indeed it is us'.[3] In May 2000, U4 organized a conference in Maastricht during which an Action Plan was prepared with the following four main components and objectives:

(a) Strengthen the international anti-corruption framework, principally the OECD anti-bribery convention. The objectives of this component were to promote adherence to and additional adoption of the OECD Convention and support efforts to curb money laundering and improve standards of corporate governance.

(b) Provide coordinated support to developing countries committed to fighting corruption. This was to be accomplished through the inclusion of anti-corruption programmes in partner country PRSPs, as well through support of the implementation of common, integrated approach programmes in specific partner countries.

(c) Improve the capacity of developing countries which are Utstein partners to protect development assistance programmes from becoming subject to corruption. For this purpose, the Utstein countries would provide support in strengthening developing country financial management and procurement systems; coordinate and strengthen sanctions against corrupt suppliers and institutions; increase transparency in donor systems and operations, and improve developing country capacity to design anti-corruption strategies.

(d) Learn from the experience of others and develop resources for anti-corruption activities. To accomplish this, they planned to establish capacities to monitor and review anti-corruption activities and exchange information.[4]

Each of the countries committed to introduce appropriate policies in their assistance programmes to implement these commitments. In the case of the UK this was done by having DfID include the promotion of domestic legislation against money laundering and bribing as an important aspect of actions in development cooperation, while the three other countries placed responsibility for the overlapping concerns of international anti-corruption activities in other government departments.

In addition, they agreed to support the anti-corruption efforts of the World Bank, enhance the support they provided to Transparency International and, as with other initiatives, promoted collaboration with other DAC/OECD members. Johnson, for example, had a meeting with the USAID Administrator in which she suggested U4 interest in working with the US on anti-corruption measures. Ultimately these efforts contributed to the DAC approving in 2006 the 'DAC Principles on Donor Action on Anti-Corruption'.

Perhaps their most lasting contribution in this area was the establishment of the Utstein Anti-Corruption Resource Centre at the Chr. Michelsen Institute in Bergen, Norway, which still exists today. The Centre's mission is to provide operationally relevant research, information, and training services to help practitioners in its donor agencies develop a better understanding of anti-corruption issues and more effective approaches to reduce the negative impact of corruption on development. Donors now include the original Utstein nations (except the Netherlands), plus Australia, Denmark, Finland, Sweden, and Switzerland.

European Aid

The EU Commission was and still is a substantial source of ODA, accounting for 11 per cent of total ODA in 1998–2002 and 10 per cent in 2015–17. The assistance is funded by contributions of the member states, some assessed, some voluntary. Its programmes had started primarily as a means of helping French colonies in sub-Saharan Africa. From 1958 to 1984 all the Development Commissioners were French, balanced by Directors General, always from Germany. Eventually, the programmes evolved with the accession of the UK in 1973 to include previous UK colonies. But there were also programmes to Latin America, Asia, the Mediterranean, Eastern Europe, the former Soviet Union, and so on, developed at different times. There was extraordinary fragmentation and ad hoc policies reflecting changing EU foreign policy priorities.

At the time the Utstein ministers appeared on the scene there were two main programmes: the first with a focus on the former colonies in the Africa, Caribbean, and Pacific (ACP) regions; and the second for Asia and Latin America (ALA) with the two together accounting for about 60 per cent of the total EU assistance budget. But there was also a programme for Mediterranean countries, aimed at creating eventually a free trade area; a technical assistance programme for countries that would be candidates for accession to the EU; a programme to support economic reform in the former Soviet Union; and a humanitarian aid spigot as well as 'functional' programmes on such topics as the environment. There were two main Commissioners and Directorates with mandates in the area: the Development Directorate and 'RELEX', the Directorate for External Affairs, but others had a role as well. The ministers did not like what they found. Clare Short said in an interview with the *Financial Times*:

> The European Commission's programmes have huge potential to do good, but they are much less effective than they should be...the Commission is the worst development agency in the world. The poor quality and reputation of its aid brings Europe in disrepute. In the midst of this sorry state of affairs, there are some encouraging signs. The new Commission is committed to a wide pro-gramme of reforms...in particular to speed the abysmally slow delivery of aid. But the EU also needs to improve vastly the quality of its programmes as well as the speed of implementation. Otherwise, we will have bad programmes delivered quickly.[5]

The DAC peer review of the EU aid programmes in 1998 was very critical as well. It recognized that the Maastricht Treaty of 1993 provided the broad, general basis for EU development cooperation, but beyond this guidance,

> to find EU's development cooperation policies applicable to any given sector or geographical area it is necessary to enter a thicket of regulations, resolutions, declarations and communications for which there is no road map...There is no coherent Commission-wide development strategy or statement on development cooperation and the policies on country macro-economic and sector approaches, project and programme identification, implementation, procurement and evalu-ation lack Commission-wide consistency and coherence.... Over the years the splintered administrative and policy culture at the Commission has tended to focus too much on procedures, inputs and operational processes and not suffi-ciently on implementation, outputs and results.[6]

> The Maastricht Treaty clearly sets out the goal of fostering the campaign against poverty in the developing countries...Although poverty reduction is said to be an overarching objective, this is not completely apparent in the Commission's operational programming...Lip service to the poverty goal will no longer suffice.[7]

From her experience as an MP ratifying various agreements with ACP coun-tries, and as representative for several countries in transition at the World Bank, Herfkens had a dismal view of EU aid and doubted that it was even worth spending energy on it. But witnessing Short's fighting spirit in the EU's Development Council, she joined the battle. Their efforts did not bear much fruit the first year.

With the Romano Prodi-headed Commission in September 1999, a new Development Commissioner took office: Poul Nielson, the former Danish Development Minister and very much on board with the Utstein agenda. He recruited as his new Director General for Development Koos Richelle, who had been Herfkens' DG and was deeply steeped in the 'Utstein' principles. They both got to work to make significant changes in EU aid programmes. And the U3 in the European Development Council was very helpful in empowering Nielson among his Commissioner colleagues, giving him the needed policy blessing for his reforms.[8]

The U3 was disproportionally influential, the more as Denmark and Sweden were in agreement with them on most issues. These five were the only ones of the fifteen EU countries which had a cabinet-level Development Minister, and they had large bilateral programmes. As a result, they tended to dominate the debate and the decisions over the majority, most of whom did not agree with the Utstein agenda.[9]

In the Development Council meeting of 11 November 1999, Nielson outlined his new policy intentions: priority for poverty reduction, diminish bureaucracy and check lists, decentralize more, complementarity with members' bilateral aid, and an integrated strategy for humanitarian aid. Short and Herfkens emphasized the importance of poverty focus, coherence, measurable results, ownership, untying, and a link to the IDGs.[10]

Nielson presented his concrete plans and proposals at the Development Council meeting of 18 May 2000. Herfkens reported to her Parliament that

> Poverty reduction is to be the overarching objective. The Commission has expertise and can have value added with a focus on integration of the developing countries in the world economy, regional integration, structural adjustment— linked to the PRSP, infrastructure, transport, food security, good governance and human rights. The challenges are: unclear division of labour among the various Commissioners; staff shortages; inefficient regulations (80 regulations must be complied with); the need to move away from projects to sector support; and from *ex ante* monitoring to measuring output and impact.[11]

Herfkens and Short were also keen on moving the Commission towards providing assistance in the form of budget support and to pay for recurrent costs in countries exhibiting strong programme ownership. This was especially important because of the traditional difficulties the EU faced in disbursing aid— attributed to so-called 'absorptive capacity' problems in poor countries but in reality often caused by myriad donor procedures. They did not want the

Commission to try to coordinate bilateral assistance of EU donors in the recipient countries as this would have resulted in yet one more bureaucratic layer. They preferred the country to do the coordinating in the context of the agreed PRSP. Wieczorek-Zeul was keener on emphasizing the 'European' dimension of the assistance. All three wanted a much larger share of the European Development Fund to go to poorer countries.

Progress was slow. In the Development Council meeting of 31 May 2001, the Commissioner compared the reform process to 'repairing a failing motor. We are at the stage that it is totally taken apart; now we need to get new spare parts and put it together again.'[12]

The reform was finally put in place in late 2001/early 2002. It consisted of the establishment of a new body, 'EuropeAid', responsible for monitoring, evaluating, and implementing all programmes. Programming would be based on multi-annual Country Strategy Papers. The number of financing instruments was reduced. More sector lending was expected to reduce the time lag between commitment and disbursements, and the Commission became, and still is, one of the largest donors of budget support.

Somewhat later a new General Affairs and External Relations Council (GAERC) was established which absorbed the Development Council. This resulted in a de facto downgrading of the Commission's development focus— although the Development DG's continued to meet, chaired by Richelle, providing the opportunity for the U4 DG's (with Sweden instead of Norway, the latter not being an EU member state), to continue cooperation even after the U4 no longer met at ministerial level.[13] Further changes were made in subsequent periods aimed at focusing the assistance more towards low income countries and LDCs—all changes that were strongly advocated by the Utstein members.

Wieczorek-Zeul, recalls that 'When I became Minister in 1998, there were all sorts of problems with EC development policy: lack of coordination and coherence, long and complicated procedures... Since then, a lot of positive things have happened. European development policy has become more focused, the aid to poor people in need reaches them faster. Those are major accomplishments.'[14] How much of this resulted in permanent changes in EU practices will be discussed in Chapter 11.

Tanzania

Coordinated pressure in meetings of international bodies was one avenue for promoting change. Equally important was the demonstration effect of working effectively together in assisting individual countries. The U4 were visiting their partner countries, all time improving their bilateral programmes in ways that reflected the values they had agreed in Utstein. But they decided to make a joint visit to Tanzania as a way of solidifying their cooperation as well as showcasing their efforts. Tanzania was chosen for a variety of reasons: it was a country in which all four had large programmes. It was a highly indebted poor country with a new government which was in the process of developing a poverty-oriented strategy and negotiating an interim PRSP with the World Bank and the Fund. And of course, it had been subjected to the most awful administrative burdens by donors with dozens of uncoordinated projects. By that time everybody working in or on Tanzania had read the Helleiner report and the dysfunctional aid relationship it described (see Chapter 2, p. 16).

The quartet that descended on Dar es Salaam on 10 April 2000 included Anne Sydnes from Norway who had replaced Johnson earlier that year after a political crisis resulted in a government change. Over two days, they met with President Benjamin Mkapa, several cabinet officers, parliamentarians, NGOs, and, in a meeting chaired by Sally Fegan-Wyles, the UN resident coordinator with the DAC group, the local representatives of bilateral aid agencies. Their message was by now standard: the government should be in the driver's seat in putting together a national poverty alleviation strategy which should be 'owned' by the government and society at large; donors should increase their collaboration and coordination; efforts should be made to reduce Tanzania's administrative burden for implementing aid programmes.

According to Benno Ndulu, who was working as a lead economist for the World Bank at the time of the ministers' visit (and had previously participated in compiling the Helleiner report and was subsequently and for more than a decade Governor of the Central Bank of Tanzania), Tanzania had already started to implement some of the Helleiner report recommendations: there were weekly meetings under the leadership of the Ministry of Finance and the donors using a public expenditure review as the heart of the policy dialogue. President Mkapa had bought in to the process which included analytical work that was fed into a joint budget framework with clear allocation of resources derived from both domestic and foreign aid. The draft budget was discussed publicly with the involvement of civil society and parliament.[15]

Ndulu recalls that the U4 visit gave powerful support to a collaborative process that had already started but some parts of the government were still wavering and not all donors were on board: 'This blessing from the highest level led to a "golden age of budget support" as even Japan feeling isolated moved its support into the budget framework.'[16] James Adams, who was at the time World Bank Director in Tanzania and who according to Ndulu deserves credit for changing the World Bank's attitude and launching a collaborative approach, said that the 'stars had already aligned, before the U4 appeared'. In partnership with Sally Fegan-Wyles, the UN Representative, he had started to organize local consultative groups to promote donor coordination: 'The U4 visit was very inspiring. It provided an extra shot in the arm and was helpful in getting more donors involved. The presence of the group was very powerful and particularly helpful as the four ministers representing progressive donors—and especially Clare with her "Old Labour" credentials—told the Tanzanians to reform and to take the initiative in capacity building.'[17]

The visit stimulated discussion on a wide range of topics of which the four most important were debt relief, health, and, in particular, HIV/AIDS, the importance of education, and a recent Tanzanian report on corruption.

On debt relief, the U4 expressed satisfaction that the decision to grant debt relief had been reached the week before and emphasized that the resources freed should be used to reduce poverty.

On education, a representative of the Nyerere Foundation, a local NGO, said that without investing in education Tanzania could not reach any level of development. But the Ministry of Education and Culture could not enrol more students because it did not have enough funds to recruit teachers. He concluded that there was a need for total debt cancellation so that funds could be used for education.[18] The ministers pointed to the IDGs which included universal primary education as a target to be achieved by 2015. They also referred to the World Education Forum that was to take place in Senegal later that month which was expected to 'highlight the need for greater commitment and stronger action to achieve primary education for all children. We recognize the constraints facing Tanzania and other countries in sub-Saharan Africa, but we believe that the collective commitment that should result from the Dakar forum will enable significant progress to be made.'[19]

Adams recalls that

unlike many countries which felt external pressure to increase education expenditures, in Tanzania President Mkapa both took ownership of the decision to increase education expenditures and was a vocal ally of the Bank's efforts to move from project support to education sector operation. We ended up with a sector loan that was quickly supported by the Netherlands and subsequently used to mobilize broader donor support for education. I particularly appreciated the Dutch support because I had personally assured President Mkapa that a sector loan would be a better instrument to attract support from beyond the Bank.[20]

Short also committed the UK to £30 million in support of primary education, conditioned on the education being provided free of charge to everybody. On this, she had to argue with the Education Minister, who, consistent with the World Bank views at the time, continued to believe in imposing user fees (see Chapter 7).[21]

The link of education to debt relief was highly relevant: the interim PRSP which the World Bank and the IMF were discussing with the Tanzanian government involved the cancellation of US$2 billion of Tanzania's debt based on a somewhat less detailed and comprehensive strategy document, but which enabled the institutions to provide up-front debt relief without waiting for the long drawn out process of completing a PRSP. This led the U4 to repeat their mantra: 'Debt relief must guarantee that the money saved should be used in health, education and other social sectors.'[22] 'And the government should include an anti-HIV/AIDS strategy in a national poverty alleviation plan that it was drawing up (in connection with the Interim-PRSP).'[23]

Shortly before the ministerial visit, the government had received the so-called 'Warioba Report', a Tanzanian initiative which exposed massive corruption in the state machinery. Some local commentators had argued that national efforts to combat corruption would not succeed without international participation.

> While the Ministers expressed willingness to help Tanzania in its fight against corruption, they made it clear that the core impetus must come from within Tanzania and not from international initiative. 'Corruption is like stealing from the poor', Herfkens said; 'There is a lot you can do in your own system', chimed in Short and, commenting on how to kick-start the local initiative, Wieczorek-Zeul advised 'to implement transparent budgeting and to involve in the battle NGOs which had a role to play.[24]

> On HIV/AIDs the U4 called at all their meetings with the Government, civil society and others for top level political commitment to more effective campaign to improve awareness and reduce the rate of transmission of the infection. Tanzanian Ministers claimed publicly that this was now getting a higher profile including in Mkapa's New Year message, but others the U4 met, made clear that top level government commitment was still lacking.[25]

Adams recalls in this connection that the Utstein visit was especially helpful:

> I had met with President Mkapa before the Utstein team arrival and as we briefly reviewed potential issues, I expressed two concerns. One was that there might be noise on economic reform from the 'left-leaning' members of the visit and the other was my concern that the Government's HIV/AIDS effort was moving slowly. In practice the Utstein team gave a forceful message on the priority of reform right up front during the visit—eliminating that issue. On AIDS the strong message from the Group to President Mkapa turned out to be timely and effective. After the Utstein visit President Mkapa provided much more forceful leadership to the AIDS effort and the program finally began to come together.[26]

The meetings with the local representatives of the World Bank, the UN and the local donor staff were extremely important: they helped in putting together the health sector loan supported by the four countries. This was an important breakthrough as Germany had not at that point financed a budget support programme, sectoral or otherwise. Providing budget support was a critical dimension of the 'new-style' aid that the U4 promoted. Project-style aid managed by the donors undermined local systems and responsibilities; and, given fungibility of resources, did not at all guarantee that programme objectives would be achieved. But most importantly, budget support contributed to the development of sustainable in-country systems and effective donor collaboration over the whole range of donor programmes.

The four ministers left a communique which focused on more effective joint working by donors. The communique repeated the by then well-known message: '30 donors, funding 1,000 separate projects and sending 2,000 aid missions annually. This is using up Tanzanian administrative capacity that should be devoted to strengthening government systems.' They committed themselves to a 'concerted effort to promote more effective joint working... to reduce transaction costs and increase effectiveness by strengthening joint programming, and harmonizing appraisal procurement, funding arrangements accounting, auditing, monitoring and evaluation.'[27]

After they left, they also sent President Mkapa a letter which said, in part:

We recognize the scale of the challenge that lies ahead for you. The issues you face are complex and sensitive. We understand too the burdens that you, as the Head of State, bear. [See Box 6.1.] But we do feel that there are some issues on which your leadership own role is particularly crucial. We hope that in the areas of HIV/AIDS, tackling corruption and pursuing the implementation of education reform you will take a more prominent public profile on these issues in Tanzania. We are ready to offer further assistance in all these areas in the context of our joint efforts to make development assistance more effective.[28]

At their second ministerial meeting in The Hague soon after their return from Tanzania, the ministers judged the visit to have been a success. A letter to their embassies describing the visit as 'best practice' resulted in joint action initiatives among the U4 in Zambia and Ethiopia. It was agreed that Norway would identify other Nordic countries' presence, particularly in developing countries, in order to develop more synergies between the U4 and other Nordics. Later evidence shows that Dutch aid money was channelled through DfID in Malawi while Swedish funds were channelled through the Dutch embassy in Mali; and Swedish funds were in due course administered by Norway in Malawi. 'Utstein'-type groups were established in several countries. For example, such a group was active in Vietnam with the participation of Sweden.[29] But early on, Germany cautioned regarding budget support that 'the results of the joint efforts need to be assessed before joining other efforts to pool financial resources in sector budget support programmes'.[30]

Box 6.1. Tanzania: radars and education

Soon after the U4 visit, Short and the UK faced a different challenge: contrary to the understandings regarding development priorities, Tanzania signed a contract with British Aerospace for the provision of an expensive radar system. The arrangement 'smelled' of corruption from the start and Short opposed it, going against her Prime Minister and the narrow interests of the UK firm. The Tanzanians went ahead anyway, although many in the country knew and appreciated her stance as she proved to be committed to Tanzania's interests rather than to those of the British export industries. Later it turned out that British Aerospace was found guilty of corruption in a UK court as they had paid a huge bribe to a Tanzanian and paid a fine. Short remembers that in the meantime DfID had made a 50 million UK pound commitment to Tanzania's primary education. She recalls that she was able to convince President Mkapa to cancel the second phase of the radar contract, else the aid intended for primary education would in effect have paid for the corrupt contract.[31]

The 'Big Tables'

The U4 efforts to spread their message to the rest of Africa found a willing and capable collaborator in the person of K. Y. Amoako, who was then Executive Secretary of the UN Economic Commission for Africa (ECA). Amoako, who knew Herfkens from the time that he was director at the World Bank while she was on the Bank's board, had invited her to address a meeting of ECA Finance Ministers in Addis Ababa on 6 May 1999. Her speech emphasized that donors had imposed unnecessary burdens on recipients, were erratic in their commitments, and undermined recipients' management and institutions. She committed to a new attitude based on partnership, so that the recipient government could be in control; and emphasized that 'reforms were needed both in making donor pro-grammes more coherent and focused on development needs, and in making recipients' public expenditures better coordinated and managed'.[32]

A few weeks later Amoako participated in the 'Tidewater' meeting of heads of aid agencies in Turnberry, Scotland, as did Herfkens, Johnson, and Short. These meetings of aid leaders, which had been going on for several decades on the personal invitation of the DAC chair (with the original conference held in Williamsburg, in the Tidewater area of the state of Virginia in 1968) permitted the participants to discuss important issues in an informal setting without staff. Amoako had attended his first Tidewater meeting the previous year in Nara, Japan, at the request of DAC Chairman Jean-Claude Faure. He found it refreshing how directly the ministers spoke to each other, so he said he jumped at the chance to return the following year to Turnberry. What happened next is best described by Amoako in his own book on African development, *Know the Beginning Well*:

> During the two-day conference, it was obvious that my participation helped amplify the African voice among the OECD ministers and decision-makers. I had met most of them the year before, but at Turnberry I felt like I was really getting to know some of them on a personal level. Our exchanges were more candid, and many ministers repeatedly sought my opinion as talk turned to Africa's debt overhang, financing for development, and trade and globalization policies. I formed a close bond with a few ministers in particular: Clare Short from the United Kingdom, Eveline Herfkens from the Netherlands, and Hilde Johnson from Norway. These women seemed locked in on finding new ways to reform the aid dynamic and I became good friends with all of them.
>
> During a coffee break, three of us were sitting around talking about the conference in general and they told me how helpful it was for them to be able to hear directly from an African so closely involved with African development policy. They said they had learned a lot just listening to me talk. And then it hit me, an uncontrollable urge to state the obvious.
>
> 'You always meet in these reclusive settings and you're all always talking about Africa, but I'm the only African here,' I said. 'It doesn't make sense.'
>
> 'So why don't you have a meeting in Africa that you invite all of us to?' one of the ministers, though I cannot recall which, shot back. 'And get some other Africans there.'
>
> It was like a light bulb went off in our heads at the same time. Of course, we should do that, I thought. So, 16 months later, we held our first Big Table meeting. The Big Table opened up a whole new way for the two primary groups of actors on both sides of the development spectrum to interact.[33]

Over the next three years ECA organized three 'Big Table' meetings and a special Big Table session at the World Bank/IMF meetings in October 2003 to discuss ways to increase aid effectiveness and broader African development issues. The Big Table concept created a dialogue between aid ministers with reforming developing country Ministers of Finance and/or Planning on a wide range of issues related to effective development assistance. The novelty was in enabling African Ministers of Finance—as a group—to candidly express their problems with donors who explicitly invited them to do so—something they did not dare to do in bilateral relations fearing that they should not be biting the hand that fed them. Among these African Finance Ministers were Luisa Dias Dogo from Mozambique, who later became Mozambique's Prime Minister; and Donald Kaberuka from Rwanda who later became President of the African Development Bank.

Big Table I took place in Addis Ababa in November 2000 with the participation of twelve African countries, nine bilateral donors (in addition to U4, Canada, France, Sweden, Switzerland, and the USA) and representatives from the IFIs, ECA, and the African Development Bank (AfDB). The topics were by now familiar: the PRSP process, the trade-offs between the speed of delivery of debt relief versus the quality of the PRSP, the needs for capacity building in Africa, and a new topic: the link between the IDGs (which by then had been transformed into the Millennium Development Goals (MDGs) (see Chapter 7) and development programmes and aid resources.[34]

Big Table II (Amsterdam, October 2001) involved the participation of a similar number of African countries, donors, and institutions. The meeting focused on African ownership and responsibility for assuring good governance practices. Several questions were again raised about the PRSP: has the PRSP increased the absorptive capacity of donor funds? How can the PRSP process help the move away from aid dependence? It was noted that a second-generation PRSP process should consider giving more resources to the good performers. Furthermore, the meeting agreed that the new development partnership required a fundamental shift from externally driven conditionalities to self-monitoring and peer review of progress towards mutually agreed outcomes. Finally, the meeting endorsed the principle of an African peer review mechanism espoused by the African leaders as a key pillar of the New Partnership for Africa's Development (NEPAD) launched earlier that year by the African Union.[35] The African peer review process was patterned after the DAC donor peer review process that had been functioning effectively for many years. Amoako, who at the initiative of Herfkens was the first African leader to address an informal DAC High Level Meeting lunch, was instrumental in making this happen.[36]

NEPAD was a topic that concerned the third Utstein Ministerial that took place in Birmingham, shortly afterwards, on 4–5 November 2001 (with Canada and Sweden joining the second-day discussions). Johnson, who by then had returned as Norway's Minister of International Development, introduced a paper which argued that in the NEPAD agenda African leaders were franker on issues such as corruption than they had been in the context of the African Union earlier; and that both the peer review process and the code of conduct of good governance were valuable steps. The peer review process has continued to this day, though several observers both from the region and from the outside have suggested that the process is not as effective as originally envisaged as it has become politicized.[37] The U4 'attached particular value to African leadership of the initiative. They favored an approach based on mutual accountability—both the Africans and the international community making commitments and then delivering on them as discussed at the ECA Big Table meetings'.[38] However, in their subsequent meeting in Germany in the summer of 2002, they expressed 'concerns about the effectiveness of the peer view process.'[39]

Big Table III (Addis Ababa, 17 January 2003) focused on 'mutual accountability between African countries and their development partners in ensuring development effectiveness. The meeting agreed on a set of commitments to be monitored by both sides of the partnership and a framework for doing so. In addition to improving aid quality and quantity, Africa's partners should also aim to ensure coherence of their aid, trade and debt policies with the MDGs' (see Chapter 7).[40] Short put this system into practice in DfID's Rwanda programme with an independent body monitoring how far both sides kept to their commitments.

It was also agreed to hold a special session of the Big Table in connection with the autumn IMF/World Bank meetings, which focused on Africa's financing needs. Such a session occurred on 28 October 2003 and had an interesting agenda: in addition to discussions about the quantity and quality of aid, it raised one new issue, the response of the IFIs to exogenous shocks; and a reiteration of an old problem: the new IMF Poverty Reduction and Growth Facility did not try hard enough to create macroeconomic space for policies and expenditures to promote growth and poverty alleviation. Both discussions led to further improvements in the IMF policies and practices in later years.[41]

This detailed discussion of the Big Tables stimulated by the ECA and the U4 is of great interest for two reasons: first, for the frank exchange of views between a number of donors and African partners of what needed to be done by the donors to improve the quality of their assistance and reduce the administrative burdens imposed on them; and on what partners had to do to improve their governance. Second, and most important perhaps, because these exchanges led in a few years' time to more formal international agreements among a much larger group of donors and recipients about how to increase aid effectiveness. The Monterrey Consensus and the Rome, Paris, and Accra agreements on aid effectiveness later in the decade owe a great deal of debt to the work initiated by ECA, the U4, and their African partners.

Fragile States

Fragility, conflict, and violence (FCV) create additional development challenges that threaten to undermine even well-conceived poverty reduction strategies. Recent World Bank estimates suggest that today two billion people may live in countries affected by FCV in thirty-eight countries, more than half in Africa.

At the turn of the last century there were conflicts both in sub-Saharan Africa and elsewhere. Yet our understanding of the interaction between FCV and poverty was quite limited. Early on, even before they formalized their collaboration, Herfkens and Wieczorek-Zeul had worked together in Macedonia/Kosovo. At the very first Utstein meeting in July 1999, it was clear to the U4 that a different approach was needed to deal with conflict and post-conflict situations than under the poverty reduction strategies being developed at the time. They decided to make Sierra Leone a pilot country for U4 post-conflict assistance and to give the UK the lead coordinating role. In 2001, they embarked on a joint visit in the Great Lakes area—the Democratic Republic of Congo, Burundi, Rwanda, and Uganda. Sudan also had high priority, but this was more related to crisis operations and peacemaking, as the war was still ongoing at the time. In all these cases the U4 tried to collaborate and learn from each other in addressing the fast moving and complex challenges in these countries.

Sierra Leone

The UK was deeply engaged in Sierra Leone before any Utstein involvement. Following several years of brutal civil war an agreement was reached in Lomé, in July 1999 that provided for the disarmament, demobilization, and reintegration (DDR) of rebel forces and the establishment of a government of national unity. The agreement was supposed to be supported by a UN peacekeeping force, which had started arriving earlier. Short immediately paid a visit to the country, to discuss how the UK could best help promote peace and democracy in the wake of the agreement; and with the extensive process of reconstruction since the civil war. She shared her findings and views on the role of development cooperation regarding peace and security at the first meeting in Utstein.[42] Alas, soon enough, rebel activity reassumed: 'a peacekeeping force was deployed, when there was not yet a peace to keep'.[43]

Nevertheless, with fits and starts, demobilization and disarmament reassumed, despite obstruction from rebel forces, and the Trust Fund for DDR needed to be replenished. Short organized a donor conference in London in March 2000, attended by many high-level bilateral and multilateral donors. At such conferences too many donors often repackage old commitments, inflating their actual contributions. Short, however, ran the pledging session with an iron fist: she only gave the floor to those with new pledges and criticized those whose pledge she thought was puny, including the representative of the European Commission. Following a break in the meeting the Commission increased its pledge. The conference yielded $175 million in new aid. Alas, two months later, by the time of the second Utstein Ministerial, the rebels had started to attack the UN forces and threatened to capture Freetown, the capital. In response to a request by Kofi Annan, the UK sent a force first to evacuate UK and European nationals who remained and then to help defeat the rebels and train the new Sierra Leonean army.

The agreed minutes of the U4 Ministerial in May 2000 state that 'the top priority now is to stabilize the situation and get Sierra Leone back on track. In this respect continued engagement of the donor community was considered vital.

Then a professional evaluation of the UN involvement should be undertaken with recommendations on how to strengthen these types of UN operations.'[44] After peace was re-established, 'DfID funded and organized police advisers to help establish a police force and the long, painful task of rebuilding ministries, resettling rebel fighters, and putting in place structures to challenge the endemic corruption began.'[45] The three Utstein partners also responded positively with additional contributions. Within two years indeed peace was established, the rebels were disarmed, the territory all under the control of the legitimate government, refugees and displaced people returned home; and the country held peaceful and competitive democratic elections. Sadly, despite considerable efforts, corruption continued to be a major problem.

The UK also prepared a strategy paper on the lessons to be learned from the Sierra Leone experience with a special emphasis on demobilization and rehabilitation. The paper focuses on four main themes: improved security; regional stability; improved governance, political development and tackling corruption; and fostering a just and inclusive economy and society. It notes that reducing poverty and inequality is essential to sustaining peace and security and suggests that Sierra Leone is passing through an intermediate phase between conflict and full peace requiring continuing efforts to improve local security and regional stability, as Sierra Leone is 'in a bad neighborhood' adversely affected by developments in neighbouring Liberia.

The strategy observes that despite the fact that donors are few in number, coordination is weak; improvement requires leadership from the government, which has been lacking, but hopefully will be forthcoming from a newly established PRSP unit.[46] It concludes with the recommendation that the UK, having invested so much, needs to continue to be engaged with substantial financial assistance 'working with other major donors, especially the Utstein Group, the EU and the IFIs'.[47]

Since then Sierra Leone has stabilized and has gone through several peaceful multiparty elections and transfers of power and is now regarded as one of the more successful post-conflict transitions. This would not have been achieved without the leadership of the UK, prompted very much by Short, who convinced Tony Blair to commit British troops to remain to get the situation under control, and whose leadership was essential for post-conflict reconstruction.

The Great Lakes

'The Great Lakes proves how development and conflict are linked.'[48] This is how Short recalls the major Utstein effort to help support the peace process through development assistance provided to parties in the longest and biggest African war. Short had previously visited the Democratic Republic of Congo (DRC), Rwanda, and Uganda many times. Uganda was already a priority country for all three ministers, and very familiar to all of them. This time, it was decided that three ministers, Herfkens, Johnson, and Short, would visit four countries, the DRC, Burundi, Uganda, and Rwanda, as well as the stronghold of the rebel RCD-Goma in Kisangani over a period of four days, 11–14 February 2002. They used the Dutch government's plane, but they were also forced to cross the Congo River in what is called a 'pirogue', an event immortalized in the lower image in Plate 4.

The trip objective was to start a process of engagement which would 'impress on the regional actors the importance of progress in the peace process through development and poverty reduction' and to 'improve understanding of the development needs of the countries concerned and to promote donor coordination including regarding humanitarian aid, peacebuilding, human rights and democratization', a tall order for one trip.[49] There were a multitude of problems: in the DRC, the young Kabila had just come to power and there was a need to promote disarmament, demobilization, repatriation, reintegration, and resettlement of armed forces as well as reconstruct parts of the country. The Rwanda-supported rebels in Kisangani had to be persuaded to stop harassing the UN troops in East Congo. And there was a need by all parties to cooperate and stop doing unpleasant things to each other: Rwanda had to withdraw from the DRC; the DRC had to stop supporting groups that were attacking Rwanda and Burundi; and Uganda had to withdraw from North East Congo and influence the rebels there to participate in peace talks. There were also tremendous domestic political and economic challenges in all the countries, including violations of human rights. The visit's main thrust was the need to take a regional perspective for stability and progress to be achieved, engaging with heads of state in all four countries.

All of this was politically complex and has proved intractable. The instruments that the Utstein group had at its disposal were persuasion, influence in relevant international organizations and forums, and, last but not least, money. The UK, the Netherlands, and Norway had substantial programmes in Uganda based on the Utstein principles, while the former two engaged in a similar fashion in Rwanda. The Dutch had contributed 110 million euros to a World Bank Trust Fund set up to help the DRC with disarmament, demobilization, and reintegration. Short, with Herfkens' help, promised to help revive a railroad from Kisangani to Kindu, provided the rebels stopped harassing the UN and permitted it to use the airport facilities in the two towns. At that time Short remembers she was trying to persuade the DRC that if they cooperated on peace issues, the UK would provide a development assistance programme.

Later, the DRC became the focus of a massive international programme, badly managed in Short's view, in which the Utstein partners did not have significant roles.[50] But after this early visit the three ministers left feeling hopeful; 'I am frightened how hopeful I am', said Short.[51] Indeed, for a while, it appeared that the UN peacekeeping operation was making progress. But eventually the situation deteriorated again. The railroad was not built because the feasibility study showed it was not cost effective compared to road transport. A road link was under consideration when Short left office in 2003.

Sudan

For many years before and after the U4, developments in Sudan had preoccupied the international community. Johnson was part of the 'troika' consisting of the US, the UK, and Norway, which pushed for and finally succeeded in securing peace in Sudan. Sudan was also on the U4 agenda, but with the UK and Norway as the most active. Johnson recalls: 'As part of the division of labour in our group, I took on more of the Sudan portfolio and Eveline Herfkens instructed her officials in The Hague and the Ambassador in Khartoum to take their cues from Norway.'[52] Both she and Short were engaged in the lengthy and tortuous negotiations that ultimately led to peace and the comprehensive peace agreement for Sudan in 2005.

It was hoped that the full implementation of the agreement would lead to a just peace for Sudan, where the country would remain united: a 'New Sudan', the term used by both sides. If this did not materialize, South Sudan was guaranteed self-determination and the right to a referendum on its independence within six years. Key to sustainable peace was the provision of peace dividends for the people. Development assistance was essential for this purpose.

Johnson's experience is presented in detail in her *Waging Peace in Sudan*, in which she writes that collective donor effort had been in preparation even before the peace process produced any results:

> We wanted to be ready in the early post conflict period in order to avoid the mistakes in other countries of an 'aid-gap' of six to ten months... The process included donor meetings with broad participation in the Netherlands in April 2003 and in Oslo in September 2004. The normal method in post conflict situations is to establish a pooled funding mechanism to avoid a 'donor circus' that imposes an administrative burden on the recipient government which in this instance was extremely weak.[53]

It was agreed early on to establish a Multi-Donor Trust Fund (MDTF) for Sudan with two windows, for Sudan and the autonomous region of South Sudan, respectively. It was not clear who would run it, the UN or the World Bank. The donors had established a Capacity Building Trust Fund (CBTF) run by UNICEF which was meant for the transition. The regional government in the South had close to no capacity and needed support. The CBTF was small but could also be used for quick impact projects until the Trust Fund would be up and running. Following lengthy discussions, the Sudanese parties finally decided that the World

Bank would administer the MDTF, but that NGOs and the UN agencies would be contracted by the regional government to help run the programmes. In the spirit of the Utstein group, a Joint Donors Office (JDO) was to be the main donor presence in South Sudan, supporting this process, engaging with the World Bank MDTF and the government. It was hoped that providing aid through a single channel would result in speedy implementation and prevent an uncoordinated post-conflict donor environment.

Collaboration with other Utstein members, particularly the UK and the Netherlands, was substantial, despite the fact that both Short and Herfkens had left their positions prior to its establishment. Other donors joining in were Denmark, Sweden, and Canada. But while these donors provided their contributions on time to the MDTF, many other donors did not deliver on their pledges from the Sudan's donor conference. A good deal of the resources did not go to the war-affected population in South Sudan but was instead redirected to Darfur which was viewed as the most urgent humanitarian crisis.

The famous gap in early post-conflict situations emerged again. A significant part of the door funding was deposited to the MDTF and sat there for several years, as the supposedly 'speediest World Bank Trust Fund' turned out to be one of the slowest. The JDO did not work as it was intended—in Johnson's view because of World Bank resistance—and could not enhance the speed of programme implementation. The UN and the World Bank would not work out their problems, with the result that the people of South Sudan continued to suffer many years after peace was established. Johnson's continued efforts to get the MDTF to move failed, and five years after its establishment it had disbursed only a third of its funds.[54] The absence of visible progress likely contributed to greater and longer instability.

An important conclusion of Sudan and post-conflict situations was the need to establish security before any development can take place and the significance of providing support to a lead donor's intervention rather than a multiplicity of donors. Another was the difficulties of UN–World Bank collaboration in fragile states. The World Bank, dependent as it is on the government's own implementing capacity, has tended to struggle in situations where the government is non-existent or very weak. This disappointing experience, and similar turf-wars later between the World Bank and the UN, prompted Johnson to champion negotiations on a crisis/post-conflict cooperation with the World Bank on behalf of the UN system (see Chapter 10).

Peacebuilding

The U4 developed significant experience in so-called 'peacebuilding' activities in various FCV countries. Peacebuilding is multidimensional and covers four separate but interdependent areas: (a) to provide security; (b) to help establish the

socio-economic foundations for long-term peace; (c) to promote the establishment of a political framework that leads to long-term peace; and (d) to encourage
reconciliation. Support must reflect this interdependence and be sustained for the
longer term. There are additional problems when the conflict results in the
refugees that spill over to neighboring countries which are unable to cope with
them (see Box 6.2).

Box 6.2. Kosovo and Macedonia: jumping over one's own shadow

In the spring of 1999, the world witnessed a calamity that has become all too
frequent in recent years: tens of thousands of refugees fleeing violence in their
homeland, running through the borders of weak neighbouring countries. This
time it was Albanian Kosovars escaping into Albania and into Macedonia,
fleeing ethnic cleansing and pursued by Serbia's Milosevic, who was trying to
prevent Kosovo's secession from what was then the Federal Republic of
Yugoslavia (Serbia/Montenegro).[55]

The West, which had shamefully sat on its hands while ethnic cleansing was
occurring in Rwanda a few years earlier, decided to act by sending NATO
troops into Macedonia and targeted bombardment of Serbia. The Macedonian
government, unable to handle the refugees, decided to close the border, causing
them even greater hardship. The war in Kosovo blocked Macedonia's trade
route to the north, and the trade route to the south through Greece was not
working well due to the continued tension over Macedonia's name. As a result,
the country was isolated with both imports and exports being adversely
affected and unemployment rising to 35 per cent.

Herfkens, who had an emotional attachment to the country, having represented it at the World Bank as part of her 'constituency' and was close to the
Macedonian leadership, flew to Macedonia on 6–7 April to offer additional
economic assistance and debt relief, as well as to try to convince the
Macedonian government to reopen the border and allow humanitarian agencies to work in the area. Short also visited the border of Albania and Macedonia
at about that same time. She writes, 'I visited over Easter. Refugees were
clustered at the border; there were reports of hunger and some deaths.
I promised the government aid and to build a camp if they would let the
refugees out of no-mans-land.'[56] Though they were focused on the same issues,
there was no 'Utstein' coordination—indeed Utstein had not yet taken place.
But, following these interventions, and those of others, the Macedonian government did let the refugees in. The international community responded
positively by raising $252 million in a subsequent donor meeting organized

(continued)

Box 6.2. *Continued*

---

by the World Bank and the European Commission in Paris on 5 May 1999.[57] The campaign against Milosevic eventually succeeded and a United Nations mission to help maintain the peace in Kosovo was established. In this setting Wieczorek-Zeul asked Herfkens to join her on another trip to Kosovo/ Macedonia using a German military aircraft on 8–9 July. They flew to Skopje for meetings with the Macedonian government which was grateful for the additional support they offered. They then visited Kosovo where they were pleased to discover that material damage was not too bad, but that there were large needs given Kosovo's historical lag in infrastructure development and huge unemployment. They announced additional assistance and together with the UK, which had separately contributed large amounts of resources, helped rebuild the two devastated countries.

When Herfkens and Wieczorek-Zeul returned to their respective capitals they wrote an op-ed published in the Netherlands in *Trouw* on 24 July 1999 in which they concluded on a hopeful note: 'At the end of the 20th century Europe's unification has proven that cooperation and economic development can overcome aggressive nationalism. Also, from the prospective of self-interest at the threshold of the 21st century Europe has the historic obligation to jump over its own shadow.'[58]

Support for the fragile states in the Balkans was not an 'Utstein' thrust. But the timing of Wieczorek-Zeul and Herfkens' joint visit was interesting: the day after they returned, they flew to Norway where together with Johnson and Short they formalized their cooperative efforts at Utstein Abbey.

In simple terms, if the donor community is blind to the needs of the security sector, it fails and the country slides back into civil war. This means that security-sector reform, including reform of the police and the re-establishment of institutions to restore the rule of law and safety for the population, must be given priority. Short says:

If you want to get financial sector reform you have to find out what and how much is legitimate, given local threats and challenges. And for this you have to get a functioning police service, you have to be prepared to finance guns for the police, as we did in Sierra Leone. But the development people don't want to touch the military. So, I had to set up a separate unit in Kings College staffed with military people in order to help us.[59]

In 2001, the UK established two 'Conflict Prevention Pools', one for Africa and one for the rest of the world. The objective of each pool was 'to improve the government's contribution to conflict prevention and peacebuilding by joining up British expertise across three ministries—DFID, the Foreign Office and the Department of Defense. The model for this was Britain's help for Sierra Leone.'[60]

Another important condition according to Johnson, following analysis of a number of post-conflict countries in a UN context, is that the largest pre-conflict donor takes the lead and is willing to bring along and coordinate with others, as the UK did in Sierra Leone, working with the UN and the World Bank on the ground. Supporting security-sector reform is essential and, of course, in all cases it is necessary to provide debt relief.[61]

In order to promote a better understanding of the problems and improve the effectiveness of the aid they provided, the four ministers commissioned a comprehensive study of their peacebuilding programmes in early 2002—just before they left for the Great Lakes. The study was coordinated by the Norwegian Peace Research Institute (PRIO). It was based on four separate studies undertaken by each country's evaluation departments, reviewed 336 projects, and was completed in late 2003.

It was by far the most thorough analysis of the aid effectiveness in peacebuilding at the time and contributed to a greater understanding of what works and what does not. The study concluded that the four countries had understood that peacebuilding is multidimensional, that there is interdependence between the different parts, and that it must be responsive to different contexts and be sustained for the longer term. The study also recognized that the multidimensional aspect of peacebuilding efforts requires cooperation between ministries and departments with different cultures.

While the joint study found that there was understanding of the complexity of the problem and the need for multiple and diverse interventions, it also concluded that none of the four countries—or for that matter other donors—had developed a peacebuilding strategy. Planning is based on relatively little analysis and there are important conceptual confusions and uncertainties. Of course, the situation is not helped by the fact that according to the study, 'there is no known way of reliably assessing the impact of peacebuilding'.[62]

The problem is compounded by the fact that the country situations do not lend themselves to clear lines of demarcation of stages: pre-conflict, conflict, and post-conflict. One should also avoid responses along two artificially compartmentalized lines of emergency/humanitarian and long-term developmental aid. There is a need for coherent approaches for countries in the twilight zone between conflict and post-conflict peacebuilding.[63]

Security sector reform was on the agenda of practically all the U4 ministerial meetings. In Birmingham, each of the original four had something to say: Short noted that 'South Africa's decision to direct military to protect politicians during elections in Burundi was a healthy sign of Africans helping each other in the security sector.' Wieczorek-Zeul reported that 'political consensus was emerging that it was necessary to strengthen the state mechanisms to ensure the stability needed for development'. Herfkens announced the setting up of a 'Peace Fund', additional to the ODA target, to help finance African peacekeepers in Africa. And Johnson reminded the meeting of Norway's programme of 'training for peace', targeting police and security officials in Southern and Western Africa.[64] Later she developed a 'peacebuilding strategy' following the study's recommendations.[65]

In the following years the international community would devote progressively more attention to these issues. Both the DAC and the multilateral institutions would develop guidelines for effective assistance in fragile states. Keller reports that

> in the Netherlands ad hoc contacts with the Ministry of Defense were trans-
> formed into more systematic policy cooperation (exchange of staff members and
> expertise; enhanced coordination in the field). This approach was first put in
> practice in Afghanistan, where the Dutch so-called 3D integrated approach
> (Defense, Diplomacy, Development) was successful and set standards for other
> donors, including the multilaterals.[66]

On the other hand there is evidence that, in Afghanistan, a lot of the old-style practices continued much to the detriment of the affected populations.[67]

Much later, Johnson, as the UN Secretary General's Special Representative for the UN mission in South Sudan, played a major role in peacebuilding in South Sudan, a tall order in the world's newest country virtually without functional institutions. Short recently wrote: 'We did attempt to learn and cooperate, but we did not get very far, and I fear that the international system is still very poor at it.'[68] We will return to the international community's increasing attention to the problems of FCV states in the last several years in Chapter 11. But some of the lessons learned early on appear to be still valid today: the best results usually are achieved when the largest pre-conflict donor takes the lead and is willing to bring along and coordinate with others, as the UK did in Sierra Leone, working with the UN and the World Bank on the ground. It also helps when the country is relatively small and the UN peacekeeping operation is effective in keeping the peace.

Looking Back

The objective of this volume is not to provide a detailed evaluation of the U4 bilateral aid programmes. Still, the obvious conclusion is that at the end of the original four ministers' tenure their 'regular' bilateral programmes were signifi-
cantly different than at the beginning: the number of focus countries assisted was smaller, there was a greater emphasis on poverty, and there was an increase in respect for ownership and thus the amount of budget support (the very positive conclusions of various evaluations regarding effectiveness of budget support will

be covered in Chapter 11) and what came later to be called 'programmable' aid— that is, assistance that could be used to fund the recipient's own priorities and programmes. After 2002/3 their bureaucracies lacked the political inspiration and cover that the ministers provided, but their senior bureaucrats continued to collaborate, and for the first years afterwards their programme directions did not retrogress. The German aid programme definitely changed for the better with Wieczorek-Zeul and her long tenure as minister helped solidify its progressive tone.

The situation in individual African countries varied: Tanzania went through several cycles of growth and poverty reduction—with the latest one likely to have upset the U4:

When Tanzania's President John Magufuli took office in 2015, he cancelled the independence day parade, curtailed international travel for his ministers and began making impromptu visits to government offices to sack tardy civil servants. Almost three years later Magufuli's crackdown on waste has morphed into a broader authoritarian assault on civil society, the political opposition and even foreign investors. In 2018 Tanzania's parliament passed an amendment to the statistics act making it a criminal offense to publicly question official statistics.[69]

Uganda, and even more so Rwanda, have made great strides in reducing poverty, but democratic deficits persist: Presidents Museveni and Kagame continue to be in power twenty years later. The DRC continues to face tremendous internal political instability which has impeded economic progress. Sierra Leone has successfully emerged from another crisis, this time stemming from an Ebola epidemic. Sudan has undergone its own revolution and negotiations to resolve the divisions in South Sudan continue on and off. Kosovo has made a lot of progress but there is still an unresolved tension over a Serb enclave, while Macedonia has finally succeeded in settling the dispute over its name with Greece by becoming North Macedonia which would enable it to become a member of NATO and the EU.

Through their individual and joint efforts, as well through their involvement in various networks, U4 made significant contributions in raising the effectiveness of economic assistance. Perhaps their most lasting contribution in this respect was the development of the concept of mutual accountability between donors and recipients. I would argue that looking back over the past twenty years the most important point is the maxim made popular by the Utstein Four: Donors do not develop developing countries. They develop themselves.

Notes

1. OECD, *Harmonization of Donor Practices for Effective Aid Delivery*, DAC Guidelines and References Series, (Paris: OECD, 2003).

2. See https://www.stortinget.no/no/Saker-og-publikasjoner/Publikasjoner/Innstillinger/ Stortinget/1999-2000/inns-199900-028/9/#a4.

3. Eveline Herfkens, speech, 21 May 2001, referencing an innovative conference programme design. On the front cover of the programme a question was posed, asking where corruption came from. On opening the programme the reader saw their reflection in a foil mirror.

4. Johan Helland, *Utstein Partners Anticorruption* (Bergen: U4 Utstein Anticorruption Resource Center, 2002), p. 5.

5. *Financial Times*, 23 June 2000, cited in Maurizio Carbone, *The Politics of Foreign Aid* (New York: Routledge, 2007), p. 34.

6. OECD DAC, *European Community*, Development Cooperation Review Series, No. 30 (Paris: OECD, 1998), pp. 11–12.

7. OECD DAC, *European Community*, pp. 14–15.

8. Koos Richelle, email, 25 March 2018.

9. Koos Richelle, email, 25 March 2018.

10. Eveline Herfkens, letter to Parliament, 2 December 1999.

11. Eveline Herfkens, letter to Parliament, 8 June 2000.

12. Eveline Herfkens, letter to Parliament, 22 June 2001.

13. Koos Richelle, email, 25 March 2019.

14. Heidemarie Wieczorek-Zeul, 'An Important Step Forward', D-C December 2005, www. inwent.org, cited in Carbone, The Politics of Foreign Aid, p. 36.

15. Benno Ndulu, interview with Eveline Herfkens, 21 November 2018.

16. Benno Ndulu, interview with Eveline Herfkens, 21 November 2018.

17. James Adams, interview with Eveline Herfkens and C. Michalopoulos, 7 May 2018.

18. *The Guardian*, 'Tanzania can fight anti-graft war effectively', 11 April 2000.

19. *Daily News*, 'EU ministers advise on promoting education', 12 April 2000.

20. James Adams, email, 11 June 2019.

21. Clare Short, comment, 17 September 2019. She also recalls raising concerns that in light of the 'fungibility' of resources, the assistance would result in helping the government purchase unnecessary military radars.

22. *The Guardian*, 'Tanzania can fight anti-graft war effectively', 11 April 2000.

23. *The African*, 'EU ministers urge donors to support poor countries', 13 April 2000.

24. *The African*, 'EU ministers hail Warioba Report', 12 April 2000.

25. German Embassy, Tanzania letter, Netherlands Archives, Tanzania, dossier 1.5.

26. James Adams, email, 11 June 2019.

27. *The African*, 'Ministerial declaration on more effective working', 17 April 2000.

28. German Embassy, Tanzania letter, Netherlands Archives, Tanzania, dossier 1.5.

29. Utstein in Vietnam from the Netherlands Archives.

30. Utstein Ministerial, The Hague, 2000, Minutes.

31. Clare Short, email, 6 November 2018.

32. Eveline Herfkens, 'Aid Works—Let's Prove It', *Journal of African Economies*, 8(4) (1999), p. 481.

33. K. Y. Amoako, *Know the Beginning Well* (Trenton, NJ: Africa World Press, 2020 forthcoming).

34. 'Africa/OECD Ministerial Consultation' (Big Table I), Addis Ababa 19–20 November 2000.
35. 'Africa/OECD Ministerial Consultation' (Big Table II), Amsterdam 14–16 October 2001.
36. Short recalls that Amoako addressed a briefing at Number 10 when Blair was about to launch his Commission for Africa: Clare Short, comment, 16 September 2019.
37. They shall remain unnamed because of the sensitivity of the subject. But, my own perception is that the DAC process has also been weakened significantly in recent periods.
38. Utstein Ministerial, Birmingham, 2001, Minutes.
39. Utstein Ministerial, Wiesbaden, 2002, Minutes.
40. UN Economic Commission for Africa, Big Table III, Addis Ababa, 17 January 2003; Special Session, Washington, DC, 28 October 2003.
41. UN Economic Commission for Africa, Big Table III, Addis Ababa, 17 January 2003; Special Session, Washington, DC, 28 October 2003.
42. Utstein Ministerial, The Hague, 2000, Minutes.
43. Netherlands Ministry of Foreign Affairs Archives, Dossier 2.
44. Utstein Ministerial, The Hague, 2000, Minutes, p. 1.
45. Short, An Honourable Deception?, p. 101.
46. Sierra Leone, Strategy Annex, UK Archives.
47. Sierra Leone, Strategy Annex, UK Archives, p. 5.
48. Stavern, 21–2 June 2018, transcript, p. 11.
49. Eveline Herfkens, letter to Dutch parliament, 6 March 2002.
50. Clare Short, email, 6 November 2018.
51. *The Times*, London, 20 February 2002.
52. Hilde F. Johnson, *Waging Peace in Sudan* (Eastbourne: Sussex Academic Press, 2011), p. 46.
53. Johnson, Waging Peace in Sudan, p. 179.
54. Johnson, Waging Peace in Sudan, p. 210.
55. Its formal name at the time was the Former Yugoslav Republic of Macedonia, FYROM, to distinguish it from the Greek province of the same name. The name issue with Greece was finally resolved in 2019, with the country now called North Macedonia.
56. Clare Short, comment, 12 August 2019.
57. See www.m.reliefweb, accessed 20 July 2019.
58. *Trouw*, 'Jumping over one's own shadow', 24 July 1999.
59. Stavern 21–2 June 2018, transcript, p. 8.
60. Ireton Barrie, *Britain's International development Policies: A History of DfID and Overseas Aid* (Basingstoke: Palgrave Macmillan, 2013), p. 110.
61. Stavern, 21–2 June 2018, transcript, p. 8. But security assistance did not mean promotion of arms exports. Both Wieczorek-Zeul and Short were especially active in blocking arms sales to developing countries.
62. Dan Smith, 'Towards a Strategic Framework for Peacebuilding: Getting their Act Together', Evaluation Report 1/2004 (Oslo: Royal Norwegian Ministry of Foreign Affairs, 2004), pp. 10–11.
63. Eveline Herfkens, speech, New York UN Security Council, 30 November 2000.

64. Utstein Ministerial, Birmingham, 2001, Minutes, para. 6.
65. Hilde F. Johnson, comments, 28 September 2019.
66. Ron Keller, email, 30 March 2019.
67. Ashraf Ghani and Clare Lockhart, *Fixing Failed States* (Oxford and New York: Oxford University Press, 2008).
68. Clare Short, email, 3 February 2019.
69. Justin Sandefur, 'Tanzania outlaws fact checking, seeks world bank aid to create new facts', *CGD*, 28 September 2018.

7

Improving the International Development Architecture

Introduction

The end of the twentieth century and the beginning of the next millennium was characterized by an extraordinary burst of international cooperation on development. As discussed earlier, this was in part due to the lessening of international tensions with the end of the Cold War. It was also a consequence of the improved understanding that ending poverty required collaborative efforts between donor and recipient, with partners in the driver's seat setting their own priorities.

For decades there had been a major communication and coordination problem between the IFIs which controlled the bulk of the multilateral resources for development and the UN, whose General Assembly and Economic and Social Council retained the moral and legitimate authority of a worldwide forum representing the global consensus on economic and social development. These two structures needed to work together in the pursuit of the common goal of waging war on global poverty.

Just around the end of the twentieth century the opportunity arose to forge a connection between the IFIs and the UN in the context of the establishment of the Millennium Development Goals (MDGs). Recall in this connection that in the summer of 1999, Annan had written to the U4 ministers complimenting them for their initiative to address world poverty, stating 'we must act to wipe out the shame of absolute poverty over the next sixteen years', that is by 2015; and they had responded positively in support of his millennium initiative. Recall also the discussion in Chapters 2 and 3 regarding the IDGs and the strong support Short and the other U4 had given to the concept. The U4 were not the origin of the MDG initiative. But they were strong supporters who used the MDGs as a vehicle to articulate aid programme objectives as well as anchor a major initiative in education.

After the attacks on the USA on 11 September 2001, many political leaders in the West, including in the USA, felt that maybe somewhat more should be done about global poverty. While the four ministers were well aware of the fact that most terrorists were not poor and most poor were not terrorists, they decided to make the most of the opportunity to reverse the decline in ODA manifested in the aftermath of the Cold War and take steps to improve the international architecture for development. The run up to the 2002 Monterrey Finance for Development Conference provided such an opportunity.

This chapter starts with a discussion of the agreement to establish the MDGs at the UN and its implications for development. Goal 8 of the MDGs (see Box 7.1)

Box 7.1. The Millennium Development Goals and Targets

Goal 1. Eradicate extreme poverty and hunger
Target 1. Halve between 1990 and 2015 the proportion of people whose income is less than $1/day.

Target 2. Halve between 1990 and 2015 the proportion of people of people who suffer from hunger.

Goal 2. Achieve universal primary education
Target 3. Ensure that children everywhere, boys and girls alike, will be able to complete a full course of primary education by 2015.

Goal 3. Promote gender equality and empower women
Target 4. Eliminate gender disparity in primary and secondary education, preferably by 2005 and at all levels of education by 2015.

Goal 4. Reduce child mortality
Target 5. Reduce by two thirds between 1990 and 2015 the under-five mortality rate.

Goal 5. Improve maternal health
Target 6. Reduce by three quarters, between 1990 and 2015 the maternal mortality rate.

Goal 6. Combat HIV/AIDS, malaria, and other diseases
Target 7. Have halted by 2015 and begun to reverse the spread of HIV/AIDS.

Target 8. Have halted by 2015 and begun to reverse the incidence of malaria and other major diseases.

Goal 7. Ensure environmental sustainability
Target 9. Integrate the principles of sustainable development into country policies and programmes and reverse the loss of environmental resources.

Target 10. Halve by 2015 the proportion of people without sustainable access to safe drinking water and basic sanitation.

Target 11. By 2020 achieve a significant improvement in the lives of at least 100 million slum dwellers.

Goal 8. Develop a global partnership for development

Target 12. Develop further an open, rule-based, predictable, nondiscriminatory trade and financial system (includes a commitment to good governance, development, and poverty reduction, nationally and internationally.

Target 13. Address the special needs of the least developed countries (includes tariff- and quota-free access for exports of the least developed countries, enhanced debt relief for least developed countries and cancellation of official bilateral debt, and more generous official development assistance for countries committed to reducing poverty).

Target 14. Address the special needs of landlocked countries and small island developing states (through the programme of action for the Sustainable Development of Small Island Developing States and the outcome of the 22nd Special Session of the General Assembly).

Target 15. Deal comprehensibly with the debt problems of developing countries through national and international measures to make debt sustainable in the long term.

Target 16. In cooperation with developing countries, develop and implement strategies for decent and productive work for youth.

Target 17. In cooperation with pharmaceutical companies, provide access to affordable, essential drugs in developing countries.

Target 18. In cooperation with the private sector, make available the benefits of new technologies, especially information and communication.

addresses structural factors preventing developing countries from making progress and highlights the question of support that the developed world is expected to extend to developing countries in order to help them achieve the MDGs. This includes the perennial question of how much aid developed countries should commit to provide to developing countries, a question which received considerable attention in the run up to the Monterrey Conference. The chapter then turns to the special efforts the U4 and the international community made to increase aid to achieve universal primary education, MDG 2; and to battle HIV/AIDS, malaria, and other diseases, MDG 6.

The Millennium Development Goals

In 1998–9 the UN was busily engaged in preparations for the Millennium General Assembly which was to take place in September 2000. In April 2000 the UN produced the document *We the Peoples: The Role of United Nations in the 21st Century* which contained its vision of the future including many recommendations aimed at reducing global poverty. The good relationship between

Kofi Annan and James Wolfensohn was critical in forging better relations between the UN and the World Bank. As we saw earlier, the two of them also drew into their discussion and worked closely with the new IMF Managing Director Köhler.

In June 2000, the IMF, the OECD, the UN and the World Bank launched a common document, *2000: A Better World for All*, containing essentially the IDGs as they had evolved within the DAC (see Chapter 2). This document which, for the first time, brought together the four institutions on issues of global poverty was viewed with considerable scepticism, if not concern, by many NGOs and developing countries, who considered the IFIs and OECD to be instruments of the rich world. This was a rather odd objection since the IDGs were drawn from the conclusions of the UN development conferences of the 1990s. Still, after extensive negotiations over the next several months, in September 2000, 189 countries endorsed the Millennium Declaration at a major meeting of the United Nations General Assembly called to mark the advent of the new millennium. The Declaration contained almost all the IDGs in some form, plus several other commitments drawn from various UN resolutions. The actual MDGs took a little while longer to settle and resulted from further negotiations between the IFIs and the UN. They were approved by the UN in September 2001 and contained specific quantitative targets, with deadlines, for eradicating poverty and reducing other forms of human deprivation as well as promoting sustainable development by 2015 (see Box 7.1).

The MDGs had some limitations: there was a fundamental difference between the first seven MDGs which laid down targets for progress in developing countries and Goal 8 which entailed the responsibilities of the developed countries: the first seven included concrete quantifiable targets and deadlines whereas Goal 8 contained many non-quantified, non-time-bound, and somewhat vague commitments by the OECD countries to provide improved market access for developing country exports and financial assistance. It even lacked references to targets on ODA volume and aid effectiveness. Only the later Monterrey Conference (discussed shortly in this chapter) put some meat on MDG 8's bare bones. And, as the MDGs were focused on measurable outcomes, they did not capture the hard to measure commitments made in the 2000 Millennium Declaration on governance, transparency, participation, and human rights.[1] Finally, there were some who criticized the MDGs for focusing too much on the 'social sectors' and less on economic growth.[2]

It was not the first time that the United Nations passed resolutions embodying lofty objectives as well as commitments by the international community to do great things in support of development only to have these objectives and commitments forgotten the moment the delegates left New York. This time it was different in several ways. First, many of the goals were time-bound and specific; second, they had been elaborated and discussed in previous UN conferences and there was already a significant international consensus about the desirability and feasibility of their achievement; third, a number of OECD countries took them very seriously and tried to focus their aid programmes to achieve them; fourth, they were not perceived to have been thrust on the South by the North and a number of developing country leaders were committed to making a serious effort to achieve them in their countries; and finally, in 2002, the UN itself established two new programmes to promote them: the Millennium Project and the MDG Campaign.

The Millennium Project involved representatives from the academic community, the public and private sectors, civil society, and the UN and other development agencies to devise a plan of implementation that would allow all developing countries to meet the MDGs. The Millennium Project presented its final recommendations in its report to the Secretary General, *Investing in Development: A Practical Plan to Achieve the Millennium Development Goals*, completed in January 2005.

In the autumn of 2002 Kofi Annan appointed Herfkens to create and lead the Millennium Campaign which continued until the end of the decade. Its purpose was to raise awareness of the Goals and promote citizen advocacy that would remind governments of their promises. Its motto was: 'We are the first generation that can eradicate poverty and we refuse to miss the opportunity.' The Campaign focused on action at the country level. To do this, it reached out beyond the usual suspects involved in the UN and the international NGOs accredited to the UN. It was the first time that the United Nations initiated an effort to build awareness of internationally agreed objectives and to inspire and mobilize citizens to hold their governments accountable for their achievement.

Despite the limitations mentioned above, especially regarding the lack of specific developed country commitments, the MDGs caught on. And their design owes a great deal to the collaboration between the UN and the IFIs. It is difficult to say how much of this can be attributed to the Utstein Group. Looking over the minutes of the U4 ministerial meetings, it is striking that the MDGs as such are not mentioned even once. Yet, they were at the heart of their focus on implementation and on what rich countries should be doing, that is, the mutual obligations/global partnership approach involving more and better aid and policy coherence in both developed and developing countries. According to Richard Manning, Clare Short's DG, who later became chairman of the DAC, 'The Ministers played a particularly important role in putting over to Wolfensohn and Camdessus the relevance of the IDGs to the area of greatest international development focus at the time: resolving the debt problems of the HIPC. Both quickly saw the value of highlighting the outcomes that the goals provided.'[3]

Johnson started an MDG campaign in Norway, aiming to mobilize civil society organizations and the public for their achievement. The MDGs were also the very core of Johnson's new White Paper, *Collective Fight against Poverty: A*

Comprehensive Development Policy. Wieczorek-Zeul regards the MDGs useful in helping move her own aid programme in new desirable directions: they helped promote a dialogue at the political level and were useful in convincing reluctant members of the Bundestag of the need of budget support: 'you need financial instruments, not projects to achieve them. And Chancellor Schröder came back from the Millennium Summit inspired and created an action plan to fulfill the MDGs.'[4] The second MDG on education did receive special attention by Utstein as a group, although it evolved from an initiative that had started earlier (discussed in 'Education for All' below).

The MDGs seemed to underpin all the U4 statements and many initiatives undertaken before and after their adoption. According to Herfkens,

The Millennium Development Goals (MDGs) brought together for the first time a shared vision on development, representing a global partnership based on a shared responsibility by all countries. Developing countries have the primary responsibility for achieving these Goals. But rich countries acknowledged, in MDG 8—to develop a global partnership for development—that poor countries cannot achieve the Goals unless rich countries increase and improve the effectiveness of their aid and change the rules of trade to foster development.[5]

The Quest for the Elusive 0.7 Per Cent Goal

There was a glaring defect in MDG 8 which refers to the developed country commitments in support of development: it is pointedly devoid of any quantitative commitments or goals or targets regarding the volume of assistance to be provided to developing countries. This is especially surprising in light of the fact that some fifty years previously in 1970 the UN General Assembly adopted a resolution stating that 'Each economically advanced country will progressively increase its official development assistance to the developing countries and will exert its best efforts to reach a minimum net amount of 0.7% of its gross national product at market prices by the middle of the decade'.

That same decade and ever since, Denmark, the Netherlands,[6] Norway, and Sweden reached, and sometimes surpassed, the target. While the UN and other international bodies continued to regularly adopt resolutions along this line, at the time the U4 appeared on the international scene, it was still only the same four countries that met or surpassed the target; and ODA had been declining in absolute terms during the 1990s. This so-called ODA/GNP goal thus became a symbol of the divergence between aspirational commitments countries make at the UN and the realities of aid financing.

Obviously, the assumptions used to calculate the target fifty years ago have not been valid for a long time. However, over the years, the 0.7 per cent target gained value as a lobbying tool for supporters of aid in developed countries domestically. Internationally, it became a measure of burden sharing albeit without results.

When Herfkens became minister, she found this situation unacceptable, and decided to propose within the EU at least to agree on a time frame over which member states would reach the goal. Some of her staff advised against wasting energy on 'pulling this dead horse'. Indeed, it would be an uphill battle, the more as, despite support from the European Development Commissioner, Poul Nielson from Denmark, among fifteeen EU members only Sweden, Denmark and, more recently, Luxembourg were able to support this. The opportunity to make progress occurred in the aftermath of the 9/11 attacks and in the context of the preparations for the Monterrey Finance for Development conference scheduled for the spring of 2002.

The Road to Monterrey

It is not entirely clear whose idea it was to have a separate non-UN Finance for Development (FfD) initiative—or when it became 'not-just-UN'. According to one source, the genesis was an ECOSOC resolution in 1997 calling for 'consideration [to] be given to modalities for the conducting of an intergovernmental dialogue on financing for development'.[7] But obviously, if they wanted to have the people that held the purses on board, the initiative could not be just within the UN.

The meetings between UN and IFI representatives discussed earlier, including the Philadelphia group, contributed to the development of an understanding on what financial issues it would be possible to agree. In early 2000, a preparatory committee was set to prepare for the 'event'. This included a bureau of fifteen UN members co-chaired by Ruth Jacoby, the Swedish ambassador for economic affairs at the UN in New York (see Chapter 5), and the Pakistani ambassador to the UN, Shamshad Ahmad with secretariat support both from the UN, the World Bank, the IMF, and the WTO. In the summer of 2000, Jacoby went to Washington DC and met with Managing Director Köhler of the IMF and World Bank President Wolfensohn who were both supportive. She wanted them to be fully onboard with the initiative and not simply attend the meeting as guests. At this point it was not clear at what level or where the 'event' would take place. But it was clear that it would not be a typical UN conference where developing countries could pass resolutions with no effect as developed countries which did not like them could simply note their reservations as the US had always done regarding the ODA/GNI target.

In the aftermath of 9/11, the changing political situation provided the opening for action on the elusive aid volume target and the upcoming Monterrey meeting created the vehicle for concrete accomplishments. In the autumn of 2001, Belgium held the EU presidency, and the progressive Belgian State Secretary for Development, Eddy Boutmans, called for an informal emergency Development Council on 10 October—outside of the usual EU Council premises. The absence of EU ambassadors, reporting back to their Prime Ministers and Finance Ministers, enabled a frank exchange and strategic plotting. Herfkens wanted the EU to agree to a time path for all members to achieve the 0.7 per cent target by 2007. Short and the UK were committed to incrementally raising the resources allocated to development, but at the time could not agree to a timeline. Wieczorek-Zeul also had a problem: she wanted a progressive increase of the ODA volume, but could not commit Germany as the Ministry of Finance was against it.

The Belgian presidency supported by the Commission decided to push for a time path to achieving the 0.7 per cent target. The summary that it presented of the informal Development Council deliberations stated that 'the present crisis should be transformed into a window of opportunity...We should seize this opportunity to set without further delay clear objectives and deadlines, for example a time path for finally achieving the 0.7 percent ODA goal.'[8] This is where the EU discussion stood when the Utstein ministers held their third formal meeting in Birmingham on 4–5 November 2001 on the eve of the formal EU Development Council meeting scheduled for 8 November.

Given the problems faced by Germany, the U4 discussion on the 0.7 per cent goal was muted:

> The Ministers discussed how best to take forward their approach to the Finance for Development (FfD) conference over the coming few weeks, including through the European Union. They noted...the need for better language on the 0.7 percent target (including possibly a timetable)...Wieczorek-Zeul reported that she was initiating a study of the 'Tobin Tax' (a tax on international financial transactions, whose proceeds could be used for development) and that the German Scientific Advisory Council on Global Change is conducting a study on other ideas for innovative financial mechanisms including a carbon tax.[9]

With Belgium having announced in advance that it would like to agree to a calendar for a time path to realize the 0.7 per cent target, Herfkens formally proposed at the Development Council on 8 November that the EU agree to a time path for all member states to achieve it by 2007.[10] Support for a time path to achieve the target was also coming from Ireland, Luxemburg, and those that had already achieved the target (the Netherlands, Denmark, and Sweden). The U4 minus Johnson (recall that Norway is not in the EU but has steadfastly exceeded the 0.7 per cent target) had breakfast that day: both Short and Wieczorek-Zeul wanted to strengthen their countries' commitment to the target but lacked the mandate to support Herfkens. They were able, however, to agree with the chair not to close the meeting until the issue was resolved, which obviously it could not.[11] France, Spain, and several others from the European 'south' were vehemently opposed: 'The most contentious issue was whether the Member States should agree on a collective target or whether they should also establish country targets.'[12]

It was decided to put the question formally on the agenda of the next meeting of their Presidents/Prime Ministers, the European Council in February 2002, and that Koos Richelle, the EU Commission's Director General, would canvass the EU capitals and prepare a report for consideration by the EU at a heads of government meeting in advance of the Conference on Finance for Development, in Monterrey in March 2002.[13] Short refused to meet Richelle as she did not have the authority to resolve the question and referred him to Gordon Brown, who, after all, held the purse. The day after the Development Council meeting, Herfkens, Johnson, and the Swedish, Danish, and Luxembourg Development Ministers published an op-ed urging agreement on a time frame before Monterrey:

> The G8 constantly makes promises, but if all rich countries—including the G8—would simply live up to their promises, we would not be concerned now about the availability of finance for poverty reduction. We call on all member states to, by the time of next year's FfD conference in Monterrey, come up with clear planning for concrete progress towards our common purpose: 0.7% GNI for ODA.[14]

Ten days later, on 17–18 November, the World Bank/IMF's annual meetings took place in Ottawa—postponed in the wake of 9/11. On his way to Ottawa, Brown made a speech to the Federal Reserve Bank in New York trying to seize leadership in the debate about the financial aspects of globalization and to promote the philosophy behind Short's second White Paper, *Making Globalization Work for the Poor*.[15] In his speech Brown proposed a new approach to poverty, including a new international development trust fund, which was to provide an extra $50 billion a year in development assistance funded by borrowing against future aid flows. This was the amount the Zedillo Report, commissioned by the UN and published in early 2001, had estimated to be needed to achieve the MDGs.

Notwithstanding its questionable feasibility, Brown's proposal made the head-lines worldwide as it would have almost doubled ODA on an annual basis. However, Brown refrained from increasing the UK's commitment towards meeting the 0.7 ODA/GNI target. This irritated the Dutch Finance Minister, Gerrit Zalm:

> Every time Gordon takes an initiative for which he takes credit he wants others to pay. I recall on the occasion that he proposed the $50 billion ODA increase before the FfD I said to him, 'why don't you first do the 0.7 before you claim compassion regarding global poverty'. Gordon insisted on sitting next to Gerrit

at dinner hoping to convince him. In the end Brown actually changed his position and agreed to a time path...[16]

The UK agreed to a time path in 2003 and achieved the target in 2013, but Brown's proposed scheme was never implemented.

Both World Bank President Wolfensohn and IMF Managing Director Köhler had personally lobbied strongly for the 0.7 per cent target, and the Development Committee also heard from Kofi Annan, who had been invited to participate in the official dinner. Indeed, the Committee communique this time contained a whole section on the Committee's views on the agenda of the Monterrey Conference. Instead of just the usual short reference regarding the desirability of 0.7 per cent, it dedicated a whole paragraph to the 'Importance of Enhancing ODA Flows' and 'recognized that a substantial increase in current ODA levels would be required if the opportunities emerging from policy improvements in low-income countries are to be realized and the MDGs to be met'.[17] However, the USA, always wary of committing to the target, dominated this forum and prohibited more concise commitments.

When European leaders subsequently met for their Council in Laeken on 14–15 December, some progress was recorded, as at least the concept of a time frame was accepted: 'The European Council notes with satisfaction the Council's undertaking to examine the means and the timeframe for each Member State's achievement of the UN official development aid target of 0,7% of GNP...'[18]

The momentum gained greatly in the run-up to the Finance for Development conference in Monterrey. Many regional and global mobilization meetings were organized, including a round table on new proposals for Financing for Development in Washington DC, in which Johnson said: 'Monterrey must move beyond the status quo. Anything else would mean letting down the millions of people who depend on us.'[19] Also, the Mexican government, having decided to host the conference, was working hard to make it a success through its representatives in the various international organizations.

US President Bush announced he was going to attend the conference. Spain, which held the EU presidency and had previously been extremely negative regarding any target, cared deeply about its image in Latin America/Mexico and changed its position. This led to the beginning of a transatlantic 'beauty contest' as European leaders agreed in their Barcelona Council on 15–16 March to a calendar for raising their collective overall ODA/GNI ratio. Specifically, they agreed that

in pursuance of the undertaking to examine the means and timeframe that will allow each of the Member States to reach the UN goal of 0.7% ODA/GNI, those Member States that have not yet reached the 0.7% target commit themselves—as a first significant step—individually to increasing their ODA volume in the next four years within their respective budget allocation processes, whilst the other Member States renew their efforts to remain at or above the target of 0.7% ODA, so that collectively a European Union average of 0.39% is reached by 2006. In view of this goal, all the European Union Member States will in any case strive to reach, within their respective budget allocation processes, at least 0.33% ODA/GNI by 2006.[20]

The Monterrey Consensus

When it was decided to hold the conference in Mexico, 'President Bush could not avoid attending this conference since his friend and neighbor President Vincente Fox of Mexico was hosting it.'[21] That meant that other governments would be prepared to be represented at the highest level. It also meant that 'Having decided to attend, the President had to have a "deliverable"—something important and attractive to announce, and the only thing that made sense was an increase in US aid, the more so because European leaders were already planning on announcing significant increases in their own aid budgets.'[22]

The US moves were welcomed by almost everybody, notwithstanding the weak link to terrorism; the headlines tell the story: The *Financial Times* headline on 15 March said 'US pledges higher overseas aid. Promise by Bush signals desire to attack conditions nurturing terrorism.' In the same article Short is quoted: 'It is very welcome that the US is committing to more aid, when many views have been expressed rubbishing the virtues of aid at all',[23] and later on, 'The single most important commitment to the cause of development is a new sense of responsibility particularly in the aftermath of September 11.'[24] And on 25 March, the *Financial Times* trumpeted: 'US wakes from 20-year slumber in development field.'[25]

Herfkens was especially active in the run-up and during the Monterrey Conference: in October 2001 she had participated in the preparatory meeting in New York and worked with her friend Ruth Jacoby to prepare agreed language regarding the 'consensus document' which it was being proposed should be agreed at the meeting. At that meeting she tabled a 'non-paper' outlining the Dutch position which highlighted three priorities for the conference: (a) compliance with the 0.7 ODA/GNI aid volume standard; (b) policy coherence at the multilateral and bilateral level; and (c) reciprocal obligations for donor and recipient countries. During the conference she co-chaired with South Africa's Minister of Finance Trevor Manuel one of the 'round tables' on 'Coherence in Development', where she talked about what the developed countries should be doing and her partner gave his view on the developing country responsibilities.

Wanting to generate pressure on the volume target, Johnson and Herfkens got the delegations of Belgium, Denmark, Ireland, Luxemburg, and Sweden, the 'G0.7', to issue a joint statement asking other developed country participants to join them in their commitment to achieve and maintain the 0.7 ODA/GNI target in order to achieve the MDGs. In order to have at least one non-European country signing up, Herfkens lobbied the delegation from New Zealand, which was very positive—but needed to check with their Prime Minister, Helen Clark, who later became administrator for UNDP. She, however, declined.

Johnson and Herfkens also organized their Prime Ministers and the Prime Ministers of Denmark, Luxemburg, and Sweden to have an op-ed published during the Conference in the *International Herald Tribune* with the title 'The rich countries will have to do better'. In an extraordinary and unprecedented public statement, the five prime ministers wrote:

> We urge the major industrialized countries to make an extraordinary effort to increase their ODA. For poverty to come down, total ODA must go up. We welcome the positive decisions on increase of ODA by the European Union and the US. These are important steps in the right direction.[26]

But there were other suggestions as well (see Box 7.2).

The Monterrey beauty contest between the USA and the EU resulted in significant actual increases in ODA over the next decade (see Appendix, Table A-1). The increases were especially pronounced for Germany and the UK and somewhat less for the USA and, as will be discussed in Chapter 10, within a few years they led to even greater time bound commitments within the EU to achieve the 0.7 ODA/GNI target.

On the question of the level of assistance, the conference was successful in putting meat on MDG 8: The consensus paragraph 42 is very concrete, stating that 'developed countries who have not done so to make concrete efforts towards the target of 0.7 of GNI as ODA to developing countries'. This famous 0.7 GNI/ODA target had been put in literally hundreds of UN resolutions to which the USA either abstained or entered a formal reservation as not accepting it. This is the first and only time that the USA did not object to it. In practice the US government promised a 50 per cent increase in American foreign aid over three years, for which it created a new multibillion 'Millennium Challenge Account' that was to provide generous financing including budget support for developing countries that were found to respect human rights, endorse democratic principles, and have coherent strategies to eradicate poverty. By creating the Millennium Challenge Corporation to channel these funds, the USA was able to implement some of the agreements on aid effectiveness, as this new outfit, as opposed to USAID, was not restricted by all kinds of congressional mandates. In addition, the USA launched a generous new programme, the President's Emergency Plan for AIDS Relief (PEPFAR), to combat HIV/AIDS.

According to one observer,

> The central feature of the Monterrey process was that it dared to reach for agreement with political commitment on a new North–South understanding on what UN delegates refer to as the 'hard' issues of international trade,

---

Box 7.2. A financial transactions tax

In the late 1990s and in the beginning of the twenty-first century, some developed countries started to explore alternative sources of revenue in order to restore declining flows of ODA. A tax of foreign exchange transactions was considered by some to be a useful instrument for this purpose. Wieczorek-Zeul announced at the Monterrey Conference that the German Development Ministry had presented a feasibility study on how such a tax would work at a side event in the meetings. She said that 'Developing countries would benefit through reduced volatility of financial flows and more stable markets. Speculative transactions could be fought off . . . and the tax would generate significant resources to be used for development purposes.'[27] The idea was also advocated by France's President Jacques Chirac, and Cuba's Fidel Castro.

Many disagreed. Herfkens was concerned that this would distract political energy from the efforts to achieve the 0.7 per cent target; and would not become reality any time soon. Opponents also argued that the tax would also curb legitimate hedging activities essential for trade; that it would not succeed in dampening exchange rate fluctuations or reduce speculation; and unless it covered all types of transactions and all countries, it would introduce undesirable distortions. The EU Commission came up with a proposal a few years back which received support from both France and Germany but failed to be launched in the end. Over the years there has been tremendous literature and controversy over the idea's feasibility, desirability, and purpose. Wieczorek-Zeul believes that a number of European countries continue to be interested in such a tax.[28] I suspect, however, that implementing such a tax on a global basis today is no closer than when it was first conceived by American economist James Tobin, who first proposed a foreign currency transactions tax in the early 1970s in response to a breakdown in the fixed exchange rate system.

---

monetary financial and development policy . . . The reform that received the most attention is the reversal of the decade long decline in ODA. The Millennium Declaration had been a grand commitment but there was little money behind it.[29]

The Economist, traditionally sceptical on the contribution of aid to development, stated that 'research on the effectiveness of aid suggests that the emphasis should be on choosing the right countries and programmes, rather than on quantity' and that 'a 50% increase in aid flows would double poverty reduction to 22%—so long as it was coupled with efficient reallocation of aid towards poor countries with good policies'.[30] In fact, ODA to Africa did double and poverty reduction was even greater—as there was some reallocation in favour of countries with good policies—but this is a story that will be discussed later.

The Monterrey Conference also adopted an impressive consensus document, twenty-three pages long with no reservations in six chapters, probably the most coherent and comprehensive internationally agreed document on finance, trade, and development. While most press coverage focused on the historic ODA increases, possibly as historic was the language developing countries agreed to regarding their own responsibilities, including for 'mobilizing domestic resources for development'. To emphasize this, the Netherlands organized a side event with the IMF and the Minister of Finance of Ghana about the need for developing countries to improve tax systems and tax collection. And Herfkens, together with the Dutch State Secretary Wouter Bos, the later leader of the Dutch Labour Party published an op-ed: 'Aid is only an addition to what countries themselves invest in their development: Increase in ODA is a benchmark for the success of the FfD conference, but not the only one. Effective poverty reduction can only succeed if developing countries ensure their own policies and governance—including tax collection—are in good shape.'[31] At the same event the Netherlands announced its first of many contributions to enable the IMF to help with capacity building on these issues, enabling Managing Director Köhler to create AFRITAC (see Chapter 5).

Perhaps the most interesting chapter had to do with measures 'enhancing the coherence and consistency of the international monetary, financial and trading system for development'. Other examples of language never agreed before at the UN were:

Para. 13.   'Corruption is a serious barrier to effective resource mobilization and diverts resources from activities that are vital to poverty eradication.'

Para. 14.   'Government should attach priority to avoiding inflationary pressures and abrupt economic fluctuations that negatively affect income distribution and resource allocation.'

Para. 43.   'Donors should harmonize their operational procedures so as to reduce transaction costs...', another concrete addition to Goal 8 commitments.

Para. 52.   'Efforts should be strengthened at the national level to enhance co-ordination between all relevant ministries and institutions.'

Para. 62.   'We stress the need to broaden and strengthen the participation of developing countries in international decision making and norm setting.'

Some of the issues that were addressed, such as the participation of developing countries in the decision making of international institutions, were to be picked up again much later in discussions on the voting rights of rising powers such as China on the boards of the IMF and the World Bank.

Most opinion regarding the outcome of the Monterrey meeting was positive: The *International Herald Tribune* said: 'There is still a significant gap between the aid pledged by rich countries and what is needed. The imperative now as aid dollars are invested more wisely, is to close the gap.'[32] *Le Monde* was more pessimistic: 'In Monterrey, States engage in minima on development assistance. Underneath a face of cohesion, profound disagreements between the Americans and the Europeans.'[33]

The *Frankfurt Allgemeine* quoted Wieczorek-Zeul, who said that the conference provided a 'positive signal for the North–South partnership' noted that the meeting was attended by and heard speeches from more than fifty heads of government ranging in views from Bush to Castro, and concluded that 'if we really want to help developing countries help themselves, we must stop the massive subsidies to our agriculture and open our borders to their exports'.[34]

Short summarized her judgement on the outcome of the Monterrey meeting in a statement to Parliament:

Monterrey was very important in that the developing world and the OECD countries agreed on what the reform agenda is to deliver to the poor of the world; that is unprecedented in human history, and very post-cold war...The preparatory process was very good and went well. But I think it would have gone sour without the commitment to more aid, and the commitment from Europe, which is yet to be delivered, but helped to leverage the US feeling then that they had to commit.[35]

Herfkens who, together with her U4 colleagues, had worked so hard to make the conference a success was happy primarily because at Monterrey the developing countries made a commitment to good governance: 'This move toward a deeper partnership, based on mutual responsibility, saved the conference from the recriminations that have marred many North–South meetings in the past.'[36]

In a statement to the Storting, the Norwegian Parliament, Johnson noted that Monterrey's likely increase of 20–25 per cent in ODA by 2004–6 could mean a reversal of the longstanding decline; she welcomed the concrete plans by the EU and the USA to step up their assistance, but cautioned that 'there is a long way to go' as attaining the MDGs will require doubling ODA commitments; and she reaffirmed her government's commitment to attain the 1 per cent ODA/GNI target by 2005.[37]

The U4 meeting at Wiesbaden in July 2002 welcomed the Monterrey results, especially what was accomplished on the aid issue. Wieczorek-Zeul emphasized the importance of Monterrey for the World Summit of Sustainable Development (see Chapter 9). Short highlighted the political importance of the G8 declaration to devote at least 50 per cent of the additional funds announced in Monterrey to 'good performers' identified through the NEPAD process—but there was some concern about how this would be received by the African countries. There was also an inconclusive discussion of the usefulness of financing development cooperation through innovative sources of finance such as taxes on foreign currency transactions or global environmental levies.[38]

The other major accomplishment of the Monterrey meeting was the extensive reference to the need for greater coherence in government policies for development both at the national and international level. This was the first and probably the last occasion in which world leaders agreed to take steps to improve policy coherence. Alas, the fragile cooperation between the IFIs and the UN already started to show cracks soon after: the Development Committee meeting in the autumn of 2002 contained rather opaque language on which institution was supposed to follow up on the Monterrey Consensus, covering up profound disagreement.[39] What happened on this score as well as other aspects of the follow up to the Monterrey meeting will be discussed in Chapter 10.

Education for All

Besides the broad objective of reducing poverty in MDG 1 and promoting larger amounts and more effective assistance in MDG 8, the U4 tended to focus their individual aid programmes on different goals. For example, it could be argued that Germany focused more on Goals 6 (combatting HIV AIDS, malaria, and other diseases) and 7 (environmental sustainability). But it is clear that, *collectively*, the U4 focused their greatest attention to achieving MDG 2, universal primary education.

The importance of primary education for all does not need to be explained to public opinion. The target was clear. Herfkens recalls an event at a school in the Netherlands where a little girl asked her: 'Why do we have to wait until 2015?' A good question, to which Herfkens had no answer.[40]

Many NGOs, including in developing countries, had been campaigning for this for at least a decade, and in 1999 had formed a powerful worldwide coalition: the Global Campaign for Education. This was before the MDGs were agreed. An earlier result of their advocacy was the commitment of several donors to spend 20 per cent of their bilateral ODA on primary education, if recipients would spend 20 per cent of their budget for this purpose. For the U4 this '20/20 compact' raised questions, as it did not seem compatible with ownership and aid being demand-driven. The last thing poor countries needed was yet more projects to build little schools, in front of which development ministers could have photo-ops, but which ignored the fact that the financing needs were predominantly recurrent (e.g. teacher salaries and teaching materials) and thus required budget support, which few donors were prepared to supply, and few recipients met the criteria to receive.

In the spring of 2000, many NGOs organized large events and a lot of political pressure for action in the run up to the 26–8 April Education for All conference, in Dakar, Senegal (mentioned briefly in Chapter 6 in connection with the Utstein ministers' visit to Tanzania). The conference was convened by UNESCO, UNDP, UNFPA, UNICEF, and the World Bank which were all represented by the head of their agencies. Many NGOs participated also, as did Short and Herfkens, who were able to convince the representatives from donor countries that the 'Dakar Framework for Action' should not only contain commitments from developing countries, but also from the donor community: 'We affirm that no countries seriously committed to Education for All will be thwarted in their achievement of this goal by a lack of resources. The international community will deliver on this collective commitment by launching with immediate effect a global initiative aimed at developing the strategies and mobilizing the resources needed to provide effective support to national efforts.'[41]

It was also agreed that UNESCO would coordinate efforts to do so. But there were doubts about its capacity to implement the scale of the programmes needed. Recall that the UK had just rejoined UNESCO after an absence of several years and the USA was still not a member. The old bickering between the various agencies—UNESCO and UNICEF versus the World Bank—in the run up and during the conference did not bode well. James Wolfensohn, eager for the World Bank to play a prominent role in the various MDGs, brought up in his speech the idea of a 'fast track' to support achievement of the primary education target by 2015. However, most delegations resented a role for the Bank, partly because of the traditional distrust of NGOs and developing countries, but also because of its lack of cooperation on an equal footing with UN agencies. Moreover, the World Bank was still demanding user fees for primary education in programmes it supported, thus effectively excluding the poorest children from benefitting.

As Utstein was all about taking seriously commitments made at international meetings, they were happy that many of their own focus countries chose invest-ment—preferably with budget support—in primary education, and/or through the commitment of funds that came available from debt relief for this purpose. This was the case in Tanzania (see Chapter 6) where, according to President Mkapa, millions of additional children did in fact attend school who otherwise would not have been able to.

However, as the Global Campaign for Education pointed out, some 'donor orphans' with credible plans might not have access to funding. Usually, donors would use multilateral channels for objectives they did not want or could not help to achieve bilaterally, but for education there was no obvious one because of the lack of cooperation between the relevant UN agencies and the World Bank. A major stumbling block was the Bank's insistence that user fees be charged for primary education programmes it supported. Since the World Bank was the primary financing agency, Herfkens asked (and funded) the Bank to prepare an in-depth study of the challenges to achieve primary education for all by 2015. The study concluded that no user fees should be charged for primary education, as they seriously impede poor children's access—and the Bank subsequently abandoned this as a requirement for its support. The study also underlined that most of the needed assistance was for recurrent costs such as teachers' salaries. By then the other actors, including UNESCO and the Global Campaign acknowledged that a division of labour was necessary to achieve progress on Education for All, based on the comparative advantage of all partners, and that this would require the World Bank to play an important role in coordinating resource mobilization and providing finance.

In a speech at the High Level Group meeting of Education for All (EfA) in Paris on 30 October 2001, Short summarized the Utstein position that developing country commitments to implement the Education for All (EfA) initiative should be reflected in four basic indicators:

(a) the development of sound national education policies linked to the poverty reduction strategies, which should *not* require the creation of separate EfA plans outside the PRSP (as UNESCO had been encouraging);
(b) the rapid abolition of user fees and other direct cost barriers to education;
(c) the resources governments are prepared to allocate to education and specifically basic primary education;
(d) concrete evidence of efforts to promote gender equality.

She concluded, once more repeating the Utstein goal to ensure that sectoral strategies fit into broader poverty reduction plans: 'We should work to ensure that the Dakar commitment on resources is incorporated into all country level negotiations on PRSPs and similar planning frameworks.'[42]

In order to follow up on the World Bank study, and to facilitate cooperation among all relevant agencies, in April 2002 Herfkens hosted a conference in Amsterdam with representatives of the Global Campaign for Education, African Education Ministers, the relevant international organizations, and interested donors including the Norwegian delegation, headed by Johnson. The conference discussed a new partnership facility to help fill the financing gaps, in a coordinated effort to help countries most at risk of facing funding shortages. Herfkens, Johnson, and Short did not want to create a 'Global Fund' for this purpose as it may have simply added another bureaucratic layer to the plethora of existing international organizations; they were also concerned not to set a precedent for such funds for each and every development goal.

The Amsterdam Conference agreed to an approach which was launched by the Development Committee two weeks later at the World Bank's Spring Meetings in Washington: the 'Action Plan to Accelerate Progress towards Education for All' proposed an Education for All 'fast track' in which about ten countries would be selected by June 2002 'for increased and immediate support, to help generate an early demonstration effect. The fast tracking would be done within the PRSP framework and implemented through a multi-donor education consortium. The technical secretariat of the initiative would be located at the World Bank, and its capacity strengthened by professionals seconded from several bilateral and multilateral agencies.

Next to Wolfensohn, and a representative from the Global Campaign, both Herfkens ('we do not want to have another generation lost because they did not see the inside of a classroom'[43]) and Johnson ('the investment that yields the highest returns is education for girls. Nothing can beat it'[44]) participated in the press conference on 10 April 2002. As Short was always happy to share the limelight and hoping that doing so would help wider UK government support for ODA increases (see above), the UK was represented by Gordon Brown. He would subsequently ensure that the G8 at the UK-hosted meeting in Gleneagles in 2005 would agree to 'support the Education for All agenda in Africa, including continuing support for the Fast Track Initiative (FTI) and efforts to help FTI-endorsed countries to develop sustainable capacity and identify the resources necessary to pursue their sustainable educational strategies'.[45]

The Fast Track Initiative continued to help low-income countries reduce the gap in four areas associated with the education sector: policy, finance, data, and capacity, involving ever more donors and international agencies. In 2011 the initiative changed its name from the Education for All Fast-track Initiative to the Global Partnership for Education. Over the last sixteen years it has allocated $5 billion in grants; its annual budget is now some US$460 million.

Health Targets and Initiatives

At the beginning of the twenty-first century several global initiatives emerged in the health sector. GAVI, a public–private global vaccine alliance, was launched in 2000, boosted by a significant contribution from the Bill & Melinda Gates Foundation. It built on the enormous achievements of the WHO headquartered Expanded Program on Immunization which had also been based on an initial contribution from the Gates foundation. In April 2001, at the African Union Summit on HIV/AIDS in Abuja, Kofi Annan launched the idea of a Global Fund for AIDs, Tuberculosis and Malaria. The two new funds were major additions to the emerging new international architecture for development.

The Global Fund, which received the support of the G8 at their Genoa meeting in July 2001, as well as private sector funding, had several characteristics that made it attractive to governments like Germany which had traditionally been wary of multilateral aid initiatives and preferred bilateral interventions: besides being multilateral, the Fund was relatively lightly staffed; the developing countries receiving assistance had to set up committees for the participatory consultation of those affected including faith groups, and, a novelty in an international organiza-tion—also those for whom the organization was created, people living with the diseases; and last, the highest decision making committee of the partnership was composed of representatives of donors and partner countries, implementing organizations, NGOs, and people living with the diseases.

The Utstein group had made health a key sector for collaboration at the local level, with a focus on health sector strategies. While they were not on the agenda at the various U4 ministerial meetings at the time, informal discussions took place. Wieczorek-Zeul was very supportive of the Global Fund from the very beginning. Some of the decision-making structures appeared to be in line with the 'Utstein spirit'. However, Johnson, Herfkens, and Short were initially sceptical that vertical stand-alone funds risked duplicating other efforts without a focus on building the health systems needed to sustain their interventions. They were also concerned that their activities would not be properly integrated into the national health sector strategies being developed and supported by both bilateral and multilateral donors.

All four ministers realized that there was a need for initiatives which could negotiate affordable drugs with pharmaceutical companies and mobilize add-itional private sector funding. And they appreciated the fact that the Fund could bring in resources from foundations and the US government that otherwise might not be available. Furthermore, none of them wanted to antagonize Kofi Annan on the Global Fund.

In the end, all U4 supported the two initiatives, hoping they would become a catalyst for significant private sector support for health in developing countries. The fact that they were multilateral fitted into the Utstein spirit and was especially helpful in gaining support in Germany. In the beginning the latter did not contribute to GAVI, while the other three did. But it became involved later, and even organized a replenishment conference.

Over time, these initiatives flourished. The Global Fund, in cooperation with other initiatives such as the US PEPFAR (see C7P47), helped countries to reduce mortality from these epidemics substantially, saving the lives of millions of people since their inception. They were also instrumental in reducing the cost of medicines to the poor as the Global Fund, GAVI, and the other international organizations were able to negotiate better deals with the major pharmaceutical companies. GAVI was also helpful in supporting research for the prevention of diseases endemic in developing countries in which global pharmaceutical companies had little incentive to invest. The U4 combined support of these global initiatives with continued efforts through bilateral assistance: Rotary International recognized all four U4 ministers for the contribution they made to defeating polio across the world.[46]

In Retrospect

Looking back at the period around the turn of the last century, one is impressed by the hectic international activity promoting international cooperation in support of development. The U4 were active participants and in some cases major initiators and drivers of change. They were able to translate initiatives they took in their own bilateral aid programmes, for example with respect to aid volume and aid effectiveness, into broader initiatives affecting the global community. They used the network which they formed to influence broader groups like the G8, the DAC, the World Bank/IMF Development Committee, and the EU, and ultimately broader conferences such as Monterrey. And it was interesting how in some cases they turned around and used the international agreements as a vehicle for overcoming domestic opposition. While there were differences among their four governments, they managed to maintain their personal rapport and good relations.

On the MDGs, Short writes:

> We joined with others to try to get the (International Development) Targets/ Goals agreed by all international institutions. The group of women ministers— known as the Utstein Group from the place of our first meeting—led the campaign. Gradually the targets were adopted by the World Bank, the IMF and EU and then, as the agreed objective of the Millennium Conference of the UN General Assembly were renamed the Millennium Development Goals.[47]

Others agreed. Hulme writes:

> In the mid-1990s, leadership and the locus of debate and compromise transferred to the OECD's DAC. The UK (Short, Brown and DfID) and Northern Europe (the Utstein Group and their agencies) took on the role of promoting the MDG idea (in the guise of the IDGs as they were then). For a short period, the Millennium Summit put leadership in the hands of the UN Secretary General. In 2001 the lead changed again and a task force from the UN, OECD, World Bank and IMF conducted the final technical and political negotiations.[48]

And the OECD:

> The MDGs have become the dominant framework for discussing development— a marker for what has been achieved and what still has to be done...That they did catch on was the result in part because the so-called 'Utstein Group' of development ministers from four European countries pushed hard for the goals in forums like the G8 and the UN.[49]

There is little doubt that the four ministers made a considerable difference in pushing for and attaining concrete commitments to raise the volume of assistance in the run-up and through the Monterrey Conference. While not every OECD country was prepared to commit to the 0.7 ODA/GNI target, several major donors did increase both their commitments and their actual assistance levels. One wonders whether this would have happened without the persistent U4 efforts, especially of the Netherlands, Norway, Sweden, and several other 'likeminded countries'. Their efforts strengthened domestic support within a number of major donors to commit to reach and stay at the target level in the future.

Finally, the U4 were instrumental in promoting global action towards the achievement of the MDGs in education and health. Their emphasis was different: Herfkens, Johnson, and Short focused more on education, Wieczorek-Zeul more on health. Their energy and efforts to mobilize resources worldwide assisted in the establishment of new institutions which have survived and flourished to this day.

Notes

1. Material in this section and the discussion of the Monterrey consensus below is adapted by permission from Springer Nature: C. Michalopoulos, *Aid, Trade and Development* (Cham: Palgrave, 2017), pp. 211–19.
2. Richard Manning, *Using Indicators to Encourage Development*, DIIS Report 2009–11 (Copenhagen: Danish Institute of International Studies, 2009), p. 48.
3. Manning, Using Indicators to Encourage Development, p. 88.
4. Heidemarie Wieczorek-Zeul, Stavern, 21–2 June 2018, transcript, pp. 3–4.
5. Eveline Herfkens, 'The Successes and Challenges in Mobilizing Support for the Millennium Development Goals', *UN Chronicle*, 45(1) (2006), p. 1.
6. The Netherlands stopped meeting the target in 2013.
7. Barry Herman, 'The Politics of Inclusion in the Monterrey Process', DESA Working Paper #23, ST/ESA/WP/23 (New York: UN, 2006).
8. Maurizio Carbone, *The Politics of Foreign Aid* (New York: Routledge, 2007), p. 69.
9. Utstein Ministerial, Birmingham, 2001, Minutes, para. 22.
10. This section, as several others in this chapter and elsewhere, is based on material provided by Herfkens in reports to the Dutch Parliament. The substance of the deliberations in the EU bodies and the formal positions of the various governments have been confirmed by Carbone, The Politics of Foreign Aid.
11. Spain argued that it was giving a lot of aid through tax-exempt private donations and that the taxes foregone should count as ODA. The matter was referred to the DAC where it was never discussed.
12. Carbone, *The Politics of Foreign Aid*, p. 69.
13. Not surprisingly, Richelle, who had previously been Herfkens' Director General, was also very supportive of the initiative.
14. *Volkskrant*, 'The fight against poverty demands action from rich countries now', 9 November 2001.

15. UK, DfID, *Eliminating World Poverty: Making Globalization Work for the Poor*, White Paper, 2000.
16. Gerrit Zalm, interview by Eveline Herfkens, 29 August 2018.
17. Development Committee communique, 18 November 2001.
18. EU Council, Presidency, 'Conclusions' European Council, Laaken 14–15 December 2001, para 54. The path was not easy: as late as the 5 March meeting of the EU Economic and Financial Council, there was no agreement on a path for attaining an EU average primarily because of objections by France.
19. Hilde Johnson, speech, 20 February 2002.
20. EU General Council, Presidency Conclusions, Barcelona European Council 15–16 March 2002 (Brussels: EU, 2002).
21. Carol Lancaster, *George Bush's Foreign Aid: Transformation or Chaos?* (Washington, DC: Center for Global Development, 2008), p. 16.
22. Lancaster, George Bush's Foreign Aid, p. 16.
23. *Financial Times*, 'US pledges higher overseas aid', 15 March 2002.
24. *Financial Times*, 'High hopes in Monterrey', 18 March 2002.
25. *Financial Times*, 'US wakes from 20-year slumber in development field', 25 March 2002.
26. *IHT*, 'The rich countries will have to do better', 21 March 2002.
27. Heidemarie Wieczorek-Zeul, speech, Finance for Development Conference, Monterrey, 22 March 2002.
28. Heidemarie Wieczorek-Zeul, email, 24 September 2019.
29. Herman, 'The Politics of Inclusion in the Monterrey Process', pp. 3–4.
30. *The Economist*, 'Help in the right places', 21 March 2002.
31. *NRC*, 'Stop belastingvoordeel voor investeerders Derde Wereld', 19 March 2002.
32. *IHT*, 'The Monterrey Consensus', 25 March 2002.
33. *Le Monde*, 'A Monterrey, les Etas s'engagent a minima sur l'aide au developpement', 25 March 2002.
34. *Frankfurter Allgemeine*, 'Handeln fur die Armen', 25 March 2002.
35. Clare Short, 'Examination of Witnesses (Questions 98–99, House of Commons Select Committee on International Development, 14 May 2000)', in Barrie Ireton, *Britain's International Development Policies: A History of DFID and Overseas Aid* (Basingstoke: Palgrave Macmillan, 2013), p. 66.
36. Eveline Herfkens, 'A breakthrough on aid in Monterrey', *The Earth Times* Monthly, May 2002.
37. Hilde F. Johnson, 'Statement to Parliament on Development Co-operation', 30 April 2002.
38. Utstein Ministerial, Wiesbaden, Minutes, p. 6.
39. Development Committee, 'Communique', 28 September 2002.
40. Eveline Herfkens, Stavern, 21–2 June 2018, transcript.
41. Dakar framework for action; still on the UNESCO (https://unesdoc.unesco.org/ark:/48223/pf0000121147) and UN (https://sustainabledevelopment.un.org/content/documents/1681Dakar%20Framework%20for%20Action.pdf) websites.
42. Clare Short, EfA speech, Paris, 30 October 2001.
43. *New York Times*, 'World Bank aims to help poor receive elementary education', 22 April 2001.

44. Hilde Johnson, opening statement at 'Education for All' conference, Amsterdam, 10 April 2002.

45. After Brown stepped down as Prime Minister in 2010, he continued to advocate for Education for All, including since 2012 as the UN's Special Envoy on Global Education and in 2015/16 as chair of the International Commission on Financing Global Education Opportunity, set up to chart a pathway for increasing investment, especially in low- and middle-income countries.

46. See https://www.project-syndicate.org/commentary/polio-s-defeat-and; Wieczorek-Zeul, email, 24 September 2019; but despite the hopes at the time, the goal of complete eradication still remains elusive.

47. Clare Short, *An Honourable Deception?* (London: Free Press, 2004), p. 89.

48. David Hulme, 'The Millennium Development Goals (MDGs): A Short History of the World's Biggest Promise', Brook World Poverty Institute, BWPI Working Paper 100 (University of Manchester, 2009), p. 46.

49. OECD, *The OECD at Fifty: Development Co-operation, Past, Present and Future* (Paris: OECD, 2011), p. 31.

8

Poverty has a Woman's face

Introduction

The global impact of four women Ministers of Development on empowering women and eradicating their poverty was varied, multidimensional, and substantial but difficult to measure with any degree of accuracy. By the time they came together gender had finally become an important part of the development discourse across the globe. But their commitment on gender issues dated to much earlier.

When the four joined forces, they made waves because they were together, they were women, they were outspoken, and they were all focused so strongly on poverty. They spoke less about gender as an abstract issue and more about poverty and the effect it had on women and their children both in immediate suffering and powerlessness. Their very existence and actions as a group had an important demonstration effect in empowering women in developing countries, especially those which they visited as a group. The impact is mirrored in the faces of the girls surrounding them in pictures taken when visiting poor neighbourhoods across Africa.

There was no explicit reference to gender-related initiatives in any of their ministerial meetings but the emphasis on women empowerment permeated their personal histories, their work in domestic politics and all their thinking and programmes. Their policies focused on eradicating poverty, increasing and improving the effectiveness of spending on education and health, and ensuring that these services provided for girls and women.

Though they did not launch a joint 'gender' initiative as such, they each took many initiatives in their national development policies to raise the profile of gender issues, increase women's empowerment, and reduce their poverty. They also worked together to support international undertakings aimed at improving women's access to education and health care, and empowering them on issues of family planning. More broadly they supported initiatives on women's rights and strengthening their status in society. This chapter starts with a short review of their efforts to empower women before they became ministers. It then presents examples of their efforts as Development Ministers at the national level as well as in support of global initiatives in which one or more of them were involved.

Before They Were Ministers

The first UN Conference on Women in Mexico in 1975 was dominated by developing countries' male leaders who railed against 'Western feminists exporting their agendas to their different cultures'. And still throughout the 1980s and early 1990s women standing up for gender issues often faced indifference, condescension, and sometimes outright hostility from their male peers, both in politics and in international forums. This did not discourage the four: all of them had a strong track record on gender issues much before they became Development Ministers.

In 1974 Wieczorek-Zeul was the first woman to chair the Young Socialists in Germany and she championed women's health issues over her long career.

Johnson, as vice chair of the Christian Democratic Youth League in the 1980s, organized separate caucus meetings for young female representatives at conferences and executive meetings. An important task was to embolden young women to take on their male counterparts in debates and give them the confidence needed to enter into leadership positions. Another important battle in which she engaged together with other female colleagues in her party was to introduce the quota system in the party's legislation, ensuring that there would be at least 40 per cent women in the executive board of both the youth league and the party, and on the lists for local and general elections.

Short, as an MP, battled the British tabloids over their photographs of topless models. She was Shadow Minister for Women, chair of her Party's Women's Committee and the UK delegate to Socialist International Women. As chair of the Women's Committee she led the move to a quota system for selection of candidates which led to a big increase in the number of Labour women MPs after the 1997 election. In late 1996, she addressed the Human Rights Commission in Geneva on women's issues.

Herfkens, at the time ambassador to the UN and WTO was in the audience and was duly impressed. During her tenure she initiated the group of women ambassadors in Geneva—which still meets. In a speech to the International Women's Leadership Conference Herfkens reported:

> throughout my career, I organized and networked with my, alas, always few female peers: forming women's caucuses and alliances results in information sharing, mutual support and friendship which is truly empowering. The degree of women's organization matters much more than their sheer numbers. But you have to have at least some female colleagues to be able to do so: as a member of the World Bank Board of Executive Directors I had to wait several years before our number doubled: from one to two.[1]

In the early 1980's the picture started to change. The World Bank launched the Women in Development Unit, headed by Barbara Herz. She developed a programme focusing on education, health, micro credit, agriculture, and women's labour force participation. In the early 1990s the programme gathered momentum with support from the World Bank President Barber Conable and Larry Summers, then vice President and chief economist. She writes:

> While some people were certainly skeptical, Larry Summers became a powerful and persuasive advocate for girls' education. He reviewed our research on the returns to girls' education—gains in productivity, fastest path to smaller, healthier, and better educated families, all because women gain voice and choice as the value of their time rises. Larry decided to focus on girls' education in his speech at the Annual Meeting (of the World Bank/IMF) which was published. He said that when all its benefits are considered, girls' education may well be the highest return investment available to developing countries. This caused enormous interest—it helped us launch a huge push on girls' education that lasts today.[2]

Herfkens recalls that while Summer's speech was certainly noticed, his repeating the same point in Pakistan had even greater impact. She feels that, despite progress, there were still many 'sceptics' on the Bank's Board where she served as Executive Director in the 1990s. Johnson, for her part, had quoted the above mentioned World Bank's research on the impact of investing in education for girls already as an MP in 1995–6, criticizing the Norwegian Labour party-led government for its abysmal lack of investments in the education sector.[3]

Programme Priorities

The U4 emphasis on women empowerment in national development strategies had two broad dimensions: first, that as women and children constituted the vast majority of the world's poor, broad poverty eradication programmes would need to empower women and girls. This could be done through 'mainstreaming' gender issues in all aid programmes—that is, ensuring that gender issues were addressed at the individual programme level; but Johnson notes, 'after realizing that mainstreaming alone was not enough we made sure we did both, mainstreaming and separate budget lines for women and gender equality'.[4]

Herfkens, Johnson, and Short used the same approach in order to support non-governmental networks of local women dealing with issues like domestic violence, female genital mutilation, and legal reform. Similarly, Wieczorek-Zeul writes:

> In my time as Minister, I had also made the promotion of women to a focal point in German development policy. Equality between men and women was both an independent objective and a cross-sectional task. Between 2000 and 2008, half of the BMZ (Germany bilateral aid agency) funds were allocated to projects that had a positive impact on gender equality. And I also increased the number of

women in leadership positions at the BMZ—from 7 per cent when I took office to 36 per cent in 2009. Even today, the BMZ still has more women in leadership positions than the Federal Ministry for Family Affairs, Senior Citizens, Women and Youth.[5]

The second and perhaps more important dimension was the support of specific bilateral and multilateral programmes to empower women. By far the most important effort in this area was the focus on education for girls. This was probably the highest sectoral priority for all four Utstein ministers. Both Short and Johnson put education for girls as the number one priority in their bilateral programmes. In a 1999 speech Short stressed:

the overwhelming priority of securing universal primary education across the world—as not just a basic human right for all children important as that is, but—equally significantly—as the absolute precondition for progress in development and the reduction of poverty. These benefits are even more pronounced in the case of girls' education. Research on the education of girls shows that women with as little as four years of education are more likely to have smaller, healthier families, to work their way out of poverty, and to send their own children to school.[6]

In a speech in 2002, Johnson again emphasized the core arguments for giving the highest priority to education for girls:

As far back as 1992, a World Bank report documented that girls' education is the development investment that yields the highest economic returns in the poorest countries. Nothing beats it. As the saying goes: 'When you educate a girl you educate the whole family.' Educating girls and women produces results in areas like family planning, health, HIV/AIDS, income generation and many more. It fulfills several strategic development goals simultaneously. We know all this. Yet, in many societies, girls are still last in line...This vicious circle must be broken.... Now it is time to use education as the prime weapon in the fight against poverty.[7]

In 2001 Herfkens stated: 'More education for girls implies they delay marriages and pregnancies and are better able to make informed choices about family planning, nutrition and health. This results in a virtuous circle of less children, better fed and educated, with a better future for all.'[8] Wieczorek-Zeul adds: 'Children of mothers who can read and write have a 50 per cent higher chance of becoming older than 5 years than children whose mothers are illiterate.'[9] The high priority they gave to this sector was manifested also through their support of the Education for All initiative discussed in Chapter 7.

1. Johnson, Short, Herfkens and Wieczorek-Zeul during the World Bank/IMF Spring meetings, April 28, 1999. Photo by Photothek.

2. Johnson, Short, Herfkens and Wieczorek-Zeul in front of the Utstein Abbey, July 25, 1999.

3. Short, Herfkens and Wieczorek-Zeul, Utstein Ministerial II in The Hague, May 12–13, 2000.

4. Herfkens, Short and Johnson on the river Congo, February 12, 2002.

5. Short, Johnson and Herfkens with President Kagame of Rwanda, February 13, 2002, photo by Roeland Stekelenburg.

6. Herfkens, Wieczorek-Zeul and Johnson, Development Committee Meeting, April 9, 2002.

7. Herfkens and Johnson with Nancy Birdsall (Center for Global Development) and Moises Naim (Editor Foreign Policy magazine), receiving on behalf of the Utstein Group, the first annual Commitment to Development Award, April 28, 2003.

8. Johnson, Short, Herfkens and Wieczorek-Zeul during their reunion in Berlin, February 21, 2019, photo by Marco Urban.

Another set of interventions of importance were efforts the U4 made to raise the earning capacity of women. Several different kinds of approaches were used to promote this objective: Herfkens writes: 'Where relevant we raised in the policy dialogue the need of legal reforms, to enable women to own and inherit property, including land, as well as obtain access to credit; and being able to inherit.'[10] DfID worked on land ownership rights for women and in particular the problem of women losing their homes and land when they were divorced or widowed.[11] Through collaboration with economist Hernando de Soto on legal empowerment of the poor, Johnson actively promoted property rights for women, an initiative which later led to the establishment of the Commission for Legal Empowerment of the Poor, co-chaired by Madeleine Albright and de Soto, in which Johnson was a member (2005–6).[12]

A further group of programmes involved assistance to smallholder agriculture which to a large degree supports women in rural communities. The vast majority of the world's smallholder farmers are women, making investment in their production an important intervention in fighting extreme poverty and promoting women's rights. Johnson, for her part, launched an Action Plan for Agricultural Development, with an aim of contributing 15 per cent of Norwegian aid to smallholder agriculture. The Action Plan covered ensuring land and property rights, support for production, and the whole value chain to markets, both local and international.[13]

Expanding developing country access to developed country markets for such products was also an important issue. Here the EU Common Agricultural Policy (CAP) was a frequent target for Herfkens who argued—unfortunately without much effect—that the CAP was disastrous, particularly for women in developing countries. They are the small farmers and labourers whose domestic markets the EU destroyed with subsidized milk powder and cans of tomato paste, and whose export potential the CAP limited through barriers on imports of products such as fruits and vegetables or cut flowers (see Chapter 9).

The other major sectoral intervention given high priority by the U4 was reproductive health. The emphasis in this sector was multilateral as all four contributed substantial resources through several global initiatives discussed below.

Multilateral Initiatives

Education for All (discussed in detail in Chapter 7) was by far the most important multilateral effort in which all four participated, but in which Herfkens, Johnson, and Short were especially involved. It was the most important because education is so critically important for women's empowerment. They were active at its very beginning, they fostered cooperation between the relevant UN organizations and the World Bank on the issue, convinced the World Bank to drop insistence on fees for primary education, and, over time helped fund the Fast Track Initiative. The Global Fund, in which Wieczorek-Zeul was especially active (and which was also discussed in Chapter 7) was also important for women as HIV/AIDS victims in sub-Saharan Africa are predominantly female.

This section addresses several other multilateral initiatives in which one or more of the U4 ministers played an important role and which were more explicitly focused on women's empowerment. These include the critical support they provided for UNFPA, the International Partnership for Microbicides (IPM), the World Bank's Gender Action Plan, and efforts in Women, Peace and Security, including the United Nations Action against Sexual Violence in Conflict.

United Nations Population Fund (UNFPA)

At the International Conference on Population and Development in Cairo in 1994, the international community had adopted an action plan to give all people by 2015 access to sexual education and family planning, protection against HIV/AIDS, access to health care for pregnancy and childbirth, and to strengthen the status of women in society. This action plan became the basis for the work of the United Nations Population Fund (UNFPA), the largest international organization in the field of reproductive health.[14] The global targets agreed at Cairo were in turn incorporated in the MDGs on maternal and child mortality. But because of opposition by the USA and a few other countries, the objectives regarding reproductive care were excluded from the targets.

In 1999 the Netherlands hosted in The Hague the Cairo-Plus Five conference aimed at reviewing progress and reinforcing the international community's efforts in the field of reproductive health. Hillary Clinton, who participated in the conference, praised 'the Netherlands for the lowest abortion and teen pregnancy rate per capita in the world, enabled by coherent policies which ensure abortions would be safe, legal and (thus) rare...'[15] Herfkens doubled spending on reproductive health to 6 per cent of its aid budget making the Netherlands the largest donor to UNFPA. It was sorely needed: at the time 78,000 women a year died because of backstreet abortions. Thus, when in 2000 UNFPA had a shortfall of some $100 million in its budget to provide condoms and the pill, particularly in sub-Saharan Africa, Short and Herfkens closed the gap by each providing an extra $50 million. The U4 in press conferences in sub-Saharan Africa and in meetings with African leaders, talked openly about the need for men to use condoms to protect women against HIV/AIDS.

Then on 22 January 2001, the first act of the new US administration headed by George W. Bush was to announce termination of its annual contribution of $34 million to the UNFPA. The US government accused the Fund of supporting forced abortions in China, an allegation that an investigation by the US State

Department could not confirm. The Executive Director of UNFPA, Thoraya Obaid of Saudi Arabia, criticized this at that time: 'With these 34 million US dollars two million unintended pregnancies and 77,000 cases of infant mortality could be prevented.'[16]

Within a few days, on 26 January, Herfkens wrote to the EU Development Commissioner, Poul Nielson, copied to Short, Wieczorek-Zeul, and the Swedish Development Minister, suggesting that the EU would publicly commit to compensate penny for penny the losses the relevant international organization including the UNFPA and the International Planned Parenthood Federation would suffer from this policy. Nielson agreed for the EU to 'bridge the decency gap', as did, obviously, Sweden (who at the time held the rotating presidency of the EU), as well as Short and Wieczorek-Zeul. Johnson was happy to pitch in. In the end the EU more than compensated for the shortfall caused by withdrawal of American funding. In addition, the EU tried to also compensate as many international NGOs as possible who were hit by the US policy. The Obama administration restored US participation in 2008, only for the Republican administration to again cut UNFPA funds in 2016.

International Partnership for Microbicides (IPM)

In the early twenty-first century poor women in sub-Saharan Africa were the fastest growing population who contracted HIV/AIDS, falling victim to men who refused to use condoms. Finding a means for them to protect themselves was an urgent challenge. The International Partnership for Microbicides (IPM), an international NGO, was founded in 2002 with the objective of developing HIV prevention products and other sexual and reproductive health technologies for women, and to make them available and accessible in poor developing countries, especially in sub-Saharan Africa where they are urgently needed. Herfkens became IPM's very first international donor. DfID and Norway soon followed. In 2008 Herfkens joined IPM's board, succeeded in 2014 by Wieczorek-Zeul, who was able to bring Germany on board as a donor. In 2020, Johnson continued the tradition succeeding Wieczorek- Zeul on the IPM Board.

The World Bank's Gender Action Plan

The World Bank had developed gender action plans in earlier periods—the first notable one in 1991. And it had published various influential studies that make the point that gender equality fosters growth and development (see p. 131). In 2006, at the initiative of Danny Leipziger, at the time vice President for Poverty Reduction and Economic Management (PREM) at the World Bank, the Bank launched its latest Gender Action Plan. Under the banner 'Gender Equality is Smart Economics' the Bank sought a partner in the G8 to solidify support and promote funding for the initiative. It found a willing partner in Wieczorek-Zeul who for many years had championed women's issues and funding in Germany's development assistance programmes. Together with the Bank she launched the initiative in Berlin through a conference on the 'Economic Power of Women' at the end of February 2007. The conference was attended by Chancellor Angela Merkel and ministers from several countries, including Denmark (Ulla Tornaes) and Egypt (Mahmoud Mohieldin).

The Gender Action Plan had a twin goal: to help empower women to be economically active and productive and to change the way Bank teams viewed the gender issue. The focus was on four issues: providing women with more productive inputs, such as in agriculture; providing women credit to spur entrepreneurship; helping women to function and be successful in the labour market; and helping women gain land titles to be used as collateral.[17] Wieczorek-Zeul continued to champion the Action Plan, including by distributing it to the members of the committee on Women's Rights and Gender Equality of the European Parliament, which she addressed on International Women's Day that year.[18]

The initiative was supported with funding from Germany, Denmark, Sweden, and the UK. Originally slated to raise $20 million over four years, it ultimately raised $70 million in total funding. The Bank prepared a major report on *Gender Equality and Development* in 2012 and is currently on its latest action plan contained in the *World Bank Strategy for 2016–2023*.[19]

The UN: Women, Peace, and Security

Conflict destroys millions of people's lives, leading to extreme poverty. Women and children are the ones most affected. Preventing and resolving conflicts is therefore of fundamental importance in combating extreme poverty. Yet, women are to a large degree excluded from such processes. This is particularly the case with peace processes aiming at ending conflict. Those who are holding the gun are usually the ones deciding the terms for silencing their guns. That belligerents are rewarded with the possibility of deciding on the terms of peace, often on issues of fundamental importance for post-war reconstruction, is a major problem.

This acknowledgement led to the engagement of several likeminded countries towards the passing of UN Security Council Resolution 1325 on Women, Peace and Security, agreed on 31 October 2000. This is considered a core UN resolution with a gender perspective, contributing to a stronger focus on the participation of women in peace processes and in peacebuilding. All U4 countries contributed to the analysis and deliberations at the UN which ultimately led to the passing of the resolution and all four subsequently organized seminars and conferences to promote its implementation. Johnson and Herfkens did, in their own way, contribute to its implementation, as they supported women groups' presence at the peace negotiations in Sudan and organized meetings for women from both parties aimed at influencing the talks and the delegations on each side during the period 2001–5. Johnson later engaged internationally to establish the Global Network of Women Mediators in 2019.

Sexual violence is used as a weapon of war. The U4 were engaged in this issue early on. Already when the negotiations on the Rome Statute for the International Criminal Court were underway in 1998–9, Short and Johnson engaged to ensure that sexual violence was included in the definition of war crimes and crimes against humanity in the convention text. This would lead to increased accountability for such violations against women and girls in conflicts around the world. The Rome statutes entered into force on 1 July 2002. At Wieczorek-Zeul's initiative, an informal EU Development Ministers meeting in 2007 issued a statement urging compliance with the statute by bringing responsible perpetrators before the International Criminal Court.

As Deputy Executive Director of UNICEF (see Chapter 10) Johnson followed up this engagement as chair of the network United Nations Action Against Sexual Violence in Conflict (in short, UN Action) in 2008–10. This was a cross-UN initiative that united the work of fourteen United Nations entities with the goal of ending sexual violence in conflict. The inter-agency network comprised UN entities from a spectrum of sectors including peacekeeping, political affairs, justice, human rights, humanitarian aid, health, gender equality, and women's empowerment. The efforts of UN Action under her tenure led to several breakthroughs in the Security Council against sexual violence in conflict, including in 2008 the establishment of a sanctions regime and the creation of a global advocate, the special representative against sexual violence in conflict. This has, in turn, led to a much stronger focus on sexual violence in conflict, both scaling up interventions of prevention, monitoring, and reporting on violations, and advocating for accountability against the perpetrators.[20]

Conclusion

Empowering women so that they can get out of poverty is a long-term, multi-dimensional struggle: it requires fundamental changes in society and culture, in politics and economics. While many of the specific targets in the MDGs were achieved (see Chapter 11), several involving gender issues were not: in particular, Goal 3, regarding the elimination of gender disparity in education, and (while some progress was made), in Goal 5, regarding the reduction of the maternal mortality rate by two thirds between 1990 and 2015. These two goals in which the least progress was made are illustrative of the challenges involved. They also demonstrate not only the need to retain a focus on fighting poverty, but also to ensure a simultaneous strong gender focus in all development work. Perhaps even more passionately than in other areas, the U4, acting together and separately, endeavoured to promote change in education, health, and economic empowerment of women.

Their legacy continues: IPM is on the brink of a breakthrough ... still trying to develop means to help women prevent HIV infections; and Education for All (now renamed the Global Partnership for Education) and the Global Fund continue their work helping girls and women.

The Sustainable Development Goals agreed at the UN to be achieved by 2030 (see Chapter 12) contain even more goals affecting gender. SDG 3 seeks to end HIV/AIDS, which is critical for young girls in sub-Saharan African countries, whose infection frequently results from sexual violence. SDG 5 asks to end all forms of discrimination against women, in all fields be they political, economic, or cultural, including their sexual and reproductive rights. SDG 10 asks to abolish inequality in all forms. That the SDGs include many more goals and indicators that would improve the lives of women is in itself an achievement.

But a recent *Lancet* study has shown that the newly re-established Trump administration policy of curbing US assistance to family planning organizations—especially those that consider abortion as a method of family planning—will likely increase abortion prevalence in sub-Saharan African countries most affected by the policy.[21] The challenges remain and may be even greater today.

The struggle continues.

Notes

1. Eveline Herfkens, speech, National School of Government/International Women's Leadership Conference, London, 4 March 2010.
2. Barbara Herz, email, 24 October 2019.
3. Christian Democratic Party, *Counter White Paper: Solidarity with the South: Major Interventions in Norwegian Development Policies (1995-6)*, p. 78.
4. Hilde F. Johnson, email, 28 May 2019.
5. Heidemarie Wieczorek-Zeul, *Gerechtigkeit und Frieden sind Geschwister* (Marburg: Schuren, 2018), p. 127.
6. Clare Short, speech, University of Nottingham, 23 November 1999.
7. Hilde F. Johnson, speech, Nordic Solidarity, Conference on Education and Development Cooperation, 3-4 June 2002, on the theme 'Education, a Weapon against Poverty?'
8. Eveline Herfkens, speech, Leiden University, 8 March 2001.
9. Wieczorek-Zeul, Gerechtigkeit und Frieden sind Geschwister, p. 126.
10. Herfkens, note, 30 June 2019; a similar point was made by Johnson, email, 28 May 2019.

11. Clare Short, comment, 19 August 2019.
12. See https://en.wikipedia.org/wiki/Commission_on_Legal_Empowerment_of_the_Poor.
13. See https://www.regjeringen.no/globalassets/upload/kilde/ud/pla/2004/0001/ddd/pdfv/210700-landbruk.pdf (*Agriculture against Poverty: The Norwegian Government's Action Plan for Agricultural Development*, 2004).
14. Wieczorek-Zeul, *Gerechtigkeit und Frieden sind Geschwister*, p. 125.
15. Hillary Clinton, Keynote Speech, Education for All Conference, Amsterdam, 9 February 1999.
16. Wieczorek-Zeul, *Gerechtigkeit und Frieden sind Geschwister*, p. 125.
17. Danny Leipziger, email, 21 May 2019.
18. H. Wieczorek-Zeul, '1957–2007: The European Union and the Advancement of Women: Women Building the Future of Europe', Brussels, 8 March 2007, Committee on Women's Rights and Gender Equality of the European Parliament.
19. World Bank, 'World Bank Gender Strategy', *World Development Report* (Washington, DC: World Bank, 2012).
20. Draft material for this section, including the relevant references, provided by Hilde F. Johnson, email and comments, 19 August 2019; UN Security Council resolutions S/RES/1820 (2008), 19 June; S/RES/1882 (2009), 4 August; followed by S/RES/1888 (2009), 30 September (paras 4, 5, and 10); and S/RES/1960 (2010), 16 December (para. 3).
21. *The Lancet*, 'The Devastating Impact of Trump's Gag Rule', 393(10189) (15 June 2019).

9

A Coherence Deficit

Introduction

Policy coherence for development (PCD) involves the systematic establishment of mutually reinforcing policy action across government departments and agencies to promote poverty reduction and sustainable development. Coherence was a central theme of the U4 from the very beginning of their collaboration. They pushed for policy coherence in their development partner countries by supporting the PRSP process and encouraging consistent developing country policies in support of poverty eradication.

Ensuring that the OECD countries pursued coherent policies vis-à-vis developing countries was in some respects an even bigger challenge. Unlike other OECD members such as the USA and France, where bilateral aid and multilateral organizations are dealt with by different ministries or agencies, the Utstein Four were at least able to control and/or influence both bilateral and multilateral assistance policies. But as we discussed in Chapter 5, the UN is typically the bailiwick of Foreign Ministries: sectoral ministries handle specialized agencies, and, most importantly, Ministries of Trade are in charge of trade policies.

Compartmentalization of national policies in developed countries can lead to incoherent policies towards developing countries. It is difficult for Development Ministers to muster the political clout to ensure that the 'development' objective is fully taken into account in policy decisions affecting their countries' foreign policy and economic or other interests. Indeed, in the Netherlands, Norway, and the UK the justification for establishing a cabinet-level position was that it enabled the minister and their ministries to interact with other ministries at the same level and participate in regular cabinet meetings. In the Netherlands, the minister's position was further strengthened by explicit reference to PCD requirements in the 1998 government coalition agreement.

There are many potential conflicts in PCD: multinationals may be exploiting developing country resources based on inequitable agreements in areas such as trade, investment, taxes, and finance; developed country defence industries may be pushing arms exports and saddling developing countries with unsustainable debts; and environmental concerns may be juxtaposed with developmental objectives. The biggest problems usually involve trade policy conflicts: aid projects aiming to increase developing country exports have often been stymied by protectionist import restrictions in developed country markets; agricultural export and domestic support for their own farmers by developed countries typically undermine aid agency efforts to increase food production in poor countries; rules protecting intellectual property have hindered public health and access to affordable medicines in developing countries; and there is an insidious link between developed country aid programmes and export promotion: all too often, aid has been used as a market distorting instrument by assisting developed country inefficient exporters through 'tying' of assistance to procurement in the donor country.

Incoherence problems arise also among various international agencies. Imagine a developing country receiving advice on its trade policy: the Planning or Development Minister will be advised by the World Bank to adopt a liberal trade policy as it is good for efficient resource allocation, will promote growth and, provided that it is accompanied by lots of other policies, poverty alleviation; UNCTAD on the other hand had traditionally espoused protectionism primarily influenced by old-style industrial policy considerations; the Finance Minister will be advised by the IMF to be cautious because trade liberalization may result in loss of tariff revenue with adverse impact on the budget; and the Trade Minister would learn from other Trade Ministers in the WTO not to liberalize anything as unilateral liberalization is regarded as giving away your negotiating chips. It is enough to give up and do nothing, or follow the advice of the last institution you spoke to, or the one that gives the most money.

This chapter will discuss U4 efforts to promote policy coherence to deal with a number of these issues. First, I will address the trade policy conflicts. Development Ministers often must wage battle with domestic protectionist interests, advocating open markets for developing countries' exports; or with developed country exporters, trying to slash their subsidies or other incentives on all sorts of things ranging from food to fighter aircraft that undermine developing country producers or priorities. Then I turn my attention to U4 efforts to promote 'untying' of aid procurement by source. This is frequently viewed as a 'quality of aid' issue. I deal it with in this chapter because Development Ministers must fight off the same donor export interests to permit developing countries to use aid money to buy goods or services from the least expensive source, thus making aid go further. The final section will discuss coherence between environment and development concerns as they emerged in the World Summit on Sustainable Development (WSSD) in Johannesburg in 2002.

Trade Policy

Changing trade policy so that it helps developing country exports at the expense of inefficient developed country domestic producers and creates policy space for economic development, is a challenging task as it brings global development considerations in conflict with powerful domestic vested interests. The U4 situation was even more complicated as three of the four countries were members of the EU where trade policy is made at the EU level: the European Commission negotiates on behalf of Member States, be it after authorization of a negotiating mandate of the EU Council, while agreements require final approval of both the Council and of the European Parliament by a qualified majority. The Utstein efforts had two dimensions: first and foremost, promoting EU policy coherence and second, promoting such coherence at the global level in connection with the workings of the WTO.

Policy Coherence for Development (PCD) in the European Union

The EU Maastricht Treaty of 1992 pledged that 'The Union shall take account of the objectives of development cooperation in the policies that it implements which are likely to affect developing countries.' In reality, however, the policy prescription of 'shall' remained for a long time a dead letter for all intents and purposes. There was the fundamental juxtaposition of narrow domestic economic interests versus global development concerns. There were additional difficulties because of different national interests within the EU: in particular, there was a North–South divide, with Southern Europe feeling more often the impact of open trade policies, for example regarding textiles, or many agricultural products competing with developing countries. Moreover, different groups of developing countries had conflicting interests: ACP countries earned large benefits from EU trade policy in certain commodities such as bananas and sugar imports, which were given significant preferences in EU markets. And there was complicated decision making involving many different EU bureaucracies with limited understanding of developing country interests.

The three EU Utstein ministers tried their best to promote more open EU markets for developing country agriculture and other exports. Dutch efforts focused explicitly on trade interests of low-income countries and the LDCs. As early as November 1998, Herfkens had started to push the EU Development Council to become a standard bearer for addressing 'coherence' issues that were on the agenda of other Councils, such as trade, agriculture, and fisheries, and to implement a resolution on coherence that the Council had passed in 1997.

Short's second White Paper argued that

> Globalization is reinforcing the need for a more integrated approach to policy making. Policies no longer fit into neat sectoral boxes and the distinction between domestic and international policy is increasingly blurred. The formulation of sustainable development strategies in a global economy requires that developed and developing countries have more joined up and coherent policies.

There is a particular responsibility on developed countries. There is no sense for example in using development assistance to support countries and then undermining this through trade restrictions and unfair subsidies. All developed countries policies towards the world's poorest countries should be consistent with a commitment to sustainable development and poverty reduction.[1]

And further, 'Getting a pro-development EU position across this wide range of trade issues is of enormous importance in securing a fairer deal for developing countries.'[2]

A particular concern was the EU Common Agricultural Policy (CAP) which obstructed developing country exports to protect inefficient EU farmers of many primary commodities through a myriad of tariff and non-tariff trade measures and protectionist subsidies. Cotton, which needs a lot of water and is a major export of several very poor LDCs in the Sahel was, and still is, being produced with generous subsidies in bone dry Spain and arid Greece. Rice was, and still is, cultivated in the Po river valley in Italy's north; sugar beet in Germany, France, and elsewhere; and the CAP shielded fruits and vegetables produced in the south of the EU from competing imports from developing countries. Moreover, the CAP had been protected from serious change by the WTO agreements which permitted continued support and even export subsidies for European farmers. Norway's farmers were equally, if not more, protected. But they produced little in competition with developing countries.

Starting soon after the establishment of the WTO, the LDCs pushed for provision of special and differential treatment for their products in the form of duty free and quota free access to developed country markets, more policy space in other areas, and assistance to strengthen their capacity to trade. The Nordics in the EU, Ireland, the Netherlands, and the UK sent a letter to the EU Development Council on 30 November 1998 advocating improved LDC access to the EU market. The same countries sent a similar letter to the Council on 18 May 2000 with the same message, but this time linked to the upcoming UNCTAD conference on the LDCs to be cohosted by the EU Commission scheduled for the spring of 2001.

In March 2001, pushed by the same group of member states and others, the EU Commission proposed a new policy according to which imports of 'Everything but Arms' (EbA) would henceforth enter the EU markets free of customs duties and no longer subject to any quantitative restrictions. There were three—albeit temporary—exceptions: bananas, sugar, and rice.[3] The Dutch had wanted fewer exceptions, and less onerous preferential rules of origin to determine what products would be considered as originating in LDCs in order to allow them to add value to imported intermediate products and inputs. They also wanted to include the HIPCs as beneficiaries—a proposal that had failed in 1999.[4] Despite opposition from several member states, the Commission proposal survived, helped along by the intervention of the Dutch Prime Minister who wrote supportive personal letters to his EU counterparts.[5]

The EU's sanitary and phytosanitary standards also became the target of Herfkens' interventions: in October 2001 she complained, in vain, that the new EU food safety regulations, which exceeded those required by international standards endorsed by the WTO could 'wipe out African exporters'.[6] Indeed, the pioneering work of Otsuki and others estimated that a 1998 EU regulation that imposed stricter standards than the international standard for the presence of aflatoxin (a toxic substance) found in foodstuffs and animal feed would cost $700 million in lost revenue for African exporters of groundnuts.[7]

The EU Commission during this period had also been engaged in extensive negotiations with the ACP countries which resulted in the conclusion of the Cotonou Agreement in June 2000. The Agreement, which covers the twenty-year period 2000–20, defines the aid, trade, and political relationships between the EU and developing countries which had been former colonies and dependencies. Its objective is 'to reduce and eventually eradicate poverty and to contribute to the gradual integration of the ACP into the world economy'.[8] It provides for preferential treatment of these countries in EU markets as well as sets up procedures for the funding and conditions of EU assistance in five-year increments—with the first-five year allotment for the period 2002–7.

Arguably, the Cotonou Agreement could be viewed as a point of reference for coherence discussions. It was not, I suspect, because there were differences among the U4. Besides Norway not being an EU member, Herfkens doubted that the Cotonou approach of establishing 'Economic Partnership Agreements' which involved reciprocal preferences would be helpful for sub-Saharan Africa;[9] Germany was not willing to challenge the Commission on trade issues and the UK was somewhere in the middle.

Herfkens presented a paper on coherence at the Utstein 2001 ministerial meeting in Birmingham which formed the basis for an extensive discussion. She introduced the paper by stressing that aid alone would not achieve the poverty target. Development Ministers should be the voice of the poor in their own governments. Given entrenched national interests, a strong commitment was needed at the top of government. This could be helped by building alliances with civil society to put pressure on governments. Contrary to the opposition many NGOs had shown towards the WTO, a WTO Round was central to future trade policy as was the balanced implementation of the Uruguay Round agreements especially as they related to intellectual property rights in pharmaceuticals and protection of biodiversity, genetic resources, and traditional knowledge.

The Dutch paper argued that coherence should be a standard agenda item at every EU Development Council. But the Development Directorate of the European Commission was not adequately staffed for this agenda. In May 2000, Herfkens had succeeded in getting agreement that the Commission would create a focal point within the Directorate General for Development to check Commission-wide issues of incoherence; and that coherence would be on every Development Council agenda. Regrettably, the focal point was soon abolished. The thinking in Brussels was that coherence should start at home: 'If Member States cannot master that at home and fail to send their Ministers for Agriculture, Trade, Development Cooperation to their various Councils with a coordinated mandate, you cannot expect a little "coherence focal point" at DG/Development to fix this.'[10]

Following the Birmingham meeting, the three EU ministers initiated a campaign to encourage the EU to open its markets for developing country exports. They did this in several ways: first, they started to push the Development Commissioner Poul Nielsen to engage more actively in defending the development case when such policies were being considered by the Commission and they sent a letter to him to this effect which was supported by Sweden.[11] Second, they continued to raise trade policy issues at the Development Council. Two prospective EU policy reviews offered opportunities for helping developing country prospects: a prospective review of the CAP and the EU External Fisheries policy. The Dutch also tried to raise development issues in other Councils: regarding agriculture, the Dutch Minister for Agriculture in the Agriculture Council opposed the EU policy on sugar as well as on sending subsidized beef surplus as food aid—but in vain.

The ministers also agreed that access to good special advice was important and noted that the UK had benefitted, as discussed earlier, by staffing up with trade specialists to the chagrin of their Trade Ministry. Herfkens reported that Otto Genee, a Dutch WTO expert, headed 'coherence' team within her ministry, including monitoring relevant issues such as the EU fishery agreements with ACP countries and regulations on sanitary and phytosanitary standards.

Genee and his team worked closely with their British colleagues and played an active role in promoting trade opening to developing countries across national boundaries in the EU in subsequent years. They created a network among interested development agencies, empowering others with the relevant information and arguments to promote coherence within their countries, using the opportunities of CAP reform and the WTO negotiations in the by then launched Doha Round. Screening procedures for legislative proposals and reporting mechanisms on PCD were created at EU and OECD/DAC levels. Alas, most other member states ducked: they either stated they did not have the staff or would not/ could not confront other parts of their government. France and Southern European countries opposed the concept as such.[12]

The World Trade Organization (WTO)

All U4 ministers supported strongly a new Round of multilateral trade negotiations (MTN) that would focus on development issues. Developing countries had been complaining, with some justification, that developed countries had not lived up to their commitments in the previous Round of trade negotiations (the so-called Uruguay Round) which had concluded with the creation of the WTO. They were unwilling to enter into a new set of negotiations on new issues such as those that had been raised by developed countries in the Singapore WTO ministerial meeting in 1997 (investment, competition, government procurement, and trade facilitation) until developed country earlier commitments, in particular on agriculture and textiles, had been fulfilled.

Short argued in a speech she gave at an UNCTAD meeting in Geneva on 2 March 1999 that 'It is in all interests that a new Round is designed to bring clear benefits to the developing countries which form the majority of the WTO. That is why I want to propose that we all work to make the next Round a Development Round.'[13]

She thereby coined the term 'Development Round' that was to become the rallying cry and indeed the basic concept around which new negotiations could proceed. It was not an easy path. The next WTO ministerial meeting took place in Seattle in December 1999 with Short giving a keynote Address on 'Trade and Development Prospects'. Unfortunately, the Seattle meeting failed to launch a new Round, partly because of bad planning, preparation, and organization by the USA, partly because of large-scale demonstrations by NGOs which had started to view the WTO trade rules as inimical to development.

Both Short and Herfkens opposed the NGOs on this: in a speech in The Hague on 16 December 1999, Herfkens said:

> In Seattle in early December we expected to hear the starting gun signaling a new development round. A series of negotiations on international trade in which the interests of the developing countries would carry real weight. And we did hear shots—but the rubber bullets and tear gas did not signal the start of anything. It was a painful experience, most of all for developing countries. The incident in Seattle was a heavy blow to anyone seriously committed to sustainable development and poverty reduction. 'Ding, dong, the Round is dead', joyous demonstrators chanted. But they were wrong. The fight is just beginning.[14]

And indeed the Seattle meeting did permit progress in an important area for the developing countries (see Box 9.1).

In a statement to a parliamentary committee on 23 May 2000, Short said: 'It is my very strong view that the WTO is the best possible chance developing countries have and the global system has of establishing equitable rules of trade and creating conditions where the poorer countries can get more benefits from international trade.' And further, 'the need for developing countries to gain from the Round has become clearer and clearer, but that it will not be a simple process'.[15]

Box 9.1. Protecting developing country rights in the WTO: The Advisory Centre on WTO Law (ACWL)

The WTO operates under a series of treaties that result in legal obligations for its members, large or small. Treaty violations are settled through the WTO Dispute Settlement Mechanism (DSM) that involves judicial procedures which permit even the smallest member to protect its rights. But using the DSM requires costly, specialized legal expertise, not easily available to developing countries, especially LDCs. The ACWL was established in Geneva in 2001, independent of the WTO, to provide developing countries with the legal capacity necessary to enable them to protect their rights and take full advantage of the opportunities offered by the WTO.

Though not a U4 initiative, the Centre owes a great deal to the support it has received from the Netherlands, Norway and the UK. Claudia Orozco, Colombia's WTO representative is credited with the original idea, aided by the Netherlands' Otto Genee and the UK's Peter Jenkins. Norway, an important WTO player outside the EU, also provided useful support. The EU Commission did not like the proposed Centre and put great pressure on its members to marginalize it by making it part of the WTO itself—which would have gutted its capacity to provide truly independent legal advice to developing countries. The USA was initially non-committal but Herfkens helped ensure that it would at least not oppose the initiative at a luncheon meeting with US WTO Ambassador Rita Hayes, the very day she was invited to join the Dutch cabinet in July 1998.

The original proposal was approved by the WTO General Council with surprisingly strong support from the USA, and Orozco and Genee were appointed to lead the Preparatory Committee. The Treaty establishing the Centre was supposed to be approved at an official singing ceremony at the Seattle WTO ministerial meeting in December 1999. As the Seattle streets had been taken over by demonstrators, the delegates were locked up either in their hotels or in the conference centre. Genee braved the crowds and managed to get to Short's hotel to obtain hers and others' signatures. The agreement to establish the ACWL turned out to be the only outcome of the Seattle Ministerial. The Centre continues to function today with a membership of eleven developed (including all U4) and thirty-five developing countries—but its services are also available to all forty-four LDCs which are either WTO members or in the process of accession.

In late 2000, Herfkens joined her own Minister for International Trade and the Swedish Ministers of Trade and Development to cooperate in writing an op-ed complaining that the EU proposals for implementing the Uruguay Round commitment to eliminate import quotas on textiles and clothing were not meaningful for European consumers and developing countries.[16] This complaint echoed similar developing country complaints that developed countries were implementing the letter but not the spirit of the Uruguay Round agreement that terminated the Multi-Fibre Arrangement under which developed countries had controlled imports of textiles and clothing from developing countries through bilateral quantitative restrictions.

Other developing countries' complaints about the results of the Uruguay Round that launched the WTO focused on the provisions for protection of intellectual property rights under the Trade-Related Aspects of Intellectual Property Rights (TRIPS) agreement. The agreement increased the monopoly protection of patents for pharmaceuticals owned by developed country companies in developing countries (with the exception of LDCs) which could result in significant increases in prices of medicines essential for the improvement of health and the fighting of pandemics like HIV/AIDS in developing countries. This problem could be addressed through compulsory licencing (the multinational is forced to licence the supply of the drug to a local manufacturer) and other provisions of TRIPS that permit flexibility in its application for the benefit of public health. When, however, South Africa tried to use this flexibility in 1997, permitting compulsory licencing under their own law for the domestic production of generic drugs against HIV/AIDS, and imports of generic substitutes from countries such as India not yet covered by patent protection, the USA and global pharmaceutical companies started legal proceedings in South Africa. This raised a global hue and cry from all those concerned with development and led to many efforts by the U4 to suggest modifications to the TRIPS agreement. In May 2001, Short established a Commission on Intellectual Property Rights tasked with producing an analysis inter alia of how intellectual property regimes can be designed to benefit developing countries in the context of international agreements and how to improve international rules and agreements that would benefit traditional knowledge.[17] Herfkens made proposals aimed at ensuring developing country policy flexibility that would enable them to obtain access to cheaper generic pharmaceuticals.[18]

A new WTO Round of multilateral negotiations was launched with much fanfare in Doha, in November 2001. The Round was based on the so-called Doha Development Agenda which was designed to address developing country concerns both about opening developed country markets for their exports as well as establishing global trade rules and policy space tailored to each country's level of development. The launching of the Round also contained a 'Declaration on TRIPS and Public Health' which confirmed the existing flexibilities available to developing countries to introduce compulsory licencing and other measures for public health and started the amendment process to correct the gap for developing countries without domestic production capacity by allowing compulsory licencing to a foreign producer.

Coherence Revisited

The World Bank Development Committee meeting a few days later gave the U4 the opportunity to welcome the launching of the Doha Round—although the meeting's communique was strangely silent on the subject.[19] On the other hand, the UN Finance for Development Monterrey meeting in March 2002 contained extensive references to the need for greater coherence in government policies for development both at the national and international level. Besides the world leaders attending, Ministers of Trade and Finance were also present. This was the first and probably the last occasion on which world leaders agreed to take steps to improve policy coherence for development combining trade and finance. Everybody seemed to agree that the new WTO Round should become a real Development Round contributing to the achievement of the MDGs. But of course, lack of coherence is not limited to rich countries (see Box 9.2).

Back in Europe policies were not living up to promises: the Dutch letter on reform of the EU fisheries policies did not yield any results. Despite U4 criticism of the lack of coherence in the renewed EU Fisheries agreement with Mauritania, the agreement was approved by the EU Fisheries Council as the required blocking minority was not achieved.[20]

Box 9.2. China's policy coherence?

In 1996 Herfkens moved from her position as Netherlands executive director at the World Bank to become ambassador in Geneva. At her last board meeting, World Bank President Wolfensohn, just returned from a visit to China, distributed to the board a coffee-table book produced by the Chinese Ministry of Finance, with beautiful pictures showing China's successful development—for which the book largely credited the World Bank. Four days later, upon arrival in Geneva, Herfkens was briefed by her staff regarding the agenda of the upcoming Human Rights Commission meeting. The Human Rights Commission had been dominated by developing countries with dubious human rights records. One of the resolutions on the meeting's agenda blamed the International Monetary Fund and the World Bank for violating human rights. Among its sponsors: China.

The Netherlands also prepared a paper on CAP reform which was cleared by Germany and the UK. Herfkens then presented the paper at the EU Development Council as a Dutch position. Despite support from Short and Wieczorek-Zeul during the discussion, nothing came of it because of unsurmountable resistance, mainly from France and Portugal.[21]

Following the agreement in Doha, the trade negotiations proceeded very slowly. As noted earlier, the so called 'Doha Development Agenda' had many implications for developing countries. One of the most important was the 'Declaration on Health' in which it was agreed that, under the compulsory licencing provisions of TRIPS, each WTO member has the right to determine what constitutes a national emergency and that public health crises relating to HIV/AIDS, TB, malaria, and other epidemics can represent a national emergency. As it was apparent that provisions for compulsory licencing (see above p. 148) may not be very meaningful for developing countries that do not have the capacity to produce the drugs domestically, the 'Declaration' instructed the WTO to find a solution to this problem. An agreement was reached at the end of August 2003, under heavy political pressure to settle the issue before the fifth WTO ministerial meeting which was to take place in Cancún, Mexico in September 2003. This introduced various reporting requirements but permitted developing countries to import pharmaceuticals cheaply in case of national emergencies.

The WTO ministerial meeting in Cancún was also to address a number of developing countries' problems, especially regarding agriculture, including phasing out cotton subsidies by developed countries, in which EU subsidies continued to undermine LDC exports, though the US policies in this area were arguably equally egregious. At a meeting of the Utstein Group in Dubai earlier in September 2003 on the fringes of the World Bank/IMF meeting in which both Canada and Sweden participated, Wieczorek-Zeul complained that 'the trade-related measures in the cotton market are irrational. The industrialized countries should be focusing trade policies on the MDGs but are in fact doing just the opposite and thereby increasing poverty.' She suggested that the EU members of the Utstein group should try to arrive at a common position and liaise on the matter before the next Council on development cooperation issues; and that at the Development Committee the World Bank should be called on to make additional efforts in its country assistance strategies to assist cotton producing developing countries.[22]

The Cancún meeting proved very contentious. The problems of four very poor producers of cotton in the Sahel (Benin, Burkina Faso, Chad, and Mali) were being ignored. Johnson and Wieczorek-Zeul had travelled to Cancún to discuss with their ministers ways of going forward, especially as the German government together with the World Bank, France, and the Netherlands had been giving assistance to cotton producers in the four countries to make their cotton competitive in the world markets. The EU Commission demurred: they pointed to the fact that unlike other governments (including the USA and China) they did not provide export subsidies for cotton. Indeed, the EU was a large importer of cotton.[23] But they neglected to say that the EU was providing huge support to very uncompetitive farmers in Greece and Spain to keep producing cotton and that without this support the EU would import much more cotton from the Sahel and elsewhere.

Besides the agreement on TRIPS, the Cancún negotiations achieved little. Neither the developed countries nor the more advanced developing countries provided preferential treatment to LDCs in the area they should have—improved market access for their exports. Recall, that the EU had put in place EbA, which provided the LDCs with duty free and quota free (DFQF) access to its markets. But the USA would only agree to provide DFQF access to 97 per cent of the tariff lines of imports from LDCs. Several studies showed that the remaining 3 per cent could include so many products that the market access improvement would be miniscule.[24] And the EU programme yielded small benefits because of rules that limited eligibility based on the product's origin. In the end, the only thing agreed, at the insistence of the developing countries, was that the negotiations would *exclude* discussion on foreign investment, competition, and government procurement, and focus solely on reducing protection in agriculture and manufactured goods.

Johnson, Short, and Wieczorek-Zeul were also active in trying to block export credits and other incentives to their domestic interests to provide financing to developing countries inconsistent with their development plans. Chapter 6 discussed the problems Short encountered in Tanzania with export financing for military sales. Johnson recalls that she was able to stop all export credits that could have qualified as ODA. And Wieczorek-Zeul remembers blocking export credit insurance for the construction of a major dam in India that was not environmentally sound, as well as blocking export financing for the military.[25]

The Untying Saga

Promotion of national economic interests under the guise of assistance to poor countries is an old story: Commonwealth assistance loans to India and Pakistan in the late 1950s were provided on quasi-commercial terms for the purchase of British goods and services, with some portion earmarked for the purchase of steel products for which there was surplus capacity in Britain.[26] Early on, the Dutch aid programme was viewed as an 'excellent source of employment for the many tropical experts who risked losing their jobs as a result of decolonization'.[27] 'Tying' aid procurement to the donor can be of obvious benefit to its export industries and technical services' companies. It can also build domestic political constituencies for development assistance with economic assistance coming from the ODA budget. But it comes at a cost which has been estimated at around 30 per cent of the value of the aid given because tying frequently involves provision of goods and services at higher costs than can be obtained on the open market. Moreover, as tied aid implies procurement without international tendering, it is very prone to corruption. Tying also tilts the kinds of products supplied: for example, in the health sector, it may result in providing sophisticated products (e.g. MRI scanners) produced by the donor when needles and bandage are more urgently needed. It can also create huge inefficiencies in running a public health investment policy when other donors apply the same methods.

Tying is a problem for bilateral assistance. Multilateral aid provided, for example, by the World Bank or Regional Development Banks is untied by source.[28] Over the years, there had been numerous efforts to conclude an agreement in the DAC to have all or parts of bilateral assistance untied on a multilateral basis. The idea behind this is that if all donors would untie their bilateral aid at the same time, their economies would benefit from each other's financing thus limiting the potential adverse impact on national producers and the balance of their international payments.

I was personally involved in leading the US team negotiating such an agreement in the DAC in 1976–7. At the time the countries most opposed were France, Japan, and Denmark. Still, we were on the verge of reaching agreement, after excluding technical assistance and food aid from the deal. But, in 1978 there was a change in government in Washington. The new authorities were concerned about the potentially adverse political impact of the arrangement on a few key constituents and the USA walked away from the deal.

Twenty years later, in April 1998, the DAC High Level meeting tasked the OECD secretariat to come up with a proposal for untying assistance to LDCs. This more limited agreement was deemed to have a chance of success, partly because it involved less than the total aid; partly because it was deemed that LDCs were especially vulnerable to the costs of tying. A proposal was developed, and it was initially expected that an agreement would be reached within a year, that is, at the DAC High Level meeting in April 1999.

This is where the matter stood when the four ministers descended on the scene. They were not the Utstein Four yet, as the Utstein Abbey meeting had not yet occurred. This was the second international meeting in which they would present a unified front (after the spring 1999 Development Committee meeting discussed in Chapter 3). Herfkens, who had just been accused of 'killing babies' because she had untied technical cooperation that had hitherto provided expensive employment for Dutch doctors in Africa, was strongly in favour of untying; the other three were equally committed with both the UK and Germany having already untied very large proportions of their aid. Norway had by then untied almost 100 per cent of its aid with only a few tons of dried fish remaining (which would soon be abolished).[29] But an agreement could not be reached: France, Japan, and Denmark were opposed—just as they were twenty years earlier. The DAC High

Level meeting communique said: 'The DAC reaffirms its support for the untying of aid to LDCs and declares its commitment to work towards a Recommendation to untie ODA to LDCs in accordance with the DAC mandate.'[30]

Short was very strongly opposed to tying aid procurement. In a blistering speech with the title 'Protectionism in Aid Procurement: Disposing of a Dinosaur', she stressed that 'the move towards more sector-wide approaches, under which donors club together to support sound programmes is undermined by the practice of aid tying'.

She gave three reasons why tying aid is bad practice:

(a) Value for the taxpayers money, since tying reduces the real value of aid by about 25%; aid is a very scarce resource and we cannot afford the inefficiency that comes with restricting procurement; (b) tying makes aid coordination more difficult: a developing country that is trying to strengthen its health sector may have to divide up procurement to fit the differing requirements of maybe half a dozen donors each with differing procurement requirements; and (c) the most pernicious problem, is that it signals that donor's major concern is not development but the next contract; as such it encourages corruption, inappropriate technology and a supplier driven mentality. And in any case it is well known that government subsidies to industry to export to developing countries—which are formally illegal under the WTO—will not sustain uncompetitive firms nor maintain jobs other than the shortest term.[31]

An effort was to be made to reach agreement at the next DAC High Level meeting on 11–12 May 2000, which was to be followed by the second U4 Ministerial in The Hague on 12–13 May 2000. The agreement was to exclude technical assistance and food aid. Still it was not possible to make a deal. The minutes of the Utstein Second Ministerial state: 'Ministers regretted the fact that the DAC High Level meeting of 11 and 12 May had not yet reached a consensus on a recommendation to untie aid. The Chairman's recommendations were considered as a way of making some progress. Efforts will be directed towards other OECD member states to respond positively to the request from the Chairman to agree to the recommendations by June 20, 2000.'[32]

Alas, no deal was made in June 2000 either. A report on the meetings in Paris on 21–2 June said that

after two days of meetings the negotiations between the members of the DAC were broken off without results, as they were not able to agree on untying of aid to poor countries. Denmark, France and Japan continue to demand that developing countries spend the aid in the donor countries...Given the lack of consensus the UK announced that it would put the subject on the agenda of the G8 meeting in July in Japan. This threatened to embarrass both France and

Japan. The pressure to eliminate tied aid is also increasing as the European Commission, including at the insistence of the Netherlands, is investigating the unfair competition resulting from this practice. There are also doubts if tying of aid complies with the competition and procurement rules in the WTO.[33]

An agreement to untie aid to LDCs excluding technical cooperation and food aid was finally reached at the DAC High Level meeting of 25 April 2001. Koos Richelle, the DG for Development at the EU Commission and a strong supporter of untying, helped forge the agreement by convincing the delegations of Denmark and Japan to agree as long as they were able to provide separate declarations about the importance of burden sharing: these countries believed that as their ODA budgets were (either absolutely or relatively) comparatively large, the cost of untying for them would be that much higher. The European Commission also made a declaration that it would try to adhere to the recommendations. In practice it did little in this respect. However, the fact that EU aid was open to procurement from all EU members, meant that the cost to the LDCs from tying was minimized as it could be reasonably be expected that companies from one or other of these countries could provide these goods or services on a globally competitive basis.

Based on the Richelle report (see Chapter 7), the Commission recommended that members fully untie all bilateral aid for procurement among the—at the time fifteen member states. Some countries (the Netherlands, the UK) wanted to go beyond the DAC recommendations and untie aid further. At the Third Ministerial Meeting in Birmingham on 5 November 2001, Herfkens was concerned that the Commission was not taking the implementation of untying seriously enough and was giving an excuse for Japan to avoid action. She thought it would be useful to extend untying to all countries with good PRSPs. Germany was among those countries that did not wish to go beyond the DAC recommendations. In the end, the ministers agreed that the EU members of the group send a letter to Prodi, the President of the Commission, and invite other like-minded EU members, such as Belgium, Denmark, Luxemburg, and Sweden to join. The UK drafted a letter which, however, Germany was unable to approve, and the letter apparently was not sent.[34]

Untying did not feature as a topic at the Wiesbaden ministerial meeting in July 2002 and subsequent meetings. The issue of untying continued to concern the EU, however. In particular the question was raised as to whether tying practices were contrary to EU provisions on competition. There were further discussions in the EU on ways to untie both bilateral and EU aid which resulted in additional progress on the issue. The Netherlands also raised the question as to whether the WTO agreement on government procurement which explicitly excludes aid from its coverage could be modified. However, this was never brought up in the WTO for lack of support among the member states.

The Environment

The complex links and tradeoffs in protecting the environment and promoting development were already highlighted by the Rio Conference in 1992. The U4 were keenly aware of the issues. They joked that on the continuum between 'saving the planet and saving the people', Wieczorek-Zeul was closer to the planet end, Herfkens and Short closer to the people, and Johnson somewhere in the middle. Early on they commissioned a paper from Johnson on what the added value could be of Utstein action on climate change—with the paper addressing also the broader issue of sustainable development in economic, social, and environmental respects.[35]

The most important event on which they wanted to coordinate positions was the upcoming World Summit on Sustainable Development in Johannesburg in the autumn of 2002. At their Birmingham meeting in late 2001, 'some shared a concern that the WSSD risked being hijacked by a narrow environmental agenda (at the expense of any poverty focus)'. Apparently this was based on a Johnson report that Annan had expressed such concerns on his visit to Norway just prior to the meeting. They agreed that it was crucial to build development issues into the process. Water and health were a priority for Norway; and water, desertification, and energy efficiency for Germany.[36]

Following up on this meeting, the responsible divisions of the U4 ministries met for a short preparatory meeting on the WSSD and subsequently Johnson and Herfkens sent a letter to the Chair of WSSD, Mr Salim, to ensure that the action programme would take adequate account of the importance of the PRSPs, but the 'poverty-environment' linkages needed to be greater stressed in the 'Political Declaration'. Furthermore, the EU Development Council decided on partnership-based initiatives in the following areas: water supply and sanitation, energy, health, and trade-related measures with particular focus on Africa—'but the plans must still be fleshed out'[37] Herfkens had wanted to include reduction of agricultural subsidies because of their potential adverse on the environment as part of the EU position in advance of the Conference, but to no avail.[38]

The preparations for the upcoming WSSD were front and centre at the Utstein Group meeting in Wiesbaden in July 2002. Wieczorek-Zeul expressed the hope that a successful outcome of Johannesburg could be that the protagonists from the environmental and development fields work together in the future. But the ministers expressed concern about the state of preparations so far and discussed how the G77 (the developing countries group) might be included more in the process and the US blocking tactics be dealt with. They also agreed that the replenishment of the Global Environmental Facility could make a considerable contribution to the success of Johannesburg and were pleased that the USA also showed signs of support for the Facility.[39]

Wiezcorek-Zeul declared that 'the access of the poor to energy enhanced energy efficiency and the promotion of renewable energies were important aspects of poverty alleviation and climate protection'. The World Bank was criticized for not being open enough in this area. Short noted that 'renewables were currently more expensive than conventional sources of energy; the only way to bring costs down for developing countries was for developed countries to increase their use of renewables'.[40] Subsequently, Germany developed an energy paper, agreed by the others at the working level which was to form the basis for cooperation with the World Bank. The paper argued in favour of small decentralized energy infrastructure investments based on renewables and other sustainable forms of energy technology. It thus aimed at poverty reduction and protection of the climate and natural resources. The paper was welcomed by the participants though there were some objections/demurrals: the UK did not wish to see ODA used for commercial investments; Norway did not want to create a separate international organization.[41]

In the end the WSSD was not captured by the environmentalists but tried to combine the fight against poverty with the fight to sustain the environment. The conference produced three major outcomes: (a) The Johannesburg Declaration on Sustainable Development; (b) The Johannesburg Plan of Implementation; and (c) a series of commitments by governments and other stakeholders to a range of activities to promote sustainable development at the national, regional, and international level.

The Johannesburg Declaration contains a series of lofty pronouncements regarding various global issues, ranging from the 'deep fault line between rich and poor that poses a threat to global security and stability' to the fact that 'globalization has added a new dimension to the challenges of sustainable development'. There was also the habitual reference to 'developed countries that have not done so to make concrete progress towards the internationally agreed ODA targets' (but not an explicit reference to the ODA/GNI target) and a grand call for 'more effective, democratic and accountable international and multilateral institutions'. A contemporary report noted that 'delays in completing negotiations on the Johannesburg Plan of Implementation left little time for full and effective consultations on the content of the declaration'.[42]

The Johannesburg Plan of Implementation is a lengthy (sixty-five-page) substantive plan of action with many new thrusts on the issue of sustainable development. Whereas Agenda 21, the action plan from Rio, focused on reducing production of toxic materials, and reducing reliance on fissionable materials for energy production, the Johannesburg Plan focused more on changing consumption patterns, including energy but also of other products affecting climate change. It also gave higher priority to production of alternative, small-scale sources of energy and to the role to be played by the private sector. Whereas Rio had discussed reforms in several sectors, for example increased reliance on public transportation, Johannesburg devoted a great deal of attention to priorities for sustainable development in different developing countries by region: the Africa plan of action alone, which focused on NEPAD (see Chapter 6, p. 90) was five pages long. And there were many other proposals drawn from conferences addressing developing country problems that had taken place since Rio.[43]

Finally, the Plan contained some new commitments, similar to the MDGs, but somewhat less concrete:

- Halving the number of people lacking access to basic sanitation by 2015 (reiterating MDG target 10);
- Halving the decline in fish stocks and restoring them to sustainable levels by 2015;
- Reducing the loss of biodiversity by 2010;
- Increasing substantially the use of renewable energies in global energy consumption;
- Setting up a ten-year framework for programmes on sustainable consumption and production.

In general, and despite some of these above targets, the Plan, while comprehensive, was mostly aspirational in nature, not that different from traditional UN conferences. There were few new concrete targets or goals, and except for the goal on fish stocks, no specific time horizons for accomplishing specific objectives. In that respect it was a step backwards from the specifics of the MDGs and the concrete actions of Monterrey.

There were, of course, many programmes and initiatives that were launched as well. One of the most interesting was the beginnings of a new initiative aimed at reducing corruption and increasing transparency in the extractive industries. Short put in a proposal for this purpose in Tony Blair's speech for the WSSD but it was not delivered because of a 'problematic relationship' with Zimbabwe's Prime Minister Mugabe.[44] Short remembers that Blair did not give the speech because Mugabe was in the room. When DfID followed up the proposal with a conference in London in June 2003, Johnson came in to support. This ultimately led to the establishment of the Extractive Industries Transparency Initiative (EITI) in which Norway and the UK participated actively. EITI was chaired by Short in 2011–16 and continues to function today.[45]

Wieczorek-Zeul felt the conference was a success, in particular because of the increased emphasis on gender issues and despite the fact that Germany failed to get the kind of commitments to renewable energy that it was seeking. Again, however, the conference was useful in motivating Chancellor Gerhard Schröder to launch a major conference on renewable energy in Bonn in 2004. As noted above, Germany had prepared a paper on this subject which was discussed with U4 partners and was then used for the conference.[46]

Johnson also felt that she was able to achieve her objectives in the WSSD pronouncements on the tension between international environmental agreements and the WTO. The conference had raised the issue of coherence between rules that relate to the environment and those that relate to trade. In earlier WTO negotiations many developed countries had advocated subordinating environmental concerns to trade rules articulated in the WTO. Developing countries had objected to this subordination earlier but had not engaged on the issue in the WSSD with the result that the draft of the Implementation Plan contained such a subordination. Johnson was joined by Switzerland in suggesting a text that environmental concerns and trade concerns should be mutually reinforcing.

Their objections to the text threatened to cause the whole meeting to break down. The EU was formally opposed to the Norwegian/Swiss proposal; as the European Commission tends to bully member states regarding anything remotely related to trade, many member states agreed with Johnson but could not openly support her position. 'We were all rooting for Hilde: she was very courageous', remembers Koen Davidse, a member of the Dutch delegation at the Conference.[47]

The South African delegation, who as hosts wanted to avoid a conference break up, also put pressure on her to drop her objection. But in the end Johnson managed to mobilize developing countries that had traditionally wished to avoid subordination of environment to trade rules to support her position, which won the day (see p. 153 of the Plan of Implementation) as the EU 'caved'.[48] Overall, the individual Utstein governments supported most of the conference specifics but had different priorities and did not play a role as a group in determining the outcome.

In Retrospect

The U4 were unique in that they were the only ministerial level network pushing for coherence in policies for development, both at international and domestic level, a somewhat astounding situation given the immense resources devoted to development globally. They essentially won the argument regarding providing assistance in the context of coherent national plans as articulated by developing countries through the PRSP process, although the emergence of new donors such as China in later periods has undermined their earlier success.

The Utstein Four were also successful in their pursuit of untying of development assistance—although again there has been retrogression recently: some of it has been the result of China pursuing the traditional aid-tying policies of OECD donors half a century or more ago; some by retrogression in OECD itself (see Chapter 11).

Overall, U4 efforts to improve policy coherence between trade and aid for developing countries did not yield significant results, but not for the lack of trying.

There were a few wins: EbA was one of them, be it that it took another decade for the Commission to acknowledge that it had not resulted in significant increase in exports from LDCs, due to the strict preferential rules of origin; after these were relaxed somewhat in 2010, EbA did make a real difference. The Cotonou agreement was also beneficial for a few products to several others. An amendment to TRIPS ensured a mechanism that allows access to compulsory licencing through imports, though the many conditions and political pressure behind the scenes have resulted in almost a non-use of the instrument.

Unfortunately, although the Doha Round was born, it died without producing the expected trade liberalization for developing country exports—although its official obituary has yet to be written. And the EU and US policies on cotton are still irrational; in the case of the latter, even after several rounds of dispute settlement where the US was found to have violated its obligations to reduce domestic and export subsidies and paid financial compensation to the complainant, Brazil.

In the EU the abolition of the Development Council was a setback for coherence for development. The expanded Foreign Affairs Council, which meets in different formats (e.g. with Defence or Development Ministers) represented a 'win' for the Foreign Ministries and may not have come about if the original U4 ministers were still in office. Still, the U4 Development DGs continued to meet, which provided the opportunity for continued cooperation at a lower level for a few years.

Finally, on issues of policy coherence between development and the environment, it is too soon to say. There has been much progress. MDG 7 already contained the commitment to 'integrate the principles of sustainable development into country policies and programmes; and to reverse the loss of environmental resources'. Johannesburg was succeeded by the Paris Climate accords, and agreement on the SDGs. However, there is some concern that in the EU the recent shift from PCD to PCSD may water down the focus on reducing poverty. And of course, the USA has declared its intention to abandon the Paris Climate accords. But on all this, the jury is still out, and will be the topic of discussion in Chapter 12.

Notes

1. UK DfID, *Eliminating World Poverty: Making Globalization Work for the Poor*, White Paper (London: DfID, 2000), p. 19.
2. UK DfID, Eliminating World Poverty, p. 71.
3. The architect of the EU Commission proposal at the time was Trade Commissioner Pascal Lamy, who later became Director General of the WTO.
4. See Constantine Michalopoulos, *Emerging Powers in the WTO* (Basingstoke: Palgrave Macmillan, 2014), p. 241.

5. Eventually EbA became part of the EU proposals in the new Round of WTO multilateral trade negotiations—see below.

6. *Reuters*, Eric Onstad, Interview-Trade Barriers block Africa growth-Dutch minister, 12 October 2001.

7. T. Otsuki, J. Wilson, and M. Sewadah, 'What Price Precaution? Europe's Harmonization of Aflatoxin Regulations and African Groundnut Exports', *European Review of Agricultural Economics*, 28(3) (2001), pp. 263–84.

8. See https//:www.Europa.eu/policies/Cotonou.

9. 'Reciprocal preferences' means that, unlike thepredecessor of Cotonou (the Lomé agreement, which involved only unilateral preferences), the Economic Partnership Agreements require that the ACP countries also provide preferential treatment to EU exporters in their own markets. This requirement has created problems in a lot of sub-Saharan Africa countries, which to this date have not all completed the required arrangements, even as discussions for the extension of Cotonou beyond 2020 have already started.

10. Koos Richelle, email, 13 January 2019.

11. Utstein Ministerial, Birmingham, 2001, minutes, first day.

12. Ron Keller, email, 13 January 2019.

13. Clare Short, speech, UNCTAD Conference, Geneva, 2 March 1999.

14. Infobulletin, Dutch Ministry of Foreign Affairs.

15. Clare Short, statement to Parliamentary Committee, 23 May 2000.

16. *IHT*, 'It's time for EU barriers to fall', 17 October 2000.

17. 'Integrating Intellectual Property Rights and Development Policy', Report of the Commission on Intellectual Property Rights, London, 2002.

18. Eveline Herfkens, 'TRIPS and Public Health: Opportunities for Doha', *Bridges*, 12 October 2001. The problems pharmaceutical companies created in providing cheap medicines for poor people in poor countries ultimately led to the establishment of organizations such as GAVI (see Chapter 7).

19. Development Committee, communique, 18 November 2001.

20. UK DfID, 'Follow-up Matrix to 3rd Utstein Ministerial Meeting in Birmingham', 14 June 2002, p. 4.

21. UK DfID, 'Follow-up Matrix', p. 6.

22. Utstein Ministerial, Dubai, 2003, minutes, p. 6.

23. Interpress Service IPS, 9 September 2003.

24. D. Laborde, 'Looking for a Meaningful Duty-Free Quota Free Market Access Initiative in the Doha Development Agenda', ICTSD, Issue Paper 4 (Geneva: ICTSD, 2008).

25. Stavern, 21–2 June 2018, transcript, p. 3.

26. Barrie Ireton, *Britain's International Development Policies: A History of DFID and Overseas Aid* (Basingstoke: Palgrave Macmillan, 2013), p. 23.

27. J. A. Nekkers and P. A. M. Malcontent (eds), *Fifty Years of Dutch Development Co-operation 1949–1999* (The Hague: Jdu Publishers, 1999), p. 123.

28. Although some Executive Directors at the World Bank have been known to try to influence procurement decisions to benefit their exporters.

29. Johnson, comment, May 2019. The UK also untied 100% of its aid at about that time, but it is not clear exactly when: Clare Short, comment, 6 September 2019.

30. OECD, *DAC in Dates* (Paris: OECD, 2006), p. 29.
31. Clare Short, speech to Adam Smith Institute, 3 December 1999.
32. Utstein Ministerial, The Hague, 2000, minutes.
33. *Financieel Dagblad*, 'Industrialized Countries in Conflict about Tied Aid to Developing Countries', 23 June 2000.
34. Utstein Ministerial, Birmingham, 2001, minutes; UK DfID, 'Follow-up Matrix', Birmingham.
35. Utstein Ministerial, The Hague, 2000, minutes, p. 5.
36. Utstein Ministerial, Birmingham, 2001, minutes, first day.
37. UK DfID, 'Follow-up Matrix', Birmingham.
38. Eveline Herfkens, letter to Parliament, 14 June 2002.
39. Utstein Ministerial, Wiesbaden, 2002, minutes, p. 2.
40. Utstein Ministerial, Wiesbaden, 2002, minutes, p. 3.
41. Utstein Ministerial, Dubai, 2004, minutes.
42. Peter Doran, 'WSSD: An Assessment for the International Institute for Sustainable Development' (processed), 3 October 2002, p. 1.
43. UN, WSSD, *Plan of Implementation*, A/Conf.119.20, 4 September 2012.
44. This is the wording from the official EITI website: https://www.eiti.org.
45. See https://www.eiti.org.
46. Utstein Ministerial, Dubai, 2004, minutes, p. 5.
47. Koen Davidse, interview by C. Michalopoulos and E. Herfkens, 5 January 2019.
48. Stavern, 21–2 June 2018, transcript, p. 9.

10

The Long Transition

Introduction

The May 2002 elections in the Netherlands resulted in a government change and the replacement of Herfkens by Agnes van Ardenne in late July. 'With Herfkens' departure the personal chemistry among the U4 was no longer the same. Van Ardenne came in with a different personality and a different approach to development co-operation.'[1] Short's resignation from the Blair cabinet in the spring of 2003—over disagreement with the Prime Minister about the UK's participation in the Iraq War—undermined further the personal dynamics of the Utstein group, although, in this instance, the programmatic differences were less pronounced than in the Dutch case (see Box 10.1).

These changes did not lead immediately to an end of U4 cooperation. There was an Utstein ministerial dinner in Doha in September 2003, and another meeting in Berlin in March 2004. Moreover, after the two ministerial changes, 'the U4 DGs, for a while, kept meeting with the old frequency and format if only because the personal bond between the DGs remained. Where possible, "Utstein co-operation" remained in place, notably on the important matter of donor coordination. However, the policy impact of the meetings was far less than before because of the lack of an overarching political level' collective drive.[2] There is a record of a final U4 meeting in Berlin in March 2005—but at the Director General level. Both Short and Herfkens continued to be active through speeches and other activities focused on development. But their impact could not be expected to be the same as when there were four coordinated ministerial voices.

Collaboration also evolved in a different direction, with a teaming up of different Utstein countries in twos and threes, with Norway and the UK being the primary drivers on donor reforms.[3] There was also the emergence of the so-called Nordic Plus group which included the Netherlands and the UK, but not Germany. And, of course, Johnson stayed in office until 2005 and Wieczorek-Zeul until 2009, pushing for implementation of the U4 agenda in different contexts and with different partners. They continued to collaborate with each other, the UK, and the Nordic Plus group on specific issues. Thus, while 'a systemic and fully fledged U4 cooperation never re-emerged on a political and ministerial level',[4] there was a transition over time. The U4 did not disappear from the international scene as much as they faded away as a ministerial group.

Box 10.1. About Utstein in 2003

Short, still an MP but on assignment as a reporter for the BBC, and Herfkens, making a speech on behalf of the UN MDG campaign were present at the WTO Ministerial in Cancun (see Chapter 9) where they were tracked down for an interview with the Dutch newspaper *Trouw*. The interview did not produce interesting insights on the WTO Ministerial where Wieczorek-Zeul was active representing Germany, but on the state of play in the Utstein group:

'Short regrets that after her and Eveline Herfkens' departure, the group cannot play its pioneer role in the field of development anymore. "When we came together a driving force emerged; that force seems to have disappeared." The end of the Utstein group? Short is afraid so. What remains of the four rebelling women, who resisted endless speeches at international conferences, now looks like a powerless club. At the recent IMF/World Bank Meetings in Dubai the group seems to have started a second life. Six Ministers, those from the original founding countries supplemented by Canada and Sweden announced that they will work towards 'broad alliances to achieve the eight UN Millennium Goals'. The six Ministers will fight for rich countries to live up to their commitments...Tough language, though van Ardenne—first as Secretary of State, later as Minister—over the last year made very contradictory statements about her participation in the Utstein Group. As Secretary of State she initially stated she would prevent being thrown out of the group despite her demotion to Secretary of State. Sources close to the group however suggested she could only play a secondary role.

Earlier this year Van Ardenne, who succeeded Herfkens claimed that she had not opted for the group from the outset, but rather looked for alliances with 'less obvious partners'. She named the US and France; with the US she saw great advantages, particularly in the field of water management. Short, the Minister who quit over Blair's policy regarding the Iraq war, laughs condescendingly at that preference. 'France and the US? Not exactly the most progressive parties in the field of development cooperation.' Van Ardenne wants part of the peace keeping in which the Dutch are involved to count as ODA. Not as much the actual deployment but for instance military training. According to an unnamed source 'the Norwegian Minister Johnson is deadly against van Ardenne's idea. And she is not the only one: international organizations worry that it might alert the US as the US spends a lot of money in Iraq and Afghanistan which it might want to qualify as ODA. It is totally out of line with Utstein principles which on the contrary sought to define ODA as purely as possible.'[5]

The OECD discussed but did not support Van Ardenne's proposal at its High Level meeting in the spring of 2004. Suma Chakrabarti, representing the UK, said best what many felt: 'Adding to ODA eligible items will make it too easy to attain ODA volume targets without real aid increases.'[6]

This chapter will review this transition roughly over the period 2003–8, discussing key aspects of international cooperation for development: The Rome–Paris–Accra accords on Aid Effectiveness in 2003–8; the 2005 MDG review and related developments; the Doha Round of Multilateral Trade Negotiations; changes in HIPC; the Doha Review Conference on Financing for Development; and other aspects of international cooperation over this period. 2008 is a useful end point for this chapter of the story, as the financial crisis that started that year changed the world in many ways, including in international cooperation for development.

New Faces, New Networks

During the Fall of 2002 the remaining Utstein Ministers and Van Ardenne met a couple of times to see if the personal and policy 'click' could be restored, but that never happened. She put less effort into the coherence agenda; was not always prepared to confront her colleagues, members of the cabinet, to address a policy incoherence; and was less devoted to a strict adherence to the sector wide approach which was at the heart of Utstein thinking. She wanted to focus more on private sector development and 'fragile' states. However, an important area where Van Ardenne and the remaining Utstein Ministers kept seeing eye-to-eye was donor co-ordination.[7]

On fragile states, Johnson recalls that Van Ardenne was very engaged on Sudan, and collaborated with her as she was in favour of strong donor coordination and supportive of donor preparations for peace. But she did not sign—or was not invited to sign, it is not clear which—a letter sent by the Utstein group to the government of Nepal in September 2002.[8]

The inclusion of Sweden in the Utstein group, combined with Van Ardenne's reduced involvement, contributed to the emergence of the Nordic Plus group, which, besides the Nordics, comprised the Netherlands and the UK, with Ireland and Luxemburg joining later. Keller, Director General for the Netherlands writes:

Parallel to the Nordic-plus group, the DGs of the original four continued to meet. For Germany this included Michael Hoffman, who was definitely much more 'modern' in his approach than the German implementing agencies which tended to remain in a 'project' mode; and for the UK Suma Chakrabarti, who continued in the same tradition as Short. In 2003–2005 this group met every three months. While these DG meetings were very useful, be it without visible results, as our Ministers did not exist as U4 by that time.[9]

The U4 did not disappear immediately or become a powerless club. It morphed into something different, more diverse and diffused, but indeed less powerful than the original.

This is confirmed by another report:

The Nordic-Plus became recognized internationally as having more efficient and better organized aid bureaucracies and focusing less on development per se and more on poverty reduction as well as social and environmental aspects of development. They have played a progressive role in debates on the international aid architecture and were instrumental in initiatives such as the 2000 MDGs the 2005 Paris Declaration and the 2015 Sustainable Development Goals (SDGs).[10]

Along the lines of the process launched by the ministers earlier in Tanzania, the group organized

a truly coordinated and fully harmonized program in Zambia, much to the chagrin of their field offices who thought that they would thereby lose power and influence. They appointed lead donors per sector, established mission free periods, unified payment terms, harmonized and simplified monitoring requirements and pooled sector expertise—all elements subsequently adopted by the Paris Declaration on Donor Coordination and Harmonization [see next section].[11]

At the field level all the multilaterals for example, the UNDP, the African Development Bank and the World Bank were fully engaged. The latter even sent a camera team to make a movie about aid harmonization. The movie was then shown to the World Bank's Board of Executive Directors as a shining example of how from then on the World Bank and bilateral agencies would proceed 'coordinated and harmonized'. Within the UN the Zambia initiative strengthened the push for internal programmatic coordination. And within the EU led by DGs Manservisi and Richelle, a strong worded instruction was sent to all EU representatives in the field to actively participate in harmonization.[12]

Aid Effectiveness

The question of how to make aid more effective had been at the forefront of U4 discussions from the very beginning of their collaboration as well as the subject of a huge number of studies, discussions, and meetings over the last half century, some of which have been referred to in earlier chapters. Effectiveness depends on actions by both the donor and the partner country. Bringing the two points of view together in a meaningful international agreement had proved very difficult.

The Monterrey Financing for Development Conference took some preliminary steps in this direction, but the most important development occurred in 2003 in the form of the Rome Declaration on Harmonization. Recall in this connection the discussion in Chapter 6 about the importance of harmonizing donor procedures in order to reduce the burden of partner countries, as well as the DAC work on donor practices' harmonization.

Meeting in Rome in February 2003, ministers, heads of aid agencies, and senior officials representing twenty-eight aid recipient countries and more than forty multilateral and bilateral development institutions endorsed a declaration aimed at harmonizing practices in ways that would produce improvements in development effectiveness. Everybody credits Richard Manning, formerly Short's DG who participated in the original Utstein meeting, for the success of the Rome meeting. At the time, he was chair of the DAC Task Force on Aid Effectiveness. In a comment on an earlier draft of this text he said: 'Your conclusions on my role are also somewhat over-flattering: my key role on the day was to knock a few heads together to ensure we ended with an agreed communique. However, I do think that the Task Force (which had strong support from the World Bank among others) did play an essential role in helping to generate the ideas on which the Rome Forum was built.'[13] The Rome Declaration contained many specifics, such as, for example:

- Ensuring that development assistance is delivered in accordance with partner country priorities, including poverty reduction strategies...and that harmonization efforts are adapted to country circumstances.
- We will work to reduce donor mission, reviews, and reporting, streamline conditionalities, and simplify and harmonize documentation.
- Providing budget, sector, or balance of payments support where it is consistent with the mandate of the donor and when appropriate policy and fiduciary arrangements are in place.

Two years later, in Paris, international cooperation on aid effectiveness reached a different level in terms of the countries participating, the range of commitments, the degree of specificity and the establishment of a follow up to monitor progress. The so-called Second High Level Forum on Joint Progress towards Enhanced Aid Effectiveness was attended by 138 countries, twenty-eight bilateral and multilateral donors, and numerous NGOs, all of whom agreed to a series of steps to increase aid effectiveness under five major principles:

1. **Ownership:** Developing countries set their own strategies for poverty reduction, improve the institutions and tackle corruption.
2. **Alignment:** Donor countries align behind these objectives and use local systems.

3. **Harmonization:** Donor countries coordinate, simplify procedures and share information to avoid duplication.
4. **Results:** Developing countries and donors shift focus to development results and results get measured.
5. **Mutual Accountability:** Donors and partners are accountable for development results.[14]

The various commitments under the five general chapters involved specific quantitative targets that were supposed to be achieved by 2010. For example, under 'Ownership', the specific target was that at least 75 per cent of partner countries have operational development strategies. Under 'Alignment', donors committed that by 2010 at least 90 per cent of them will use country public financial systems and country public procurement for their assistance. Under 'Harmonization', by 2010, 40–66 per cent of donor missions to the field should be joint with the host country. Finally, it was agreed to monitor progress by the joint group of donors and recipients of the DAC Working Party on Aid Effectiveness organized under DAC/OECD auspices. The results of the Paris agreement were subsequently communicated and reconfirmed by the UN Summit on the MDGs that was convened in New York in September 2005 (see the following section).

By the time of the Paris meetings, both Herfkens and Short had left office but Johnson and Wieczorek-Zeul were still around and attended. Johnson remembers that in the run-up to the meeting and during the Paris deliberations, she worked actively with DfID's Permanent Secretary Suma Chakrabarti, the right hand of the Development Secretary, as well as with the representatives from the Netherlands and Germany. For the first time several African finance ministers were present, at the insistence of the U4 and other likeminded countries. They also helped in requesting stronger commitments by the donors at the meeting. The Nordic Plus group reportedly put together 'a concrete joint action plan for harmonization of their aid practices'.[15]

The issue over which there was the most resistance was the commitment to the use of country systems, and there was also some noise on untying. The resistance was greatest by the most project-oriented donors such as the US as the proposed text ran against their unwillingness to accept budget support and other aid channels making use of partner country systems. The controversy almost made the meeting to collapse. We had mobilized several developing countries, who also made their case and I recall we would not agree unless the text was part of the communique, and I believe we threatened to leave without consensus.[16]

The deadlock was broken by Japan, which suggested 'preliminary' targets for some indicators to be agreed at the meeting, while others were left for technical work and agreement by September 2005. The USA accepted this idea in principle, and it was hammered out in textual language in a small side meeting with the USA, EU, and some others, including a couple of developing countries.[17]

> The Forum reflected two important shifts in development thinking: 1) Action was needed not just on the part of donors, but also partners. Thus the initial focus on 'donor practices' became a commitment to 'mutual accountability'; and 2) change was seen as a process that would take time but was to be monitored. Two additional Forums were agreed: one in 2008 to monitor progress, and one in 2011 to review actual achievements by 2010.[18]

A third High Level Forum on Aid Effectiveness was held in Accra on 2–4 September 2008 with the participation of a very large group of developed and developing countries, multilateral institutions, global funds, and civil society organizations broadening the range of stakeholders involved in the discussions and the setting of the aid effectiveness agenda. Wieczorek-Zeul was again there. Bert Koenders of the Dutch Labour Party, a close friend of Herfkens and Johnson and an admirer of the Utstein efforts, had succeeded Van Ardenne as Development Minister and attended the meeting for the Netherlands.

Koenders writes: 'I remember it was Douglas Alexander and myself being unhappy with soft and according to us sloppy language on which politicians were not at all properly consulted and the meeting therefore threatened not to get sufficient political message.'[19] Manning reports that both the UK's and the Netherlands' representatives at the meeting thought the language regarding the use of budget support and the use of country systems was too weak and threatened to block agreement at the last moment—but that they were able to go along after 'minor drafting changes' were made to the text.[20] Whatever the judgement as to whether the changes made were minor or not, the conference proposed many improvements in three aspects of implementation: developing country ownership, aspects of partnership, and delivering results.

In the 2009 Development Co-operation Report, DAC Chair Eckhard Deutscher said that the Accra conference marked 'key breakthroughs on a number of fronts', specifically:

- Agreement to use country systems as the first option when delivering aid;
- Agreement to make aid more predictable and transparent, and thus to allow partners to better budget, plan and implement their development strategies;
- A fundamental change whereby donors will determine the conditions placed on aid jointly with partner countries and on the basis of their own development plans;
- Clear and substantial progress on untying aid.[21]

It does not take a great deal of comparison to note the similarities between what was agreed in Paris and Accra and the Utstein principles and action agendas several years earlier. Ownership, use of local systems, harmonization and simplification of procedures, results oriented, had all been emphasized and promoted, including in the DAC, by the Utstein group for several years previously.

The UN Millennium Plus-5 Summit

The UN has traditionally organized follow up meetings five years after major conferences in order to assess progress in meeting the original conference objectives. This was also the case with the MDGs. The UN Millennium Plus-5 Summit was important both because it would give an opportunity to review the progress made towards achieving the MDGs as well as because it created the opportunity for the international community to mobilize additional resources in support of the MDGs.

Annan had appointed Herfkens as executive coordinator to create and lead the Millennium Development Goals campaign in the autumn of 2002. Recall from Chapter 7 that the campaign was intended to encourage citizens to hold their governments to account in developing countries for the commitments they made to achieve the goals, and in OECD countries for their commitments regarding aid levels, aid effectiveness, and trade, as agreed at Monterrey. Under Herfkens' leadership the campaign focused in developing countries on helping to strengthen constituencies for pro-poor inclusive and transparent policies and advocacy for the implementation of promises already made, to achieve Goals 1 to 7 (see Box 7.1). In rich countries the focus was on more pro-development policies, as committed to in MDG 8, and elaborated in Monterrey, such as increased and more effective aid, debt relief, and better trade opportunities.

The campaign partnered with local civil society, often already engaged in development, and reached out to other actors, parliamentarians, local authorities, faith-based organizations, youth networks, the scout movement, unions, and popular media like MTV, fostering the use of the MDGs as a common rallying framework aimed at legislators and governments to encourage them to implement policies aimed at achieving the MDGs. It was active in countries as disparate as Brazil, Indonesia, and Mozambique. It was not active in China and elsewhere where prospects for government policy change based on advocacy by civil society did not appear especially promising. And it was not always welcomed: the USA and India governments discouraged campaign activities in their territory, although in the end the campaign was active in both countries through partnerships with local NGOs and parliamentarians. In developed countries, the focus was on encouraging civil society to promote more and better aid, debt relief, and more trading opportunities as formulated in Goal 8 and elaborated at Monterrey.

Campaigns were initiated in 'lagging' countries, including Germany; not in those countries where constituencies were already strong enough, as they were at the time in the UK, the Netherlands and the Nordics, though Herfkens did address the parliaments in these countries.

In connection with the upcoming UN summit, the EU Commission, through DG Development had proposed that member states would agree to a collective target of achieving an ODA target of 0.56 per cent of GNI by 2010 and 0.7 per cent of GNI by 2015. Individual country targets were also proposed, with the targets for the 'old' member states (EU15) substantially higher than for the 'new' members. These targets were significantly more ambitious than what had been agreed in Barcelona in advance of the Monterrey meeting a few years back.[22]

The Commission proposal was viewed by Denmark, the Netherlands, and Sweden as the minimum acceptable: in their view it did not seem fair that developing countries were supposed to achieve their goals by 2015, while developed countries would still have (part of) their cheque in the mail. The proposal was also supported by Belgium, France, Finland, Luxemburg, Spain, and the UK, all of whom had set specific timetables to achieve the 0.7 per cent target. Italy, Portugal, Greece, and Germany originally resisted the new targets because they were running budget deficits at the time. Wieczorek-Zeul wanted to make the commitment but she was initially blocked by the German Minister of Finance. However, as she had beforehand agreed with Chancellor Schröder that she had the leeway to go along with the EU Commission proposal, she was able to commit the German government—which she did—and told the Finance Minister afterwards.[23] The Commission proposal was approved at a meeting of the European General Affairs and External Relations Council (GAERC) on 24 May 2005. The commitment for the ten new members was weaker: instead of 'undertake to increase', they only committed 'to strive to increase'; but the package for the Millennium Summit included two additional EU commitments: first, to make concrete progress in policy coherence for development, in twelve sectors, including trade, environment, agriculture, fishing, and social dimensions of globalization; second, to increase ODA to Africa so that it would receive at least 50 per cent of the agreed increases.[24]

The MDG campaign, being aware of the importance of the issue, had large campaigns in support of the 0.7 per cent targets in Germany, Italy, Portugal, and Spain, whose ODA performance was lagging. Both Wieczorek-Zeul and Köhler give credit to the campaign for promoting support for increasing ODA levels. Köhler recalls in particular that he, who was at the time President of Germany, wanted to support the campaign. As a symbol of his commitment he placed his signature—bending on his knees to do so—on a banner in support of the 0.7 per cent target at a Millennium campaign event in Bonn's ancient centre,[25] and invited the campaign to participate in the annual garden party at his residence. He said recently: 'The Millennium Campaign transformed an unknown set of goals into a truly global brand that mobilized political will for development like few times in history.'[26]

In 2005, the UN Summit took stock of progress in achieving the MDGs and reiterated everybody's commitments to their achievement. At the time prospects looked pretty good for achieving the poverty objective especially because of rapid growth in China and India. Prospects in achieving the other goals appeared mixed.[27] But there were encouraging signs, especially as sub-Saharan African countries had started to grow very rapidly since the beginning of the century.

It is difficult to assess the campaign's impact in achieving the MDG objectives. By working with and through untraditional actors, it was clearly successful in creating constituencies for the MDGs across society in countries where it ran campaigns, making politicians pay attention. And through partnerships with networks of local authorities, unions, parliaments, and youth movements, it also had an impact in countries where it did not have a local campaign. In 2008 an OECD pamphlet jointly sponsored by the UN and the MDG campaign with the title *Reaching Our Development Goals: Why Aid Effectiveness Matters*, summarized in popular form the main themes of the Utstein Principles. As opposed to earlier goals and targets formulated at the UN over the decades, the MDGs became widely known worldwide, and were discussed in many national parliaments. On 15–16 October 2006 the campaign mobilized a record twenty-three million people worldwide to 'stand up' for the MDGs. The record reached 173 million in 2009. In many developing countries it played a role in moving governments to articulate policies and programmes and align budgets aimed at achieving the MDGs.[28]

Herfkens focused her own attention on the developed countries in Europe where she gave numerous speeches using the MDG campaign platform to promote the familiar Utstein themes on three issues: aid volume, aid effectiveness, and policy coherence, as a means to achieve the MDGs.

In an address to the G8 parliamentarians in Berlin on 30 May 2007 she raised again inter alia the aid volume question:

At the G8 summit, in Gleneagles, which was hailed as an historic summit for Africa, G8 leaders promised a substantial increase in development assistance with an additional $50 billion; and a doubling of aid to sub-Saharan Africa by 2010. Two years down the line, total aid is decreasing again and excluding debt relief, aid to sub-Saharan Africa is stagnant, and no poor country—strong performers included—has seen the increase in aid that enables it to achieve the Millennium Goals by 2015.

As EU President Germany fostered agreement that within the EU all member states, which have not done so, will submit plans how to achieve the EU commitment of 0.56% by 2010. What is needed in [the G8 summit at]

Heiligendamm is a similar commitment regarding the Gleneagles promises, taking a frank look at the facts and renewing the resolve, providing timetables of annual increases to actually meet and monitor the Gleneagles promises.[29]

Short echoed some of Herfkens' concerns about progress in meeting ODA commitments. In a 2008 speech 'Make Poverty History', she noted that a lot of recent increases in ODA reflected debt relief to Iraq and Nigeria.[30] But her main focus lay elsewhere. She was most concerned that the existing pattern of resource utilization and consumption in both the developed and developing world would make it impossible to achieve the MDGs. She argued that climate change and environmental considerations would make it impossible for developing countries to replicate the developed countries growth pattern. Changes were needed and such changes required strengthening of multilateral cooperation.[31]

Coherence Revisited: The Doha Round Continued

Following the contentious Cancun Ministerial, the WTO multilateral trade negotiations continued in fits and starts over the next two years with a focus on liberalizing trade in manufacturing and agriculture. The EU Common Agriculture Policy (CAP) continued to be a major problem. Herfkens continued to attack this policy which clearly had adverse implications for poverty eradication. In a July 2004 speech she said:

> As a Development Minister, I was very frustrated that we were very successful in helping poor farmers in Tanzania to increase their milk production. But at the end of the day, the local factory did not buy milk from the local farmers because Dutch milk powder was so cheap that no local farmer could compete. This is also the case for the women that grow tomatoes in Ghana who cannot compete with the Italian tomato paste. The cost of our sugar regime to Mozambique equals one-third of total ODA to this country. So, we are destroying markets on which poor farmers depend. Two-thirds of the world's poor live in rural areas and depend on agriculture. We have to change our Common Agricultural Policies, which, moreover, are not in our own interest either. Our consumers and taxpayers pay for transfers from poor people in their own country to rich people in their own country while hurting poor farmers in the developing world.[32]

In order to energize the negotiating process, developed countries decided to sweeten the deal by offering developing countries more aid—this time related to trade. Thus, at the 6th WTO Ministerial in Hong Kong in 2005, there was a major 'new' initiative on aid for trade. This was not at all new. Weaknesses in the very wide range of institutions, infrastructure, and skills that are needed for effective integration in international trade define the very essence of underdevelopment and exist to some or other degree in practically all developing countries and are obviously most pronounced in LDCs. It was not the lack of assistance per se which was the problem, but that it had been supply driven, not effectively coordinated, and the reforms supported were not 'owned' by the recipient countries.[33]

The 2005 WTO Ministerial in Hong Kong agreed to establish two task forces: one to develop proposals for an Enhanced Integrated Framework (EIF) for helping LDCs; and another to develop proposals for increased 'aid for trade' more generally. Consistent with the lack of policy coherence between trade and aid institutions that has characterized international cooperation on this issue, governments pursued these proposals outside the actual WTO trade negotiations. This may have been a good thing, as the WTO trade negotiations stalled, and the aid-related initiatives may be the only major tangible and lasting result of the Doha Round.

A small technical assistance facility for the LDCs with an annual budget of a few million dollars was set up in the WTO in 2009 adding to the international fragmentation of aid giving. As to aid for trade for other countries which were not LDCs, there was a flurry of promises by many bilateral donors, but these were not in most cases additional to what these donors were already doing. Perhaps the only result from this initiative was increased attention to aid for trade by the World Bank and the Regional Development Banks.[34]

Debt, Finance, and International Financial Institutions (IFIs)

Debt

Debt issues continued to be at the forefront of international concerns in the post-2002 period. In 2002, following another debt crisis in Argentina, IMF staff put together a proposal for establishing an international Sovereign Debt Restructuring Mechanism. The purpose of the proposal was to achieve a more consistent private sector participation in debt restructuring and facilitate the prevention and management of debt-related financial crises.[35] In January 2003, Wieczorek-Zeul sent a letter to Johnson, Short, Van Ardenne, and Sweden's Karlsson, arguing that the discussion of the topic so far had focused on purely legal/procedural issues and that the 'objective of using debt restructuring to foster sustainable economic and socially equitable growth in the debtor countries had been receiving grossly inadequate attention'. The letter went on to seek the support of the Utstein ministers in proposing that the development objective be made operational 'by seeking the involvement not only of the IMF but also of the World Bank, UNCTAD and local and international nongovernmental organizations in drawing the debt sustainability analyses that serve as a basis of debt restructuring'. It concluded by noting that the debate had been dominated by Ministries of Finance and central banks and that only 'if we engage in parallel efforts to give these [development] aspects greater weight we might stand a chance of succeeding'.[36]

The IMF initiative failed because of opposition from the USA. But the letter was indicative of the continued interest of the Utstein group to use debt relief as an instrument in the fight against poverty.

In 2006 the HIPC initiative was expanded and modified into the Multilateral Debt Relief Initiative which allowed for 100 per cent debt relief on eligible debts to the IMF, the World Bank, and the African Development Bank. In 2007, the Inter-American Development Bank decided to provide additional debt relief to the five HIPC countries in the Western hemisphere. At present the IMF website continues to highlight the fact that eligible countries must ensure that 'for debt reduction to have a tangible impact on poverty, the additional money needs to be spent on programs that benefit the poor'.[37] The Utstein battle-cry of 1999 is still alive.

The Poverty Reduction Strategy Paper (PRSPs)

By the middle of the 2000s decade the World Bank had accumulated enough experience with the use of PRSPs to undertake a major evaluation. The results of this evaluation were summarized in a volume and discussed in a conference organized by the Bank's Operations Evaluation Department (OED) in October 2004.[38] The OED evaluation of the PRSPs found them to have made an improvement in four areas: (a) they were much more clearly the government's own document; (b) they helped improve the poverty diagnosis and poverty focus of development strategies; (c) they promoted a greater involvement of a broader group of stakeholders in the development of poverty reduction strategies; (d) they provided a constructive framework for donors' dialogue with the government,[39] exactly what the U4 had hoped to achieve.

But the review also concluded that the PRSPs were falling short in several ways, along the lines of the concerns the U4 had expressed:

- Early on they relied too much on the staff of the World Bank and the IMF which did little to improve partner ownership;
- Some of the earlier country strategies were standardized documents not reflecting individual country circumstances;
- The quality of the joint (IMF/World Bank) staff assessments varied significantly, with weaknesses in the treatment of private sector and partnership issues;

- Stakeholders in individual countries were not aware of conclusions of the staff assessments and did not participate actively in development strategy implementation.

Herfkens was a conference participant and focused her remarks on how the PRSPs could help achieve the MDGs, especially poverty reduction. She noted progress in ownership and participation but thought that it would be useful to have more inputs from groups such as parliamentarians and labour unions. She was critical of the fact that PRSPs focused too much on social expenditure: 'you cannot lift people out of poverty just by improving education and health ... To reduce the number of poor people growth must be equitable, labor intensive and pro-poor.'[40]

The evaluation concluded that the Bank 'should consciously avoid processes that discourage local ownership' and should try to persuade rather than prescribe policies. 'If the policy makers are persuaded, conditionality is not needed; and if they are not persuaded, conditionality does not work.'[41]

The World Bank and the Wolfowitz Affair

Wolfensohn's successful ten-year tenure as World Bank President, during which he played a major role in focusing its programs on reducing global poverty, ended in 2005. During his time, he had also been successful in working with NGOs who had previously been critical of the Bank's 'neoliberal' stance. The appointment of Paul Wolfowitz to succeed him was controversial from the beginning, partly because several European governments did not particularly like his role in the US invasion of Iraq during which he served as Deputy Secretary of Defense. The controversy continued when he brought into the World Bank a number of close associates from the Bush administration and was later fuelled by some of his policy priorities: it was alleged that one of his appointees ordered the deletion of references to family planning in a report on Madagascar—an allegation that was denied; and many in the Bank thought that his emphasis on terminating World Bank assistance to certain countries on the grounds of government corruption was too harsh and resulted in unnecessarily penalizing populations in extreme poverty. A number of NGOs started, again, to question the usefulness of the World Bank.

Short, in keeping with the Utstein emphasis on multilateralism, came to the World Bank's defence in an article with the title 'The World Bank: The Alternative Is Worse'. She said that an

odd alliance of forces ranging from anti-trade NGOs to the US Republicans are united in their condemnation of the World Bank ... In reality, bilateral aid from

individual countries is often inefficient, politically manipulative and bureaucrat-
ically expensive. World Bank interventions are usually of higher quality and
greater effectiveness ... As the UK Labour government ceases to be social democrat, right wing governments advance across the world and [now that] Paul
Wolfowitz has become the President of the World Bank there is a danger that the
Bank's focus on poverty reduction may be weakened. But if the Bank were closed
down the effects of this shift to the right would be worse. The Bank is the world's
leading development institution which employs many of the world's brightest
development experts. It is the leading center of expertise and analysis on development. It could be improved but development would be a much less effective
effort without the Bank.[42]

In the spring of 2007 an anonymous letter to the World Bank's board of
executive directors alleged that, contrary to staff rules, Wolfowitz had ordered
the promotion and increased cost of living pay increases to a staff member who
had agreed to accept a temporary external appointment so as to avoid a conflict of
interest with the President with whom she had a personal relationship. The board
appointed an ad hoc committee of its members, chaired by the Dutch executive
director, Herman Wijffels, to investigate the matter. The ad hoc committee issued
a preliminary report to the board on April 12. The report did not address the
substance of the accusations, but solely noted the procedures that had been
followed and the involvement of the board's ethics committee in the decisions
which resulted in the external appointment and promotion of the staff member in
question. The events that followed had an interesting 'Utstein' twist, although by
then only Wieczorek-Zeul was left from the original four. But Hilary Benn who
had been Parliamentary Under-Secretary of State under Short, was the UK
Secretary of State for Development and, as noted above, Koenders was Minister
for Development Co-operation in the Netherlands.

The Ad Hoc Committee report was to be discussed at the informal lunch of the
Development Committee which was to meet on 15 April. Wieczorek-Zeul recalls
that she had asked Wolfowitz to resign in a private meeting she had with him prior
to the Development Committee meeting. She also recalls that the evening before
the meeting, the EU and other European members met at the *La Perla* restaurant
to discuss strategy.[43] All were of the view that the President should be asked to
resign but that for 'diplomatic reasons vis-à-vis the US', this point should be
addressed in a separate meeting with the US Treasury Secretary Paulsen.

Bert Koenders recalls that during the Development Committee lunch, everybody was aware of the 'elephant in the room' but nobody wished to raise the
subject of the ad hoc committee's report on the President. He finally took the floor
first—as the ad hoc committee's chair was the Dutch executive director—and
raised his concerns, and others followed. In the end the Development

communique noted the subject but softly: it stated that 'we must ensure that the Bank can effectively carry out its mandate and we endorse the Ad Hoc Committee's report and ask it to complete its work'.[44]

Following the lunch meeting, all the European members, including heads of Central Banks and Ministers of Finance, trotted over to meet with Paulsen at his office. 'Wieczorek-Zeul took the floor for the EU to express everybody's concern about the allegations against Wolfowitz and their implications for the World Bank's reputation; and that Wolfowitz's resignation was necessary. Hillary Benn followed with the same message. And then Paulson asked, "Is there another position in the room?" None other existed and that convinced Paulsen.'[45]

The ad hoc committee issued its final report on 14 May. It concluded, inter alia that 'the provisions in Mr. Wolfowitz's contract requiring that he adhere to the Code of Conduct for Board Officials and that he avoid any conflict of interest real or apparent, were violated.'[46] Its two recommendations were modest: It asked the Executive Directors to consider first 'whether Wolfowitz will be able to provide the leadership needed for the World Bank to operate in the fullest extent possible in achieving its mandate'; and second that they 'undertake a review of the governance framework of the World Bank.'[47] Still, the end was swift. Wolfowitz resigned on May 18. The Bank's announcement, absolved him of any fault and stated blandly: 'A number of mistakes were made by a number of individuals in handling the matter under consideration and that the Bank's systems did not prove robust to the strain under which they were placed.'[48] Press reports at the time noted that the pressure for Wolfowitz's resignation came from France, Germany, and the Netherlands.[49] And there was a report that Thomas Scholar, the UK Executive Director at the World Bank at the time, negotiated the final agreement on behalf of the Bank.[50] This was not exactly Utstein, but clearly the collaboration continued.[51]

UN Reform

In 2003 Johnson, while still a minister, addressed the Chief Executives Board for Coordination (CEB) of the UN, the UN Secretary General's highest body, and challenged heads of UN agencies to deliver on UN reform. She warned that donor countries would soon use the willingness to work together as a conditionality for support. When she later became Deputy Executive Director of UNICEF in 2007, UN reform was one of her highest priorities. In that capacity she played an important role in two issues that had concerned the Utstein partners earlier on: first, UN reform, and second, the relationship between the World Bank and the UN system at the country level, in particular in crisis/post-conflict settings.[52]

Delivering as One

Regarding UN reform, over time it became apparent that the effort faced challenges at the country level, not least with the UN funds and programmes and specialized agencies, and UNDP's coordination role. Johnson was representing UNICEF in the UN Development Group (UNDG), where the key agencies driving reform were UNDP, UNICEF, the World Food Programme (WFP) and UNFPA. The group championed a number of initiatives to push for the UN system to deliver as one at the country level. *Delivering as One* (see Chapter 5) in particular required the establishment of a firewall between the coordinating function of UNDP and its own programmes. The UN undertook a formidable evaluation of *Delivering as One* in eight countries in 2011, an effort championed by Johnson and colleagues. The evaluation was intended as a tool for pushing through more forceful reforms of the UN development system at the country level.

The results of the evaluation were that the programme had achieved moderate success. *Delivering as One* had shown in practical ways how national ownership and leadership in the operational activities of the UN system can be strengthened. However, challenges remained in planning, monitoring and evaluation, and reporting concerning the *One* programme. There was room for improvement in strengthening the horizontal accountability and transparency of the UN system at country level for the achievement of results, as well as for the efficient use of resources. *Delivering as One* had not met the expectation that transaction costs would be lowered. Challenges also remained in the area of simplification and harmonization of business practices: 'Bolder measures may be required to put the UN system on a more comprehensive track of reform, including: rationalization of the number of UN organizations, reform of mandates and governance structures and funding modalities, and a new definition of the range of development expertise expected from the UN system.'[53] The current Secretary General of the UN, Antonio Guterres, has since then taken this recommendation forward with a groundbreaking comprehensive reform on the UN development architecture, separating the Resident Coordinators from UNDP,[54] and linking the deliverables directly to the Sustainable Development Goals (see Chapter 12).

The UN and the World Bank

The issue of coherence between the World Bank and UN agencies continued to bedevil cooperation at the country level. This was particularly prevalent in conflict-affected countries or in the context of large-scale natural disasters. There was a need for financial mechanisms through which donors could channel assistance, given the unreliability of national systems when in crisis. The Utstein ministers had been among the strongest proponents for pooled funding mechanisms, particularly in crisis-ridden countries. They were also among the largest contributors to such funds throughout their tenure. One of them was the Afghanistan Reconstruction Trust Fund, established in 2002, administered by the Word Bank, and where Herfkens, Short, and Johnson channelled a major part of their assistance to the country. Several others were to follow.

Administering a Multi-Donor Trust Fund (MDTF) gave a lot of profile internationally. Donor conferences would be organized on a regular basis, and the administrative agency would have a lot of influence on the international response. This resulted in turf fights between the UN and the World Bank, an experience Johnson had felt firsthand when the MDTF for Sudan was to be established during the peace talks in 2004. In the field, the problems with the compatibility of the two systems contributed to painfully slow disbursements in the MDTF in Sudan and Southern Sudan up to 2008, with particularly devastating consequences for the Southern region.[55] Other examples were to follow. One of the main issues was that the World Bank treated all other agencies, including the UN, as 'implementing agencies', a term interpreted as subsuming the UN under Bank authority. This led to tension and conflict.

Johnson came to UNICEF as Deputy Director in 2007, from her position as senior advisor to the President of the African Development Bank (ADB) where she helped develop ADB's Strategy for Fragile States and established the Fragile States' Facility. In this context she had also worked with World Bank colleagues on the issue. In 2008 Johnson was tasked with negotiating a separate crisis/post-conflict cooperation agreement with the World Bank on behalf of the UN-system as a whole.[56] The agreement established the principles of collaboration between the two institutions in crisis/post-conflict settings and contained an Operational Annex establishing procedures for cooperation. This contained a separate *Fiduciary Principles Accord* which involved an agreement for mutual recognition of each other's financial systems, a key issue which had created problems of collaboration and delays in places like South Sudan. According to the *Accord* the UN agencies would have equal standing as the World Bank and not be defined as its 'implementing agencies'.

Although the agreement was signed by new UN Secretary General Ban Ki-Moon and new World Bank President Robert Zoellick and disseminated in both institutions, it was not really implemented on the ground. UN agencies continued to face the same problems with Bank officials in many countries, and were confronted with the same fiduciary issues, preventing effective cooperation. One of the biggest tests of the *UN–WB Partnership Framework Agreement* came when the earthquake in Haiti hit in 2010. Johnson was in charge of UNICEF's global humanitarian operations during this time. One of the worst turf fights between the two institutions took place when the decision on administrative agent of the Haiti Reconstruction Fund was to be taken. Johnson reports that she was astounded at the Bank's behaviour during this time, disregarding the consultative process that had been agreed on in the UN–Bank agreement on the establishment of MDTFs.

Relations between the UN and the World Bank continued to be challenging. Over time, pooled funds have come out of fashion, however, with fewer donors being interested in channelling funds through Multi-Donor Trust Funds. Working relations between the UN and the Bank also improved at the country level, and reports from both institutions now indicate that a more constructive modus operandi has been achieved.

Carrying the Banner Alone

In the years after 2005, Wieczorek-Zeul was the only one standing to carry the Utstein banner forward as a minister. Her eleven-year tenure in that post was by far the longest of all her colleagues in that position.

As time passed, the challenges increased. The environment for international cooperation deteriorated as the political good will dominant in the OECD around the beginning of the century evaporated in the clouds of the continuing Iraq War. China emerged as an important new power on the world scene: its impressive economic growth was fuelled by rapidly expanding international trade which helped reduce poverty for many millions; and contributed to establishing its government as an important aid donor, especially in Africa. At the same time, global and European attention also shifted to sub-Saharan Africa, starting with the Africa Action Plan adopted by the G8 in Kananaskis in 2002 and followed by the establishment of the African Partnership Forum and the EU–Africa Summit in Lisbon in 2007.

Wieczorek-Zeul soldiered on sometimes in collaboration with the former Utstein group, as was the case in Wolfowitz affair discussed above, sometimes alone. Her focus, as with the other Utstein ministers continued to be sub-Saharan Africa.

Early on, in a show of great political courage and moral fortitude, she took it upon herself to ask the forgiveness of the people of Namibia for the atrocities committed by the German colonial authorities in their country a century ago. The gesture had not been done before and has not been repeated since. Such a gesture has been extremely difficult for former colonial powers throughout the world. Passages from the speech which she gave in Okakarara, Namibia, on 14 August 2004 (the 100th anniversary of the Herero uprising) are reproduced in Box 10.2.

Wieczorek-Zeul participated actively in all the G8 meetings on Africa, including as personal representative of the German head of state. At the Gleneagles meeting in 2005, the G8 had committed to doubling ODA flows to Africa by 2010. The 'Conclusions' of the African Personal Representative Joint Progress Report in 2007 stress that

---

Box 10.2. Namibia

'Today I want to acknowledge the violence inflicted by the German colonial powers on your ancestors particularly the Herero and the Nama. I am painfully aware of the atrocities committed: in the late 19th century, the German colonial powers drove the people from their land. When the Herero, your ancestors resisted, General von Trotha's troops embarked on a war of extermination against them and the Nama... The atrocities committed at the time would today be termed genocide and nowadays a General von Trotha would be prosecuted and convicted. We Germans accept our historical and moral responsibility and the guilt incurred by Germans at that time. And so, in the words of the Lord's Prayer that we share, I ask you to forgive us our trespasses.'

Heidemarie Wieczorek-Zeul, Okakarara, Namibia, 14 August 2004.

Growth and development in Africa remain the prime responsibility of African leaders. We are convinced that a clear link exists between good governance, sound policies aid effectiveness and development success. Growth in Africa is not yet sufficient for the fulfillment of the MDGs and the reduction of absolute poverty. The scaling of aid to ensure compliance with the commitment to double aid to Africa by 2010 needs to be accompanied by stronger efforts of all actors, including the private sector.[57]

The meaning of the last comment is unclear as the private sector by definition does not provide ODA and in any case private donations had actually increased manifoldly since 2000. Actually, ODA performance to that point was somewhat patchy as a lot of new ODA increases were the result of debt relief.

The report the following year noted significant progress in aid volume: ODA increases to Africa of $12 billion were almost half the target of $25 billion to be reached by 2010.[58] Africa was making progress, with growth rates in the first seven years of the twenty-first century almost double the rates achieved in the 1990s. The report pointed out that these figures were higher than the world average but were 'strongly linked to the global trend of rising prices for primary goods and thus subject to price volatility', and went on to assert that 'Under the leadership of the African Union, regional cooperation and integration are deepening and a number of Africa's own initiatives including the Africa Peer Review Mechanism [see Chapter 6] are accelerating Africa's political and economic transformation. If Africa maintains this momentum, the continent has the potential to make irreversible progress towards peace stability and prosperity.'[59]

And what about Poverty?

After all these conferences and meetings and reports in support of measures to eradicate poverty and meet all the other MDGs the questions remain: was there a real improvement in the lives of millions of poor? And to what extent did the climate of international cooperation and the U4 efforts contribute to this improvement? The answer to the first question for the first two decades of the twenty-first century is a qualified 'yes'. Some clues for the answer to the second, a much harder question, are presented below.

During the first decade of the millennium the world witnessed increased globalization and impressive growth in output and trade. Both China and India grew very rapidly, lifting hundreds of millions of people out of poverty. Many countries in sub-Saharan Africa also joined the parade of fast-growing economies. Brazil also grew impressively, and moreover did so while decreasing income inequality.[60]

The growth in trade reflected two main factors: increased demand and rising prices of raw materials led to a very rapid (13.8 per cent per annum for the period 2000–10) increase of developing country non-manufacturing trade. Sub-Saharan Africa's was only slightly slower (12.3 per cent per annum).

The growth of manufactured exports in the developing world was prompted by the expansion of global value chains. Developing countries benefitted from large investments by both multinationals and local entrepreneurs in assembly or production of final consumer goods based on the importation of intermediates. This resulted in an annual rate of growth in manufacturing exports of 11.1 per cent per annum for the period 2000–10. Sub-Saharan Africa's growth was even higher at 13.0 per cent per annum. The growth benefitted greatly from the reduction of barriers in trade resulting not from the Doha Round—where negotiations went nowhere, but from the implementation of reductions negotiated much earlier under the Uruguay Round, including, finally, the termination of the quotas limiting developing country textile exports.

The expanded HIPC programme no doubt had a positive effect on stimulating growth in the many poor countries participating in it: the substantial reduction in resources devoted to servicing debt had a positive impact in many participating countries including in sub-Saharan Africa. Developing country policies also improved and, though measurement is difficult, the impression is that donor aid practices improved as well.

The impressive growth in incomes was accompanied by a somewhat disturbing trend of increasing income inequality in many countries, including China and India. Only some countries in Latin America were showing increasing equality— albeit starting from significant inequality levels. Learned studies of the relationship between globalization and poverty have continued to accumulate evidence that the links are complex and country specific:

- The poor in countries with abundant unskilled labour do not always gain from trade reforms.
- The poor are more likely to share in the gains from globalization when there are complementary policies in place, such as policies that increase labour mobility or provide farmers with credit, technical know-how and other inputs.
- Globalization produces both winners and losers among the poor but is also associated with greater inequality.

Whatever the facts and ambiguous conclusions of two-fisted economists, by 2008 public opinion on globalization was turning decidedly negative. The report of the Commission on Growth and Development cites the Pew October 2007 Survey of Global Attitudes which indicated that 'enthusiasm for further opening of the global economy is flagging in many advanced economies and some developing countries as well. Only countries in east Asia buck the trend.'[61]

While most of the discussion of the impact of globalization on poverty had focused on the problems of the South, there had been some rumblings in the North: the Dutch election in 2002 reflected increased anxiety about immigrants whose conservative culture resulted in intolerant attitudes within the normally tolerant Dutch society. The concerns of parts of the British public about the impact of the 'Polish plumber' were voiced as early as 2003 when Poland's entry into the EU opened up immigration from other EU countries.

But none of these voices had been loud enough to stymie the globalization onslaught. In retrospect, the turning point was the financial crisis that hit the developed world in 2008. And it was not the charitable concern about globalization's impact on the poor in developing countries that started to turn the tide, but its perceived impact on some parts of the lower-middle class in the North, exploited by populist politicians.

The Doha Finance and Development Conference

A follow up to the Monterrey Conference on Finance and Development was scheduled to convene under UN auspices in Doha in November 2008. Wieczorek-Zeul writes:

UN Secretary General Ban Ki-Moon commissioned two people as facilitators to prepare the conference: For the perspective of the developing countries, the at that time South African Finance Minister Trevor Manuel, who was also Chairman of the Development Committee of the World Bank, and me as the representative of the 'donor countries'. We took up our work with commitment and met near Wiesbaden to prepare our work.[62]

Her notes for the meeting with Manuel on 25 May 2008 have survived and make interesting reading: Under the heading 'Making Doha a success', the following ten points are made and reproduced here:

- Monterrey conference was a resounding success. Together with the Millennium Summit (and MDGs) laid foundation and created political commitment to new global partnership.
- Success of the Doha Review Conference on Financing for Development will depend on: first, high level participation, i.e. heads of government from both developed and developing countries; second, MDG High Level event in September in New York will have to be geared towards the Doha conference.
- The active involvement of the World Bank was a first for a UN conference. In my opinion it contributed considerably to Monterrey's success. I have written to President Zoellick to make sure that the Bank will again actively engage in the preparatory process and at the Doha conference.
- Monterrey consensus has to be fully reconfirmed. Recall responsibilities of all partners.
- Reconfirm MDGs as our common goals (Am myself particularly concerned that we do not reach MDGs 3, 4 and 5).
- Discuss new challenges to financing for development such as climate change and food security.
- Reconfirm ODA commitments (EU and G-8).
- Advance innovative financing instruments (emissions trading, ticket tax, debt swaps such a debt2health).
- Need stronger progress with regard to gender equality and women's empowerment.
- Support developing countries in mobilizing domestic resources. Required is not only solid growth but also functioning taxation systems.[63]

Continuing on this issue in her memoirs she writes:

as the financial crisis began to develop increasingly in the course of 2008, starting in the USA, some people, including Trevor Manuel, hesitated whether the conference should actually take place as planned in December 2008. The argument was that the conference could not succeed in such a tense situation. My counterargument was that postponing the conference would in fact mean that it would never take place in the foreseeable future. We insisted that from 29 November to 2 December 2008 the conference actually started and ended with the Doha Declaration on Financing for Development.[64]

Manuel's speech at Doha stressed the links to Monterrey:

The visionary commitments we made at Monterrey continued to resonate, because they depended on a new spirit of cooperation. Each of us needed to take action, not because 'the other side' demanded it of us. Not because non-compliance would result in sanction or reprimand. We took action because we knew that adherence to our agreements and implementation of these actions was in our own very best interest.

Monterrey was an historic moment, made possible because the old zero-sum politics of cold war blocs had collapsed. The dead-weight of 'group think', which had held back consensus for more than a generation, finally lifted. In its place we were able to build a new partnership based on solidarity, mutual respect and collective action.[65]

Coming so soon after the Lehman Brothers default it was indeed remarkable that the Conference took place at all. The meeting was attended by lower-level officials—that is, ministers rather heads of government. Wieczorek-Zeul writes: 'the heads of the World Bank and the IMF didn't join. But Pascal Lamy, at that time head of the World Trade Organization (WTO), did come and did take part in the talks. I gave him much credit for that.'[66] The problem with the IFIs was that unlike Monterrey, the UN had dominated preparations for Doha at the staff level.

Wieczorek-Zeul's speech was very different than the talking points in May. By the time she gave the speech the financial crisis was in full force, so her intervention was far more passionate:

The financial crisis has pushed an additional 40 million people into poverty [probably a serious underestimate—but then at the time it was difficult to appreciate the crisis' magnitude and duration]. Year after year an unbelievable 18 million people die because they are poor. If billions of US dollars can be mobilized to save the banking sector, then the international community surely should be able to mobilize the billions needed to save the world from hunger and poverty.[67]

She went on to call for a Global New Deal from Doha with following elements:

- Reliable international governance structures with developing countries having a real voice;
- Civil society involvement;
- Empowering women which is needed for MDG achievement;
- Addressing the emerging humanitarian crisis which would require huge investments, some of which could be financed by innovative mechanisms;
- Establishment of reliable rules for global financial markets—'we must no longer tolerate casino capitalism';
- Fairer structures in world trade including eliminating export subsidies.[68]

The worsening financial situation prevented a 'New Deal'. Nevertheless, the meeting produced another well balanced and fully agreed document. The *Declaration* reiterated all the donor aid commitments of the Monterrey meeting and, having the benefit of the Paris Agreement on aid effectiveness, added all the right things about donor and recipient responsibilities. It contained the by now standard recommendations regarding the Doha Round of multilateral trade negotiations in ways that would benefit developing countries, and repeated the admonishment for increased coherence between aid and trade policies.[69]

Sadly, this was not to be. The 2008 financial crisis put a brake on progress everywhere. The chair summary of the Africa session of the G8 meeting the following year, with which the African leaders associated themselves, said:

> the economic and financial crisis is hitting hardest the poorest and risk jeopardizing progress made in health, the eradication of hunger and poverty. Leaders underscored the need to act swiftly to restore growth and implement adequate measures to protect the most vulnerable. G-8 countries reiterated their commitments, including those made in Gleneagles and more recently at the G20 London Summit to support African efforts towards promoting development good governance and achieving the Millennium Development Goals.[70]

Unfortunately, donors mired in financial crises and recessions started to backtrack on aid commitments:

> 'The impact on the economies of the "West" was enormous. On the other hand, the consequences for the fragile economies of developing countries were disastrous in many cases. The financial crisis is therefore a further example of how the poorest of the poor have to bear the misconduct of the richest of the rich.'[71]

Almost at the same time as the preparations for the Doha Conference, the President of the UN General Assembly, the Nicaraguan Miguel d'Escoto, asked Wieczorek-Zeul to become a member of an international commission that would deal with the impacts of the financial crisis on developing countries and draw up recommendations for action. The commission was to be chaired by Joseph Stiglitz. D'Escoto's initiative aimed at a report at UN level that would lead to a decision by the General Assembly. UN Secretary-General Ban-Ki Moon had no interest in promoting that issue. She agreed to join the commission—in her private capacity.[72]

Wieczorek-Zeul ended her tenure as Federal Minister in the fall of 2009. One of her last speeches addressed the UN Conference on the World Financial and Economic Crisis and its Impact on Development in New York in June 2009. The 2008 financial crisis was indeed an epochal event whose aftermath has cast a cloud over the global economy for the last decade. Its impact on development cooperation to eradicate global poverty was profound and lasting. It is the topic of Chapter 11.

Continuing Progress

There was no formal termination of Utstein. Cooperation continued following the end of ministerial-level meetings. But it occurred at different levels and in different forms and settings. Despite some deterioration of cooperation at the political level, the OECD countries and their developing country partners have made significant progress in both increasing the volume and the effectiveness of economic assistance for development. They have done so through a series of agreements whose important new feature has been a true donor–recipient partnership. And there has been increasing international attention to poverty eradication in sub-Saharan Africa, the region facing the greatest challenges in achieving the MDGs.

It was not surprising that the Utstein views would find expression in these agreements. James Adams, who had earlier been World Bank Director in Tanzania (see Chapter 6) and subsequently was World Bank Vice President for Operational Policies, remembers that on 'aid effectiveness the U4 set the agenda. The Rome declaration was basically a codification of the U4 approach. And Richard Manning should be very much credited for this.'[73]

Paul Isenman, who at the time of these conferences was a senior official at the OECD confirmed:

The Utstein Group was a powerful force in the DAC and the development community, because: they knew what they were talking about; were unified; were (and were seen to be) trying to do the right thing rather than push narrow national interests; represented a significant portion of total aid; and were very persistent and very forceful. In consensus-based organizations, fighting back against such a committed and persistent group that was on the side of the angels was not easy. They catalyzed and initially led very impressively a process, from pre-Rome to Paris and beyond, that was to bring about significant changes in the behavior of both donors and developing countries.[74]

Much less was achieved in terms of improved coherence between aid and trade policies. The Doha Development Agenda was nowhere close to being achieved, despite some initiatives regarding the LDCs.

Global progress in achieving the MDGs was impressive, with China and India leading the way. But there was significant progress elsewhere as well, including sub-Saharan Africa. All this came to a screeching halt in late 2008 due to a financial crisis emanating from excesses in the USA and Europe, which has cast a pall on the international economy in the following decade.

Notes

1. Ron Keller, email, 3 March 2018. Initially, Van Ardenne did not receive a cabinet-level appointment; but it was later extended to her as well.
2. Ron Keller, email, 3 March 2018.
3. Johnson recalls that she went on a joint visit (with the UK and Sweden) to Mozambique to promote the implementation of the Paris agenda, much along the same lines as the U4 visit to Tanzania: Johnson, comment, 26 May 2019.
4. Ron Keller, email, 3 March 2018.
5. *Trouw*, 'Resurrection of the stubborn Utstein Group', 27 September 2003.
6. OECD, summary record of 42nd High Level meeting 15–16 April 2004, DCD/DCA/m2004/5/prov.
7. Ron Keller, email, 3 March 2018.
8. Clare Short, letter to Sher Bahadur Deuba, prime minister of Nepal (on behalf of Utstein-Johnson, Karlsson, Wieczorek-Zeul), 14 September 2002, UK DfID Archives.
9. Ron Keller, email, 29 December 2018.
10. Jan Orbie and Simon Lightfoot 'Development: Shallow Europeanization?', in *Foreign Policies of EU Member States*, ed. Amelia Hadfield, Ian Manners, and Richard G. Whitman (London and New York: Routledge, 2017), p. 208.
11. Ron Keller, email, 14 February 2019.
12. Ron Keller, email, 29 December 2018.
13. Richard Manning, comment, 21 April 2019.
14. OECD, *The OECD at Fifty: Development Co-operation, Past, Present and Future* (Paris: OECD, 2011).
15. *Development Today*, "The Nordic Plus Group Launches Ambitious Goals for Harmonization", 4, 2004.
16. Hilde F. Johnson, email, 3 January 2019.
17. Richard Manning, comment, 21 April 2019.
18. J. Brian Atwood and Richard Manning, 'DAC High level Forums on Aid Effectiveness', in a volume on the history of the DAC, ed. R. Carey (forthcoming), p. 6. The authors also indicate that in the end the USA introduced a reservation with respect to the use of country systems.
19. Bert Koenders, email, 10 April 2019.
20. Richard Manning, comments, email, 24 April 2019.
21. DAC Development Cooperation Chairman's report 2009; Atwood and Manning report that Brazil dissented from the report on the grounds that aid practices in South–South cooperation need not follow the same patterns as those that guide North–South aid relationships.
22. Barrie Ireton, Britain's International Development Policies: A History of DFID and Overseas Aid (Basingstoke: Palgrave Macmillan, 2013), p. 77.
23. Heidemarie Wieczorek-Zeul, email, 14 May 2019.

24. Ireton, Britain's International Development Policies, p. 79.
25. Horst Köhler, interview by Eveline Herfkens, 20 February 2019. His wife Eva was also very supportive and made several speeches for the campaign.
26. Horst Köhler, email, 27 June 2019.
27. World Bank, *Are We on Track to Achieve the Millennium Development Goals?* ABCDE Conference, ed. F. Bourguignon, B. Plescovic, and A. Sapir (Washington, DC and New York: World Bank and Oxford University Press, 2005).
28. Herfkens left the campaign in 2008 and was not replaced. The campaign continued with a much lower profile under direction from the UNDP.
29. Eveline Herfkens, speech to G8 parliamentarians, Berlin, 30 May 2007.
30. Clare Short, 'More aid and less justice will not make poverty history', speech, Oxted, UK, 20 February 2008.
31. Clare Short, 'The dangers of a broken multilateral system in a divided world', speech, University of Bath, UK, 23 February 2006.
32. Eveline Herfkens, speech, Conference on Financing the MDGs, EU parliamentarians, Brussels, 15 April 2004.
33. For an extensive discussion of the issue, see Constantine Michalopoulos, *Aid, Trade and Development* (Cham: Palgrave, 2017), pp. 218–20.
34. Michalopoulos, Aid, Trade and Development, pp. 231–2.
35. Anne O. Krueger, 'A New Approach to Sovereign Debt Restructuring', Washington, DC: IMF, April 2002).
36. Heidemarie Wieczorek-Zeul, letter to Utstein (Johnson, Short, Van Ardenne, Karlsson) on sovereign debt restructuring, 13 January 2003.
37. See http//www.imf.org.hipc.
38. Ajay Chibber, 'Overview', in *Reform and Growth*, ed. Ajay Chibber, R. Kyle Peters, and Barbara J. Yale (New Brunswick, NJ and London: Transaction Publishers, 2006).
39. Victoria Elliot, 'The Poverty Reduction Strategy Initiative', in Chibber et al., *Reform and Growth*, p. 143.
40. Eveline Herfkens, 'Comments', in Chibber et al., *Reform and Growth*, p. 162.
41. Ajay Chibber, 'Overview', in Chibber et al., *Reform and Growth*, p. xxiii.
42. Clare Short, 'The World Bank: the alternative is worse', *New Statesman*, 8 May 2006.
43. Heidemarie Wieczorek-Zeul, email, 14 May 2019.
44. World Bank, 'Report of the Ad hoc Group', 11 April 2007, downloaded from *The Wall Street Journal*, 18 May 2007.
45. Heidemarie Wieczorek-Zeul, email, 14 May 2019.
46. World Bank, "Report of the Ad hoc Group" (R2007-0089) May 14, 2007, p. 48 accessed from online.WSJ.com, March 4, 2019.
47. World Bank, "Report of the Ad hoc Group" p. 52.
48. *WSJ*, "Wolfowitz" May 18, 2007; *NY Times* "Wolfowitz Resigns Ending Long Fight at World Bank" May 18, 2007.
49. *Al Jazeera*, 'Wolfowitz to Resign from World Bank', 18 May 2007.
50. *The New York Times*, 18 May 2007.
51. Robert Zoellick was chosen as World Bank President in July 2007.
52. This section is based in part on materials and drafts provided by Johnson in May 2019.
53. Evaluation of 'Delivery as One', p. 85.

54. See https://undocs.org/a/res/72/279 https://undocs.org/A/72/L.52.
55. Hilde F. Johnson, *Waging Peace in Sudan* (Eastbourne: Sussex Academic Press, 2011), pp. 210–11.
56. UN–World Bank, *UN–WB Partnership Framework Agreement for Crisis and Post-Conflict Situations* (New York: UN, 2008).
57. G8, *Africa Personal Representatives' Joint Progress Report on the G8 Africa Partnership* (Bonn/Berlin: Federal Ministry for Economic Cooperation and Development, 2007).
58. G8, *Joint Progress Report on the G8 Africa Partnership* (Bonn/Berlin: Federal Ministry for Economic Cooperation and Development, 2008).
59. G8, *Joint Progress Report.*
60. This section is based in part on Michalopoulos, Aid, Trade and Development, pp. 233–5.
61. World Bank, *The Growth Report* (Washington, DC: World Bank, 2008), p. 91.
62. Heidemarie Wieczorek-Zeul, *Gerechtigkeit und Frieden sind Geschwister* (Marburg: Schuren, 2018), pp. 158–68.
63. Heidemarie Wieczorek-Zeul, 'Notes: Meeting with Trevor Manuel', 25 May 2008.
64. Wieczorek-Zeul, Gerechtigkeit und Frieden sind Geschwister, pp. 158–68.
65. Trevor Manuel, speech, Financing for Development Conference, Doha, 30 November 2008.
66. Wieczorek-Zeul, *Gerechtigkeit und Frieden sind Geschwister*, pp. 158–68.
67. Wieczorek-Zeul, speech, Financing for Development Conference.
68. Wieczorek-Zeul, speech, Financing for Development Conference.
69. UN, *The Doha Declaration on Financing for Development* (New York: United Nations, 2009).
70. G8 Summit (2009), chair summary.
71. Wieczorek-Zeul, *Gerechtigkeit und Frieden sind Geschwister*, pp. 158–68.
72. Wieczorek-Zeul, *Gerechtigkeit und Frieden sind Geschwister*, pp. 158–68.
73. James Adams, interview by E. Herfkens and C. Michalopoulos, 7 May 2018.
74. Paul Isenman, interview by C. Michalopoulos and E. Herfkens, 2 May 2018.

11

The Legacy in Troubled Times

Introduction

The deep crisis which afflicted the developed countries in 2008 ushered in a new era whose implications are not yet fully understood. The prolonged recovery in the USA combined with stagnation in several Eurozone countries led many to agree with Larry Summers that 'growth challenges are not so much a matter of the lingering effects of the crisis as they are of structural changes in the global economy that contributed to the crisis and the problems in its aftermath'.[1] The rising prominence of China, a leading global power and aid donor, together with the re-emergence of Russia with a similar system of state capitalism, have raised questions about the prospects of liberal democracy, and the multilateral global institutions that Europe and the United States helped build in the last seventy years. Further questions were raised by Brexit and the protectionist President of the United States who in his inaugural speech stated that 'Protection will lead to great prosperity and strength.'

In 2015 the UN was able to celebrate the achievement of substantial progress in meeting the MDGs and to set up a new set of Sustainable Development Goals (SDGs), to be achieved by 2030. But the crisis led to very large declines in international private financial flows to developing countries. Tight budgets in several European countries also resulted in reductions of their aid flows. While overall flows of ODA were not affected, its quality deteriorated and its distribution was heavily influenced by aid allocations to conflict management, peace and security activities in a few countries with civil strife such as Afghanistan and Iraq, as well as refugee assistance in the developed countries themselves raising questions as to the definition of ODA. Changing developing country needs as well as changing developed country attitudes towards economic assistance, led to a variety of new aid practices and forms of collaboration which affected aid effectiveness.

The U4 continued their advocacy for development and poverty eradication in different settings: Short was until 2010 an independent MP. Johnson, following her stint at UNICEF, became Special Representative of the UN Secretary-General and head of the United Nations Mission to South Sudan and later served as Secretary-General of Norway's Christian Democratic Party. All four were members of various impressive global commissions and boards of international NGOs. Herfkens was a member of the ILO/WHO Social Protection Advisory Group,

Johnson of the UN High Level Independent Panel on Peace Operations, Wieczorek-Zeul of the Commission of Experts of the President of the UN General Assembly on Reforms of the International Monetary and Financial System. Herfkens, Wieczorek-Zeul and Johnson all became successively members of the IPM board, while Herfkens was vice chair of the board of the International Centre for Trade and Sustainable Development and a founding board member of the African Center for Economic Transformation. Short was chair of the Extractive Industries Initiative, of the Welfare Association (which focuses on the needs of Palestinian refugees), and of the Cities Alliance, which focuses on urbanization. This chapter will review international cooperation for development as well as the U4 aid programmes during the past decade in order to gauge the relevance of the U4 legacy to the continuing challenges of development.

2008 and Its Aftermath

In the immediate aftermath of the financial turmoil in 2008, world trade declined in absolute terms. The above-mentioned UN Commission of experts which was chaired by Joseph E. Stiglitz and of which Wieczorek-Zeul was a member, was set up to present proposals for addressing the crisis. Its main conclusion was that: 'Our global economy is broken. This much is widely accepted. But what it is precisely that is broken and needs to be fixed has become a subject of enormous controversy.' The Commission recognized that global cooperation was ever more needed to prevent developing countries from suffering from a crisis that was not their doing. It proposed the establishment of a global panel on systemic risk (composed of economic experts representing different regions and views) that would provide regular reports on financial market developments and propose appropriate regulations.[2] There were a lot of mutterings about fixing the capitalist system and its tendency for financial excesses leading to turmoil that hurts the weakest. In fact, few fundamental changes in the international architecture were attempted. By and large, the world stuck to the traditional 'muddle through' approach in dealing with crises.

In 2010 trade picked up again and in the next few years it appeared that, while the recovery in the USA was slow and several Eurozone countries faced debt difficulties, the international economy had weathered the financial shock pretty well. To be sure, there was some increase in protection and the Doha Round continued to be moribund, resulting in rumblings that multilateralism was on the wane. There were no major reversals of the trade order such as had occurred in the aftermath of the great depression, although recent developments are increasingly worrying. And over time concerns started to arise regarding whether the market system and capitalism more broadly inevitably tend to result in inequality of income and wealth.

The Millennium Development Goals (MDGs) at 2015

The post-2008 slowdown in trade, finance, and growth of the world economy did little to slow down the developing country progress in achieving the MDGs. Building largely on the momentum gained in the early 2000s, when their own policies were improving and globalization was galloping forward, developing countries achieved great progress in meeting them. The overall poverty reduction goal was achieved, as was the target for clean water. But even for the goals that were not met, considerable progress was made, a first for the UN, which reported that 'As we reach the end of the MDG period, the world community has reason to celebrate.'[3]

In a speech that year at an ODI conference marking the MDG achievements, Herfkens echoed the prevailing celebratory mood:

> Let's celebrate the more than a billion additional people who today have access to clean water; the billion people lifted out of extreme poverty; the additional tens of millions of kids in primary school today; the millions of babies who are alive today; . . . let's celebrate that the biggest leaps forward were made by the poorest countries, particularly in sub-Saharan Africa; let's celebrate and congratulate *developing* countries—as most progress was made for the Goals for which they have the primary responsibility; and let's acknowledge and celebrate that the Millennium Goals brought about the most successful anti-poverty movement in human history . . . [4]

At the same time, major development challenges remained. Although there was significant progress on overall targets, millions of people were left behind. The rather ambitious gender targets (for maternal mortality and girls' education), despite significant progress in girls' primary education, went largely unmet. While sub-Saharan Africa probably made the biggest relative gains, large numbers of people were and still are living in extreme poverty without basic services. Inequality has increased in many countries and big gaps still exist between the poorest and the richest households, and between men and women.

In the fall of 2015 the UN adopted a new set of goals for the world community to achieve by the year 2030.[5] The Sustainable Development Goals (SDGs) (seventeen in number), include reducing income inequality and addressing climate change; they are aspirational in nature and extremely ambitious—the elimination of poverty, hunger, and illiteracy for all. That the world community could agree on these goals following the post-2008 economic doldrums was in itself a major achievement. They represent humanity's challenges for the future and will be discussed in detail in Chapter 12.

Underneath this mixed set of news and relative calm, a substantial storm had been brewing. In part this was linked to the perceived impact of globalization, nowadays not so much on the poor in developing countries, but on developed country groups left behind. In the USA the collapse of social capital has combined with low labour mobility to result in a decay of local communities that leaves a scar far deeper than the unemployment rate.

But it has not been simply the failure to address the distributional issues that resulted from globalization, as that does not explain the rise of populism in Northern Europe, where good social welfare policies protected against globalization's downside. Large inflows of refugees fleeing the Middle East conflagration, violence in Central America, and poverty and conflict in Africa, have raised fears of cultural identity loss both in Europe and in the United States. In both settings, the rise of populism has been driven by rising xenophobia and fears about the impact of large numbers of refugees and other immigrants on traditional cultures and values, although tellingly, the greatest anti-immigration sentiment has been in areas with the fewest immigrants. In other places, such as the UK, rising rents and house prices, growing inequality, and loss of dignity have helped create a bitter mood. The result has been Brexit, and the rise of illiberal political parties and regimes on both sides of the Atlantic, not exactly a great environment for international cooperation to eradicate global poverty.

Aid and Debt

Still, economic assistance to developing countries had been largely maintained. Total ODA in 2017 was slightly higher than in 2008. As private sources of finance declined, ODA's importance as a source of 'development finance' actually increased. But the allocation of large increases of ODA to countries with civil wars as well as the inclusion of assistance provided to refugees and other expenditures in the donor country as part of ODA, tended to distort the actual benefits for recipients. Recipient programmable aid, which countries can use to finance their own programmes and priorities, actually declined in absolute terms between 2009 and 2015 and even more as a share of the total. Perhaps the most positive development was the continued increase in the importance of grants by private voluntary agencies and foundations which rose both in absolute amounts and in their share of the total.

Overall, ODA levels in three of the four U4 countries have kept up better than most. Both Germany and the UK maintained levels very close to the 0.7 per cent GNI/GNP target, although their impact on poverty has been diluted by the inclusion in the ODA levels of substantial expenditures on refugees. ODA levels relative to GNI have been maintained close to 1 per cent in Norway. Only in the Netherlands have they declined since 2016: in November 2012 the new coalition government, which included the Labour Party—traditionally a staunch supporter of ODA—without much political ado dropped its commitment to the

0.7 per cent target after thirty years of adhering to or surpassing it (see Appendix, Table A-1).

The original U4 agenda to eradicate poverty had pushed for changing the distribution of ODA to favour LDCs and other low-income countries which had less access to private sector flows and could less easily shoulder debt on hard terms. By and large these efforts succeeded in three of the four countries—the exception being Germany which continued to allocate about a third of its assistance to higher middle income and high income countries, much as it had done in the previous twenty years—while its share of allocable aid to LDCs had actually diminished (see Appendix Table A-2). By contrast the share of Netherlands and UK aid to LDCs increased consistently over the whole period while that to other developing countries declined. Norway's share of aid to LDCs had traditionally been higher than the others and fell somewhat over the period; but the share of Norwegian ODA to other low-income countries increased, resulting in little overall change to the combined total going to LDCs and low-income countries.[6]

The other major change in the distribution of ODA has been the significant increase directed to fragile states. The amount directed to these countries has exceeded 50 per cent of total ODA in recent years; and an even larger proportion of humanitarian assistance. Fragility, of course, has many dimensions: economic, political, security, social, environmental, and, as will be discussed later in this chapter, there are questions as to whether it provides a meaningful framework for thinking about allocating assistance for development.

In the meantime, aid fragmentation continued unabated, increasing the implementation burden for recipients, especially LDCs about whose governance donors are presumably worried. The number of developing countries with over forty official donors went from zero in 1990 to over thirty in 2012, with the average project worth slightly more than half a million euros.[7]

New donors have emerged and contributed to aid fragmentation. China was at the centre of the establishment of two new multilateral financial institutions. First, in 2012, with the participation of Brazil, India, Russia and South Africa it set up what was originally called the BRICS Development Bank, which later was renamed New Development Bank with an initial capitalization of US$50 billion, distributed equally among the five founding members, with headquarters in Shanghai.[8] China was also behind the establishment of the Asian Infrastructure Investment Bank (AIIB) which was launched in late 2015 with a capitalization of $100 billion and a membership of fifty-seven countries, including several from the OECD but not the USA and Japan. Its new global initiative, 'Belt and Road', is intended to expand funding for transport infrastructure throughout both Asia and Europe. The new institutions reflect both the changes in the global economic importance of China as well as some of its frustration and that of other emerging powers about the lack of progress in changing the power structure of the Bretton

Woods institutions which continue to be dominated by the USA and the EU countries.[9]

The debt problems of HIPC appeared to have been solved, so much so that in 2015 the World Bank closed its office that followed the issue. The step was probably premature as debt to China by a number of HIPC soared and started to cause worries about the need to start new relief measures. In 2018, thirty-four low-income countries that were recipients of IDA credits were assessed to be at high risk of external debt distress or in actual debt distress.[10] Transparency in developing country credit transactions deteriorated as new donors such as China provided funding with repayments tied to production or exports of raw materials. Moreover, according to World Bank President Malpass, some of the new credits contain non-disclosure clauses preventing the debtor from publicly disclosing the loan's terms and conditions, making it impossible to assess issues of debt sustainability or the need for debt relief.[11] A key issue that has emerged in recent years is how to involve China in collaboration with other donors to address the emerging problem.

Aid Effectiveness

The discussion in earlier chapters suggests that while the U4 made significant contributions in several aspects of international cooperation for development, including pushing for and attaining higher levels of aid and the achievement of the MDGs, by far their greatest contribution lay in promoting approaches and policies that made economic assistance more effective. This involved their own bilateral programmes, the multilateral institutions in which they participated, and, through the international agreements on aid effectiveness reached in Rome, Paris, and Accra, the broader international community. How did their approach stand up in light of the changing international economic and political environment of the past decade?

To answer this question it is useful, first, to summarize once more the main elements of their approach based on the Utstein Principles and their practices as they evolved over time. Then their aid performance will be examined including through the peer reviews of their programmes in the DAC. Finally, the international community's actions in implementing the commitments on aid effectiveness made during the first decade of the twenty-first century will be assessed.

The U4 Approach

The central element in the U4 approach to aid effectiveness was the balance of commitments between development partners.

The developing countries had to:

- Develop comprehensive, coherent plans to eradicate poverty; such plans should give priority both to raising the incomes of the poor and to providing them with access to services that address their basic needs in such areas as health and education;
- Mobilize their own resources for development as aid could only be supportive and supplementary to domestic resource mobilization;
- Development plans had to be 'owned' both by the government and the population, which was supposed to participate in elaborating them;
- Developing country governments should be in the driver's seat in carrying out the plans but also be accountable to the people for their successful implementation;
- Governments should adhere to basic human rights and eliminate corruption.

For their part, donors were supposed to:

- Give priority to allocating assistance to governments who made the above commitments to eradicate poverty;
- Simplify and coordinate their assistance programmes to minimize the administrative burden assistance activities place on recipients;
- Use the recipients' systems to implement assistance programmes—and help strengthen such systems where necessary;
- Provide assistance in the form of budget support, where appropriate, in order to facilitate implementation as well as strengthen public sector management;
- Promote coherence between their aid and trade policies, including by untying their aid so that bilateral aid funds would be used to obtain goods and services from the most competitive source globally, without restricting procurement formally or informally to the donor.

On the old issue as to whether to focus development assistance, that is, ODA, on poor countries or poor people, the U4 had a simple answer: obviously aid must focus on poor countries, as only aid in support of a country's own effort is sustainable ('donors do not develop . . .'); but by focusing aid on countries with a well thought out PRSP, including a commitment to eradicate poverty and achieve the MDGs, such aid would help lift poor people out of poverty. Of course, humanitarian aid to deal with emergencies was a separate story.

The U4 were aware that not all developing countries would be able to meet these criteria, and that assistance should be tailored to individual country circumstances. They were painfully aware that developing countries, especially in sub-Saharan Africa had perceived IMF and World Bank programmes in the 1980s to be driven by standardized formulas; and while they promoted the use of PRSPs as instruments for the articulation of comprehensive plans to fight poverty, they were keen to avoid their use of 'cookie-cutter' approaches. They were also aware that the development process was complex, that key institutions suffered from different kinds of weaknesses, and that progress did not follow a linear path but was full of stops and starts. Still, many of the elements of their approach summarized above found their way into the international commitments of the Paris Declaration and other international meetings in the 2000s.

The Peer Reviews

What is the evidence as to whether the U4 practised what they preached? The answer to this can be found in part in the OECD/DAC peer reviews conducted of their individual programmes as well as other broader evaluations of their approach. The DAC peer review process subjects member aid programmes to periodic reviews every five years.[12] This involves 'examiners' from two DAC members plus the OECD Secretariat reviewing a submission by the country on programme priorities and developments, and presenting a summary of conclusions and recommendations.

The peer reviews of the U4 programmes in the early 2000s were full of references to concepts articulated by the U4 ministers in their meetings, speeches, and other pronouncements. The emphasis on poverty eradication, the achievement of the MDGs, collaboration with other donors, 'ownership' by the partner governments, as well as increased attention to social services and the use of budget support characterized the reviews of all four countries over the period 2001–5.

The UK peer review for 2001 states:

> to improve aid effectiveness and maximize development impact, the United Kingdom is delivering an increasing share of its aid in collaboration with other donors through development frameworks in support of partner country-led poverty reduction strategies, most notably Poverty Reduction Strategy Papers (PRSPs). This explains a number of features of the British aid program including a move away from stand-alone projects, the pooling of bilateral funds and the untying of aid.[13]

For the Netherlands the 2001 review on the issue of 'Ownership and Poverty Focus' says: 'The Netherlands builds its approach to development co-operation on three principles: ownership, utilization of domestic resources and poverty reduction. As is true with several DAC Members, it promotes the use of country-owned strategies, in particular, the Poverty Reduction Strategy Paper (PRSP), as a framework for implementation, monitoring and evaluation, donor co-ordination and policy dialogue in priority countries.'[14] The 2006 review emphasizes that the Netherlands has a long-standing commitment to partner country-led approaches to poverty reduction going back to the mid-1990s. This translates operationally into 'on-budget where possible, off-budget where necessary'. The Ministry of Foreign Affairs (which includes Development Cooperation) considers budget support as the most effective form of aid since it ensures that recipient countries assume responsibility for implementing their own development agenda and contributes to a better alignment of aid with policy and systems of partner countries.[15]

For Germany, 'the most remarkable policy innovation since 1998 in German development co-operation was the Cabinet approval in April 2001 of the 'Program of Action 2015 for Poverty Reduction'. This establishes global poverty reduction as an overarching task in development co-operation and an important element in all national policies.'[16] Perhaps the only critical comments were those in the 2005 review which admonished the government to increase budget allocations to low-income countries.[17]

And finally, the 2004 review of Norway stressed that:

Norway is now engaged in sector-wide approaches and involved in direct budget support initiatives where the conditions are sufficiently sound. In Zambia it is pooling financial resources as well as technical assistance with other willing partners in the education sector without specific earmarking, although twinning arrangements are utilized. The guidelines on budget support for developing countries, approved in August 2004, provide a good indication of the conditions under which this aid modality can be used.[18]

Later peer reviews started to appear more critical and less focused on the earlier U4 themes. Germany's 2010 review stated:

The Coalition Agreement signed in October 2009 reiterates this commitment to development coherence. However, policy coherence also depends on embedding the concept within the various government departments and setting clear priorities for its implementation. There is considerable scope for the German government to deepen its commitment to the MDGs by making international development a more tangible goal of other government policy areas.[19]

The program is still weak in its use of country public financial management systems, common arrangements or procedures and joint missions. It needs to build on the progress made in implementing the aid effectiveness Plan of Operations by making greater use of partner country systems and adapting aid instruments to partner country-led program-based approaches.[20]

The 2015 review praises Germany for being at the forefront of using ODA to leverage private sector investment for sustainable development. Germany also stands out for its commitment and innovative approaches to financing climate change action and for efforts to improve the quality of its aid, for example by improving efficiency and better tailoring programmes to local conditions. The review finds that Germany's stated aim to focus on the poorest countries is still not well reflected in its aid flows. The share of its bilateral aid going to LDCs fell to 24 per cent in 2013, its lowest level of the last five years, and the top two recipients of German aid are China and India. This disconnect is in part because Germany's aid allocation criteria and instruments are not fully aligned with its goals. For example, an emphasis on good governance as one of several criteria for providing aid to a country may conflict with Germany's aim to help fragile countries. A rising share of concessional loans in its portfolio means more ODA is going to middle-income countries and less to the poorest. OECD Development Assistance Committee Chair Erik Solheim, said: 'As its aid budget grows, Germany should also strive to make good on its aim of prioritizing those countries that are most in need.'[21]

For Norway, which in 2008 adopted a 'holistic' approach to development, the 2008 peer review warns that 'Norway will need to ensure that its core focus on poverty reduction and the MDGs is not diluted.' The review further notes that the programme is placing greater emphasis on fragile states, UN reform, and aid to Africa, but stresses that Norway 'needs to develop an overall approach to policy coherence'.[22] The 2013 review re-emphasizes the priority Norway gives to combating poverty and its focus on fragile states, as well as the continued heavy use of partner country systems for the delivery of the bulk of its assistance. But the review also notes that as more money is being given to global initiatives, the remainder of the funding is starting to be spread more thinly: only one third of the funding goes to the top twenty recipients compared to 46 per cent in the early 2000s.

The UK peer review in 2014 outlined a substantial shift in the programme focus which 'involved a new approach to attract private investment that so far has succeeded in maintaining a pro-poor focus' and that 'DfID is committed to engaging in fragile and conflict affected states, as this responds to the need to protect UK interests'. But the review also noted that there has been less emphasis in the use of country systems and a need for the new 'value for money' approach to minimize the use of spending targets. Finally, in a worrisome comment suggesting a reversal of the earlier UK emphasis on untying aid, it urges that the 'the UK should ensure that there are no unintended impediments to foreign suppliers winning contracts'.[23]

The Netherlands peer review of 2017 exudes similar concerns about the dilution of earlier programme priorities. The review notes a government policy document, 'A World to Gain' published in 2013, which identified fifteen partner countries. However, it raises concerns that 'Budgets are increasingly managed from the Netherlands with limited opportunities for national governments input into decisions'—whatever happened to the earlier emphasis that the partner government should be in the 'driver's seat'? The review also recommends an 'increase in its use of or strengthening of country systems' and 'the need to avoid further fragmentation'.[24]

Two main conclusions emerge from reading these peer reviews: first, that the emphasis on poverty eradication was retained—at least in principle; second, that a lot of the earlier emphasis on certain key elements of aid effectiveness advocated by the U4 such as government ownership, use of partner systems, budget support, and policy coherence, was considerably diluted.

The Global Conferences

These two main conclusions are confirmed by a review of the experience with global conferences focusing on aid and aid effectiveness. As noted in Chapter 10, in November 2008, The *Doha Declaration on Financing for Development* reiterated all the donor aid commitments of the Monterrey meeting which, having the benefit of the Paris Agreement on aid effectiveness, added all the right things about donor and recipient responsibilities. Coming so soon after the Lehman Brothers default it was remarkable that the meeting took place at all, and it would not have happened without Wieczorek-Zeul's insistence and personal efforts. It contained the by now standard recommendations regarding the Doha Round of multilateral trade negotiations in ways that would benefit developing countries and repeated the admonishment for increased coherence between aid and trade policies. The problem was that donors mired in financial crises and recessions started to backtrack on aid commitments.[25]

Recall that the Paris and Accra Agreements had set up a system of quantitative targets on aid effectiveness to apply to donors and recipients, and a time horizon for their achievement. These were monitored by the DAC and showed progress in some areas, for example in the coordination of technical cooperation, but except in Latin America there had been little progress in the use of country systems for the implementation of aid programmes.

A Fourth High Level Forum on Aid Effectiveness was scheduled for Busan, Korea on 29 November–1 December 2011. This Forum was to be sponsored jointly by the OECD and the UNDP and included not only the traditional bilateral and multilateral donors but also new bilateral donors like China and Korea, and the major private voluntary agencies. The UNDP was brought in to provide a forum for the involvement of new donors, especially China, an important objective of DAC Chairman Brian Atwood. T. Abdel-Malek and Bert Koenders (see Chapter 10) the co-chairs of the working party asked for advice from a small group of people involved in process from the outset, which included Amoako and Herfkens. On the eve of the conference they posed the question as to whether aid was being delivered in a more effective way than in 2005. The two co-chairs said: 'The answer is clear: progress has been made, but globally donors and developing countries have fallen short of the goals they set for themselves for 2010. The findings from monitoring and evaluating the implementation of the Paris Declaration make for sobering reading.'[26] In fact, only one of the thirteen targets—improving technical cooperation—had been met. The co-chairs, after noting that the targets were still meaningful, recommended that 'Busan can and should aim to ensure deeper political commitment—coupled with concrete actions to follow through.'[27]

The opposite happened. The meeting at Busan weakened both the commitments, especially by the donors, and the monitoring mechanism of aid effectiveness. It produced a new entity, the Global Partnership for Effective Development Co-operation (GPEDC) and a new document which reaffirmed the major principles articulated in earlier meetings such as recipient government ownership and using country systems for implementing aid programmes. However,

> the new donors questioned the legitimacy of the OECD/DAC...and did not want to be shoehorned into these Western dominated institutions and agreements. In addition, many traditional donors, who were never fully on board with the Paris Declaration took advantage of the presence of the new donors to weaken their commitment. Thus, the UNDP was mandated to be involved in the follow up. Alas, given the UN's *anxiety not to offend* its rich country members, this put an end to the scrupulous monitoring of individual OECD/DAC member commitments.[28]

The commitments and monitoring were weakened in a variety of ways:

- There were no more timeframes for achieving the various targets;
- Several of the donor targets were completely eliminated, including the targets for programmable aid, the target for shared analysis and joint missions, and the target for mutual assessment;
- The targets for using recipient systems were combined and only averages reported for all targets, thus masking individual donor performance for each target;
- Most of the baseline information was to be obtained from recipient data; consequently, donor performance was based only on a fraction of their overall aid.

All this sounds very technical, but without these specifics donor performance could not be evaluated; and they could not be subjected to future criticism about not meeting their commitments.

James Adams, in a recent communication, writes:

DAC fouled up by making the process 'all inclusive' reaching out beyond donors to civil society and other outside groups. This decision took all the pressure off donors, the impetus behind the lead up to Rome and Paris. Next, donors clearly did not appreciate the criticism that was implicit in the Rome–Paris process and were very happy to move to broader issues. Finally, there has been no effective replacement for the Utstein group to keep the pressure on donors through the Rome/Paris follow up or any other process.[29]

There was yet another conference in Mexico City in April 2014, this time labelled 'First High Level Meeting of the Global Partnership for Effective Development Co-operation: Building towards an Inclusive Post-2015 Development Agenda', with the long title reflecting the paucity of results. The meeting was attended by a variety of bilateral and multilateral donors, philanthropic organizations, trade unions, civil society organizations, and so on and so on. Its main outcome was to request that a new study of aid effectiveness be undertaken based on the new monitoring. It produced another communique from which the following paragraph is quoted to indicate how unfortunately general, full of platitudes and purposeless the process has become:

> We encourage continued progress in ensuring that all stakeholders and voices are duly acknowledged and the necessary space is given and expanded to enhance inclusive and democratic ownership of the development agenda, including through women's empowerment, in the spirit of openness, trust and mutual respect and learning from the different and complementary roles of all partners.[30]

A study by the Center for Global Development (CGD), based on data from 2012 for thirty-one donors, including many of the new ones, showed that the quality of ODA had improved in that there were 'visible and significant gains in fostering institutions and in transparency and learning. However, there has been almost no change in maximizing efficiency or in reducing the burden on recipient countries'; moreover, 'the quality of aid of non-DAC donors is less than for DAC donors'.[31] A new study of the Global Partnership was produced in 2016 but because of the problems with the monitoring, noted above, it is impossible to say whether donor performance has improved or not.[32] The latest report, produced in 2019, shows further deterioration in most of the measures monitored. The best that can be said about it is that a global entity, albeit toothless, is still looking at the issue of monitoring aid effectiveness.[33]

Financing for development was the subject of yet another UN conference held in Addis Ababa, in 2015. It is fair to say that very little progress was achieved. There was yet another document referring to the earlier commitments, of which the most important was probably the reiteration of the importance of developing country own domestic resource mobilization and addressing corruption which had already been made at Monterrey. The two new elements were an emphasis on public–private partnerships and addressing illicit financial flows through tax havens.[34] But it is difficult to avoid the conclusion that in the aftermath of 2008 nothing much has really happened either to increase the level or improve the quality and effectiveness of development assistance or strengthen the coherence between trade and finance.

Changing Politics and Policies

The above review of the evolution of aid policies in the U4 and more broadly during the decade following the 2008 financial crisis suggests that significant changes took place in all their programmes. Was it because the previous approach was proven wrong? Did the development challenges change? Or were there other reasons for the programmatic changes that were in evidence during this period?

Budget Support and Results

One of the key features of the U4 approach was the use of budget support. The U4 did not invent budget support: the USA provided what was then called 'program' loans to India in the late 1960s. The World Bank provided a very large number of structural adjustment and sector loans in the 1980s and 1990s which involved budget support conditioned on partner performance, often co-financed by bilateral aid including the U4 countries, adhering to the World Bank conditions attached. The U4 provided budget support only for countries which had already met policy conditions and used it as an instrument to promote government ownership and the use of country systems as well as to strengthen public sector management capabilities and accountability to the population. The emphasis was controversial from the beginning, especially in Germany. Project-based assistance was re-emphasized starting soon after 2008, even though there was strong evidence that budget support was working.

In 2006 the international community produced a massive multi-country evaluation of budget support in seven countries (Burkina Faso, Mozambique, Malawi, Nicaragua, Rwanda, Uganda, and Vietnam), assessing aid amounting to over $4 billion for the period 1994–2004. The study was sponsored by a steering group consisting of nineteen bilateral agencies, including the U4 and all major donors such as France, Japan, Sweden, and the USA, as well as the World Bank, the EU, the IMF and the Inter-American Development Bank. It was, and still is, probably the most authoritative study of budget support ever produced.[35]

The report starts with a summary statement of the expectations and reasons for providing Partnership General Budget Support (PGBS), the partnership concept being integral to the donor–recipient relationship which is a necessary condition for aid effectiveness:

> PGBS was a response to dissatisfaction with the effectiveness of earlier aid instruments. Its origins are closely linked to the HIPC initiative and to the introduction of PRSPs as a focus for collaboration between donors and partner countries. There is a wide range of expectations from general budget support. These include: improved coordination and harmonization among donors; alignment with partner country systems and policies; lower transaction costs; higher allocative efficiency of public expenditure; greater predictability of funding; increased effectiveness of the state and public administration as general budget support is aligned with and uses government allocation and financial management systems, and improved domestic accountability through increased focus on the government's own accountability channels.

The overall conclusions and recommendations of the synthesis report are as follows:

- 'PGBS has been a relevant response to certain acknowledged problems in aid effectiveness.
- PGBS can be an efficient, effective and sustainable way of supporting national poverty reduction strategies.
- Provision of discretionary funds through national budget systems has produced systemic effects on capacity, and particularly capacity for public finance management, that are posited in the evaluation framework. Moreover, these effects are government-wide in nature.
- PGBS tends to enhance the country-level quality of aid as a whole, through its direct and indirect effects on coherence, harmonization and alignment. This makes PGBS a particularly valuable addition to the array of aid instruments in use.
- As regards poverty reduction, it was too soon for the ultimate effects of PGBS inputs during the evaluation period to be manifest. PGBS is a vehicle that assists in implementing a poverty reduction strategy. Its ultimate effectiveness in reducing poverty is bound up with the quality of the poverty reduction strategy that it supports.
- It is important not to overload the PGBS instrument. However, the team found in all cases a capacity to learn from experience, which suggests that PGBS could become more effective, and have a broader scope, over time.
- The evaluation also considered possible unintended effects of PGBS. Corruption can undermine all forms of aid; systemic strengthening of public

finance management, which PGBS supports, is an important part of a broad anti-corruption strategy. All of these potential adverse effects, however, also represent risks that need to be taken into account in the design of PGBS (and other aid).

- The evaluation team also found that PGBS, as presently designed, is vulnerable to a number of risks, including political risks. These threaten its ability to operate as a long-term support modality. Its sustainability depends on making it more resilient.'[36]

There were additional evaluation studies showing similarly positive results: in 2008, a Netherlands evaluation report of Dutch assistance to Africa for the period 1998–2006 concluded that budget support led to improvements in public financial management, enabled increased allocations to social sectors, and strengthened partner's ownership. In terms of the policy dialogue, it resulted in greater attention to health services in rural areas, more focus on primary education and participation of girls, and the direction of more social services to poor districts.[37]

Also in 2008, there was an Oxfam study considering the effects of budget support on the MDGs on health and education in eight of the countries that received some of the largest amounts of the EU general budget support (Ghana, Kenya, Madagascar, Mali, Mozambique, Niger, Rwanda, and Zambia), The report shows that government spending on education has increased by 31 per cent (1999–2005) with significant increases in primary school enrolments in all but one of these. The study reported an equally positive story concerning health care. Of the top ten recipients of EC budget support, seven increased their public health expenditure on average by 46 per cent (2001–4). In all seven there has been an increase in life expectancy. In five of them there has also been a fall in maternal mortality rates. 'The evidence does show that where it is giving large amounts of budget support, headway is being made in reducing poverty.'[38]

Finally, in 2010 there was another EU Commission study which concluded that aid recipients that had received relatively high General Budget Support have performed better, often significantly so, in all four MDGs assessed (covering primary enrolment, gender parity in education, child mortality, and access to water), as well as in terms of improvements in the Human Development Index, in the period 2002–7.[39]

These findings are instructive because they address in detail all the various concerns that have been expressed about budget support. In retrospect, two of the most important concerns proved to be critical to its declining use as an aid instrument: first, the fact that its impact on poverty reduction could not be easily measured. This proved to be a serious problem as donors over time again started to focus more on specific measurable short-term results from *their* aid interventions.

The second had to do with the political risks associated with budget support. The concern appears to have been with respect to the political changes in the developing country partners. But, as we will discuss below, the main problems appear to have arisen with political changes in the donors. These resulted only in part because of the inability (or shall we say unwillingness) of parliaments to understand that funds are fungible,[40] that is, that project funding, where donor money can be 'traced', might just free up public resources which can be spent on other less desirable purposes, and thus the continued illusion that the direct accountability of aid-financed projects is more important than ensuring that all resources available to developing country governments are used effectively. Moreover, despite good intent and the brilliant campaigning work they do, many powerful NGOs in the OECD, which have considerable influence with politicians and the media, have a blind spot on budgetary aid and prefer funding for their projects rather than long-term investment in institutions and systems needed for long-term capacity building. Finally, continuing prominence has been given to the issue of corruption, notwithstanding the fact (and that there was no evidence) that corruption was more pronounced in budget-support programmes compared to other more traditional project-based approaches. On the contrary, strengthened financial management and procurement systems tend to mean less corruption. These issues indeed may have been fig leaves covering up more fundamental political changes in major donors.

Politics

Measurability of results combined with changed political attitudes appeared to have been present in the evolution of thinking and the policy changes in the UK's economic assistance programmes. This has been detailed in a relatively recent analysis prepared by ODI for the twenty years 1997–2017. The analysis reviews DfID's evolving policies under various Secretaries of Secretaries, starting with Short. For the period following 2007, the review says:

> From 2007 the story shows an erosion of the new agenda carved out under Clare Short in order to justify the 0.7% commitment. The bankruptcy of Lehman Brothers in 2008 marked the start of the financial crash. The UK economy began to suffer, yet DfID's budget grew, and commitments to 0.7%, and country- and sector-spending targets, were maintained. As the financial crisis set in, public support for aid declined. During New Labour's final three years, the new Secretary of State Douglas Alexander and the ministerial and civil service leadership of DfID felt the department lacked the control and evidence to support its spending. Voices from Whitehall and Westminster also insisted that the project level accountability apparatus was insufficient. As a result, civil servants deepened results-based management (RBM) reforms. These were focused on the

project management process—and cohabited awkwardly with the ongoing public adherence to the Paris Declaration.

Andrew Mitchell, following five years as shadow Secretary of State for International Development, was appointed in May 2010 in the new Conservative–Liberal Democrat Government. He immediately positioned results, evidence, value-for-money and transparency at the center of aid management. The next Secretary of State, Justine Greening, was appointed in September 2012. She continued these reforms, while also increasing the role of private finance, preferencing UK-based contractors, and a further and stronger emphasis on the national interest. Despite this, the last five years demonstrate that some civil servants within DfID are beginning to find a path towards more flexible programming, albeit within the basic constraints of deep political pressure and the results agenda.[41]

The DfID story is telling and reflects what was happening throughout the aid world, especially in Europe. Government concerns about being able to show results so as to maintain high levels of ODA in the face of budget constraints, combined with an increasing focus on the national interest and an ideologically driven effort to involve 'the private sector', undermined commitments made in the Rome–Paris–Accra declarations on aid effectiveness and reversed some of the initiatives pursued by the U4.

In Norway, the shift away from budget support was initially caused by perceived political risks related to concerns about either corruption and financial management issues or political developments in several important partner countries. Following Johnson's departure as minister, budget support had no strong defenders in Norway's political debate: 'Ministers in charge of development cooperation, Erik Solheim (2005–12) and Heiki Holmås (2012–13) were not particularly focused on aid effectiveness.'[42] Budget support was replaced less by project funding and more by large volumes of aid channelled through global funds, the latter following a focus on quantifiable results. Starting in 2013 the Conservative minority government eliminated the Development Minister position and finally ruled out budget support as a tool of development assistance. The increased emphasis on conflict-affected countries also made Norway one of the largest contributors of humanitarian assistance worldwide, and a preference for aid channelled through multilaterals or NGOs and not through government channels.

Similar considerations appear to have prevailed in the Netherlands, the more as the merging of aid with trade in 2012 enabled the trade bureaucrats to ensure aid served Dutch commercial interests (see later in this chapter).

The results of the shift away from the Rome–Paris–Accra agenda and the reduction in budget support have been documented by a recent African Center for Economic Transformation (ACET) report on external finance for development in six sub-Saharan Africa countries (Burkina Faso, Ghana, Rwanda, Tanzania, Uganda and Zambia):

General budget support remains the preferred aid modality for recipient countries, followed by sector budget support. But with coordination problems among traditional partners—the platform for coordinating general budget support has broken down—there are no clear directions forward. With the drop in general budget support, on-budget aid is also on the decline, and not all project aid (on the rise) is on budget. Nor has technical assistance been leveraged enough by countries—it is poorly embedded in the country systems and procedures. Momentum is lacking in implementing Paris Declaration targets for predictability, untied aid, and use of country systems. Tensions exist between representatives on the ground, who want to be more responsive to country needs, and home offices, which tend to move more slowly and can be inflexible.[43]

Donor Contradictions

The same political developments and the search for certainty in results led to what two very experienced aid practitioners mentioned earlier, Paul Isenman and Alex Shakow, called donor 'schizophrenia'. In a wonderful article penned in 2010 the two of them addressed the incompatibility of the emerging surge in donor support for sector-focused 'Global Funds' especially in health with the Rome–Paris–Accra agenda for aid effectiveness:

> The Paris Declaration (2005) and the Accra Agenda for Action (2008) is based on the recognition that, especially in the longer run, it is what countries, not donors, do that matters. Donors can create hothouse programs that bloom brilliantly for a time and then wither away. Thus, the emphasis is upon country ownership, alignment of development assistance in support of country programs, a complementary harmonization of aid among donors and reduction in transaction costs, more focus on results, and on accountability of donors as well as of developing countries.[44]

At the same time, 'there was a view, particularly among civil society organizations (CSOs), that there was a need to break the mold of development orthodoxy. Existing international institutions were seen, depending on whether it was the World Bank, UNICEF or WHO, as some combination of too bureaucratic and slow, powerful and arrogant, and unwilling to give a seat at the table to CSOs.'[45] GAVI and the Global Fund had great global appeal to publics, CSOs and political leaders because they were supposed to, inter alia:

- be evidence-based, sharing cutting-edge technology and good practice globally;
- give a key governance role to civil society and the private sector;

- show quantifiable results;
- have the ability to bring off massive short-term change unlikely to be achievable otherwise;
- create 'financing' rather than 'implementing' agencies, thereby requiring fewer staff;
- be nimble and adaptable, not weighed down by the baggage of accumulated rules and political interference found in the World Bank or UN agencies.

The appeal of global funds to civil society and world-famous public figures and artists, and to political leaders, has led to explosive growth in their financing, In contrast, it is more difficult to gain public or political understanding of the longer-run benefits of the Paris–Accra approach...But, global funds have significant disadvantages when viewed from the perspective of the health sector as a whole.

GAVI and Global Fund grants are an excellent way to promote research and innovation. But they are ill-suited to long-term support and system-strengthening. Another source of tension is between relatively short-term financing and the 'moral mortgage' of long-term obligations for recurrent cost financing of staff, medicines and vaccines. In addition, global funds have set up their own processes, which has meant that governments need to 'align' with the systems of global funds, while Paris–Accra calls for the contrary. The widely admired leanness of their staffs (at least initially) has meant less capacity to work with developing countries or donors on strengthening or overseeing programs on the ground. Also, the lack of country staff has made collaboration harder for governments and donors.[46]

The way forward according to Isenman and Shakow was to combine the strengths of the Rome–Paris–Accra approach with those of the Global Funds by, inter alia, taking steps to:

- Learn from, and be better partners with, global funds as they have much to offer, including the focus on results, involvement of civil society and the private sector, transparency, and
- capacity for adaptation and innovation;
- Not underestimate the importance of the issues discussed above for aid-dependent countries with weak capacity;
- Support the changes global funds are making to respond to the Rome–Paris–Accra agenda for action, but recognize that much more is needed to help bring about that change;
- Get more serious about 'thinking twice' before establishing new earmarked funds and use existing institutions where possible to implement them.[47]

Of course, as discussed above, governments' commitment to the Rome–Paris–Accra agenda on aid effectiveness had waned, while the Funds have continued to function and indeed play an increasing role, especially in the health sector. Is the fact that as originally conceived they were not in line with the thinking about aid effectiveness of any relevance today?

A recent CGD assessment concluded that the Global Fund ranked seventh in aid effectiveness, behind several multilateral agencies but higher than all U4 present bilateral aid programmes.[48] Another study found that increased aid from the Global Fund was associated with better control of corruption, government accountability, political freedom, regulatory quality, and rule of law. This relationship held true even when controls were introduced to account for other factors that might explain the difference, like a country's wealth, relative political stability, and level of corruption at the start.[49]

Thus, there is considerable evidence that the funds are making progress in addressing concerns about their contribution to systemic strengthening. Moreover, the channelling of aid money to the Global Fund and others seems preferable as they are at least multilateral and as such preferable to bilateral interventions in which the partner country has a limited role.

But the rising importance of the Funds has also given rise to questioning the validity of the approaches to aid effectiveness embodied in Rome–Paris–Accra. For example, the CGD paper noted above argues that

> The aid effectiveness agenda was defined in a different era, when most aid was government aid to government of stable low-income countries. The principles that were adopted were sensible for aid in that context, but aid now is for different purposes, in different places, given through different channels and with different instruments. To modernize measures of effectiveness we are going to need principles that are differently calibrated for different kinds of aid. Some donor agencies should be more specialized and concentrated, some should not. In some countries it would be more effective to work through country systems, in others not. The country-led approach might make sense for public services but not for supporting private enterprise.[50]

The article does not spell out what these changes are or what these new principles will be. Clearly, many aid partners, including in Africa, have made such great strides in institutional development that their systems can be relied upon more confidently now than twenty years ago. And of course, as the authors suggest, 'the country-led approach might make sense for public services but not for supporting private enterprise'. But is it not the case that disease eradication is a public service requiring a country-led approach? And is it not the case that the development of functional and sustainable national health systems are key to their success?

U4 views on global funds tend to differ today as was the case twenty years ago. Wieczorek-Zeul had long been an ardent supporter of the Global Funds. In a recent communication she wrote:

> The question, whether or not at the time the Global Fund and GAVI were fully in line with all the philosophical perspectives and guidelines on international aid, is quite academic. Had it not been for the Global Fund we would have failed to achieve MDG 6. In short: if the house is on fire you don't argue about minor things that are not by the book—you extinguish the fire. So the evidence is overwhelming that the Global Fund and GAVI are falling in line with the ideas of aid effectiveness over the years of transition—when they were able to develop from emergency response to sustainability.[51]

Both the hopes and some concerns of the other U4, discussed in Chapter 7, came to pass:

> The desperation around the spread of HIV and AIDS and child survival made us think the Global Fund and GAVI were worth a try, particularly if they could negotiate affordable medicine, first and foremost anti-retrovirals, with the pharmaceutical industry, and mobilize additional resources from the private sector—which they did. We would not have achieved as much on combating HIV and AIDS without the mobilization of resources and expertise contributed by these Funds. UNAIDS could not have achieved the same, even with a significant increase in donor funding; and their multilateral nature makes them preferable to the spreading of bilateral initiatives. At the same time, they did contribute to aid fragmentation, and while they have made progress in integrating their efforts with and strengthening of the health systems in partner countries, there is evidence that significant challenges remain in this area.[52]

I recently posed the question to Isenman and Shakow as to whether, ten years later, their views on the issue have changed. Isenman's response was:

> I think what we said did not get the balance far off. Global funds are here to stay even though fungible donor financing of economy-wide and sectoral national plans and public expenditure programs is preferable in principle. In practice, those national plans particularly of low-income countries, have often not had sufficient quality, ownership or focus to serve as the basis of sectoral budget support. In addition, the global funds have clearly generated far more financial or political support in donor countries among political leaders and parliaments, NGOs, the media and the general public than broader sectoral or overall programmatic financing. And it is likely to be all the more so in

today's world not just of declining aid but of populist nationalism and declining commitment to helping those beyond national borders. So implementation of our recommendations (or an improved version thereof), focusing on how to reduce conflicts and increase synergies between global funds and support of national sectoral programs, remains quite relevant, if difficult to achieve.[53]

In 2018, at the request of Chancellor Angela Merkel of Germany, the World Health Organization President Nana Addo Dankwa Akufo-Addo of Ghana and Prime Minister Erna Solberg of Norway, produced the report *Global Action Plan for Healthy Lives and Well-being for All* which contains the recommendations of twelve international agencies providing assistance to the health sector globally—including the WHO, the World Bank, the Global Fund, GAVI, and UNDP—as to how to achieve the third Sustainable Development Goal, ensuring healthy lives for all by 2030 (see Chapter 12). The report in a way reflects the collective wisdom of all the major international institutions active in global health today. It concludes that ensuring healthy lives for all requires acceleration of global efforts. The specific recommendations include one which states that 'there is a pressing need to enhance the effectiveness of Development Assistance for Health' and another which calls for 'the full commitment of governments and participation of all stakeholders'. The report is also replete with references to 'adopting a collective action approach' and 'strengthening the collective impact for action'; the need to align joined-up efforts with country priorities; harmonize operational policies; the importance of domestic resource mobilization and decent fiscal management in low income countries; as well as with an emphasis on gender equality and empowerment of women and girls as a prerequisite for progress. There is one reference to the new slogan of 'maximizing investments and delivering "value for money"' (see below), but for the rest the recommendations are very much in keeping with the Utstein approach.

In the meantime, over the last decade, bilateral donors have essentially abandoned the Paris aid effectiveness agenda, especially as it relates to budget support for homegrown health strategies. Thus, on balance, there is little doubt that the Global Funds are an important and legitimate part of the assistance portfolio, a point that Isenman and Shakow made almost ten years ago and is still valid today. They deserve continued support *pari passu* with continued efforts to strengthen their performance in line with the recommendations of the WHO report cited above. The appointment in May 2019 of Donald Kaberuka (former Finance Minister of Rwanda, at the time an effective participant in the Big Tables (see Chapter 6), which 'midwifed' the Rome/Paris/Accra agenda, and former President of the African Development Bank), as Chair of the Board of the Global Fund, promises that the challenges to create the needed synergies will be given high priority. Similarly, the leadership of Ngozi-Okonjo-Iwela with her experience at the World Bank and as Nigeria's Minister of Finance and Foreign Affairs, as Chair of the Board of GAVI is also likely to be of great benefit to this unique organization.

Results-Based Financing

The question is still of interest as to why some of the approaches the group espoused, for example with respect to budget support, faded away, despite evidence that it worked and, in some respects, there was retrogression through the revival of projectized lending and what is called the results-based agenda.

'The basic premise of the results agenda, that the focus should be on what aid can achieve, is surely uncontestable. It is built around domestic political realities and genuine accountability concerns. Despite this, the results agenda has often failed to create the space for a detailed conversation about what aid can achieve in different places.'[54] One of the issues of interest in this connection is the role played by the measurability of results in influencing aid decisions. Recall in this connection that the U4 were among the first to focus on developing outcome indicators (see Chapter 6) and all in favour of specifying quantitative targets and measuring donor and recipient commitments. 'What is measured matters': the MDGs enabled focus on neglected issues as maternal mortality and gender in general. Indeed, the U4 were probably in agreement with the statement by the management guru Peter Drucker that 'what's measured improves'.

The problem was that in the post-2008 world the commitment to eradicate global poverty became progressively weaker and was substituted by concerns about how to make aid more effective in supporting the national interest. Herfkens views this as simply lack of political will by the leadership at the time, and the collapse of the 'development' constituency in many countries. Johnson agrees, but notes that 'political leadership operates in context and the political climate following the economic crisis became more inward inward-looking'.[55] Short takes the view that: 'there is now a lack of ambition and defensiveness about development that leads to results-based management. The claim is that this is more effective aid because it is measurable. There has been a similar focus on measurable results in public sector management in the UK, which has led to lower quality of service and reduced morale. But helping countries build their own systems is the more sustainable and effective approach. It is very regrettable that this has been lost.'[56]

It is in this context that one must look at the UK emphasis in 2010 on giving priority on activities that give 'value for money'. To do this requires of course the capacity to measure the results of aid interventions in some meaningful quantitative way. Yet, results are lasting when there is institutional change involving the transformation of societies. This is a messy and uncertain process with unpredictable twists and turns frequently involving messy political compromises. How much easier it would then appear to return to the pre-Utstein approach by focusing on activities that have clear and measurable benefits like immunizing x number of children or building y number of schools or a highway z miles long, without taking into account whether the country has the capacity to pay and train health workers and teachers or maintain the highway once it is built. This easily leads to illusions of certainty—what Pablo Yanguas calls the 'banality of certainty' and caused former USAID Administrator Natsios to complain in the face of massive reporting requirements to Congressional and other watchdogs that 'those development programs that are most precisely and easily measured are the least transformational and those that are most transformational are least measured'.[57]

It is interesting in this connection to compare the U4 approaches to anti-corruption with some of what came afterwards in the illusory pursuit of value for money. The U4 first priority was to help set up processes run by the developing country itself, as in Sierra Leone for the period 2000–8. The focus was strengthening partner countries' financial management institutions and systems, improving control of all financial flows, not just of the individual donor. Secondly they established the anti-corruption institute in Norway that trains aid workers and developing country professionals on the issues which is still in place. In contrast, Yanguas argues that these so-called 'anti-corruption strategies that DfID began using in 2010 had nothing to do with tackling the challenges faced by the developing countries but instead focused exclusively on ensuring that not a single aid pound was misappropriated along the way'.[58]

Still, the last decade witnessed an increased use of 'results-based financing' (RBF) including through bonds and other similar instruments in health and education. The World Bank reports that RBF has been extensively tested in Africa and has shown good results as a promising approach to achieving universal health coverage: 'They have increased coverage as well as improved quality of services while targeting resources to vulnerable populations.'[59] Development impact bonds have also been used in education, and *Instiglio* reports that the project involving the world's first development impact bond has been completed in India with positive results including 160 per cent achievement of the learning outcome target.[60]

There is extensive literature on the benefits and challenges faced by all these programmes. A key issue is whether the targets are set by the country itself or by the financing entity. The US PEPFAR programme appears to be an extreme case of donor-dominated decisions: 'Targets are set from above, i.e. the Global AIDS Coordinator's Office in DC. In country personnel have some role in setting direction but ultimately country strategies need to address these global targets.'[61] By comparison, 'DfID employed methods that are much more difficult to quantify. The empowered judgement of field staff was a hallmark of all three projects in the health sector in South Africa in 2009–2011. DfID focused on working through the national government and influencing policymakers.'[62]

The other concern is whether these sectoral approaches can be added up and result in economic and societal transformation. Results-based aid faces some serious dangers in this respect. The CGD invitation to the meeting to discuss 'Impact Bonds' ends with the following: 'Avnish will anchor the conversation on Instiglio's practical experience and involvement in various outcomes funds which seek to improve results in various sectors, such as *poverty alleviation* [emphasis added] and health'.[63] Here we are back to the early 1990s when poverty alleviation was viewed as a sector. It is as if the aid community has learned nothing over the last twenty years.

Fragile States

The last reason that must be considered for the decline in the use of approaches and aid instruments championed by the U4 and the Rome–Paris–Accra accords on aid effectiveness is the rise of importance of so-called fragile states. Recall in this connection that the U4 were among the first to recognize the special challenges posed by countries in conflict or post-conflict situations (see Chapter 6). This work contributed later to the development of DAC guidelines on the issue. Some of the main conclusions of the DAC report were to (a) recognize the specific context of the situation, as the problems tend to differ; (b) adopt the principle of 'do no harm'; (c) focus on state building; and (d) recognize the links between political, security, and development objectives.[64]

The formation of the g7+ (a group of twenty small, fragile, post-conflict economies, ranging from Afghanistan to Timor-Leste, and Yemen) in 2010 and the publication of the 'New Deal Engagement in Fragile States' lead to its endorsement by the Busan conference. The 'New Deal' calls for country-led peacebuilding and state building activities prioritized at the country level by each government and its development partners. The new approach requested that donors' assistance adhere to the principle of mutual accountability, with an agenda similar to the core messages advocated by the U4 years before.

Classifying states as fragile has been politically controversial in the UN. As a result, the development community has increasingly used definitions such as 'conflict-affected states' or situations of 'fragility'. The latter is also seen as capturing the variety of causes that can lead to fragility, including the environment and climate change. This led the OECD to establish a definition of fragile states as those with economic, social, political, security, and environmental fragility. The result is a list of fifty-six countries which account for receiving more than 60 per cent of bilateral ODA. The bulk of the countries on the list are also on the list of LDCs—thirty-seven of the forty-eight LDCs are considered fragile. The rest of the countries on the fragile list are low income with very few exceptions: oil exporters Libya and Venezuela as well as Syria all facing civil war situations. One author talks about different developing countries finding themselves at one point in the continuum between fragility at one end and resilience at the other. But it is not clear how this continuum is different from that of a continuum that measures overall social, political, and economic development. Unfortunately, there is no agreement about what constitutes 'fragility'. The World Bank has a much narrower list of thirty-six fragile countries using different classification criteria.

A recent study of donor practices in fragile versus stable states yielded some telling results. The study identified three major elements of quality of donor practices: those involving the use of partner country systems, including the provision of programmable aid; donor cooperation in providing aid; and stability of aid over time. The study concluded that using the World Bank definition of fragility, donor practices in fragile states were significantly inferior to their practices in stable ones. However, the study found that using the broader OECD definition, which included many more countries, there was no significant difference in donor practices between the two country groups. Interestingly enough, of the seven countries in which the study on budget support cited earlier showed that such an instrument was helpful and successful, five (Burkina Faso, Malawi, Mozambique, Rwanda, and Uganda) show up on the OECD list as 'fragile' while only one, Mozambique, is included in the World Bank list.[65]

I suspect that the OECD uses a broad definition of fragility because it is helpful in rallying public support for economic assistance. It also appears to be a concept around which the OECD can demonstrate that the community of Western donors is focusing their assistance to address an important development issue. It reminds one of the situation in 2005 when OECD donors were championing 'aid for trade' in connection with the Doha Round and adopted such a wide definition of what constitutes 'aid for trade' that more than half of their ODA fell into that category, while the World Bank had a much narrower and more meaningful definition.

None of this should be interpreted to mean that there are no fragile states which deserve special consideration in programme design. If indeed fragility is an important criterion and has increased over time, then one could argue that some of the things that the U4 had been pushing for, such as using the country systems and budget support, would decline in importance as 'fragile' countries by definition have serious weaknesses in government management and systems requiring more hands-on involvement by donors and project-based aid—notwithstanding the g7+ admonition that the developing country should be in the driver's seat. At the same time the SDG 'leave no-one behind' commitment cannot be achieved without a significant focus on fragile states. A large portion of the world's extreme poor are in countries of fragility, whether affected by conflict or other disasters. SDG 1 on extreme poverty cannot be achieved without succeeding there.

The Brookings study actually showed that the quality of donor performance did not vary over time; that is, it was worse in fragile states both in the early part of the period and later on. The number of countries categorized as fragile by the World Bank was relatively stable over the period 2007–14 but has increased somewhat in the last few years. Nevertheless, while it may have been a factor, especially in recent periods, one should not exaggerate the presence or recognition of greater fragility as an excuse for donors not adhering to the Rome- Paris–Accra commitments on aid effectiveness.

In fact, the contrary is in many cases true. 'Do no harm' should imply refraining from old-style bad donor behaviour. Ownership of your own development is as fundamental for aid to succeed in these countries as in others. Donor coordination is even more critical when institutions are weak. Focusing on system strengthening and building state institutions through sector approaches is equally important. Pooled funding was used in order to 'minimize harm' as well as reduce financial risk to individual donors precisely in these situations. The 'New Deal' proposed by the g7+ group never really got beyond the declaratory stage and was not implemented by donors. Not much progress has since been made in developing new modalities. The approach to fragile states and situations continues to be fragmented and plagued by many of the same problems dominating old donor practices.

Coherence

The importance of policy coherence both for donors and partners has been recognized in all global conferences in the last twenty years. The facts on the ground tell a different story. On the aid side, the World Bank and the IMF have continued to play a role in coordinating ODA and other forms of assistance. But the emergence of China as an important donor—even as it was continuing to receive large amounts of ODA itself, with a primitive aid policy harking back to OECD practices of fifty years ago, involving totally tied debt-creating aid aimed at benefitting Chinese enterprises, has strained the capacity of these institutions to play their traditional coordinating role.

The PRSPs were continued through mid-2013. But new procedures were set up by the Bank in 2014. A directive labelled 'Country Partnership Framework' became effective on 1 July 2014. The new procedures call for the Bank to produce such a 'Framework' every several years in consultation with the partner. The Framework is based on what is called the 'Systematic Country Diagnostic' that assesses constraints to achieving the goal of ending extreme poverty. The new documents have dropped the pretence that the country initiates the development strategy, a key element of ownership—although of course early PRSPs had been criticized as have been done essentially by the Bank. All the documents are now formally being done by the Bank in consultation with the partner country. So, in practice, the Bank continues to have country strategies, country programmes based on country analysis of poverty constraints—the initials are different, the slogans updated, but the substance is similar to that of the 1990s, that is, before the Utstein ladies descended on the scene and said the country should be in the driver's seat.

Most recently the G-20 Eminent Persons report came up with what the authors appear to consider a novel recommendation that each developing country ought to 'build effective country platforms to mobilize all development partners' and that such a platform 'must be owned by its government'.[66] It all sounds like the international community may finally be rediscovering the wheel after it buried it a few years back.

Over the last decade we have also witnessed a progressive incoherence between aid and trade, as well as between addressing environmental concerns and promoting development. At the national level, for a time there was hope that coherence would improve as two of the U4 countries which had been at the forefront of the issue, the Netherlands and the UK, had taken important steps to integrate aid and trade policies. The Netherlands integrated the Trade Ministry into Development with their aid minister holding the top job; and the UK established a section in DfID with expertise in trade and development which worked with the Trade Ministry to influence UK trade policy perspectives. Unfortunately, the opposite has come to pass: as countries have moved away from using their trade policy as an instrument for promoting global development, national trade interests have started to become paramount and influence aid decisions, as suggested by the aid reviews of both countries.

On policy coherence for development (PCD) within the EU, progress has been made, at least on paper. Over the last decade all EU policy documents regarding development refer to it. For example, the joint statement by the European Council, Parliament, and Commission, titled 'The New European Consensus on Development: Our World, Our Dignity, Our Future' of June 2017 contains several articles, reaffirming the EU commitment to PCD, 'which requires taking into account the objectives of development cooperation in policies which are likely to affect developing countries'. The text acknowledges (para. 109) that PCD is crucial for achievement of the Sustainable Development Goals (SDGs): 'The Consensus will guide efforts in applying PCD across all policies and all areas covered by the 2030 Agenda, seeking synergies, notably on trade, finance, environment and climate change, food security, migration and security. Particular attention will be given to combating illicit financial flows and tax avoidance, and to promoting trade and responsible investment [para. 110].'[67] However, to what extent this leads to concrete changes in, for example, trade and agriculture policies remains to be seen. Over time fewer resources in ministries have been devoted to developing coherent positions and screening legislative proposals. PCD reports, especially at

EU level, have become exercises in self-congratulation of how coherent EU policies are, with little to no independent evaluation.

At the international level the discussions of the Doha Round continued—one cannot call them negotiations—and resulted in two new agreements: on trade facilitation and information technology. But nobody was willing to engage in serious negotiations on critical issues such as agriculture, and nobody was willing to take the onus of killing the Round. And thus the WTO continued, hobbled by the lack of Justices in its Appellate Body—due to US interference—and weakened from time to time by the announcement of negotiations for the establishment of various 'Mega-Regional' agreements in different parts of the world. The 2016 US election produced a President with puerile understanding of economics who, supported by a coterie of bigoted acolytes, decided to use tariffs as a new WMD—a weapon of mutual destruction against the economies of friend and foe to achieve whatever goal seemed to him would make headlines when he got out of bed each morning. Early on, he also took the USA out of the Paris climate accords, be it that many relevant states in the USA continue their efforts. His actions have shaken the global trade architecture that had been so painfully built up over the course of several decades and cannot be excused by the fact that China has also undermined the same architecture. In this setting, talking about coherence between aid and trade policy for development is only a pipe dream.

Assessment

In April 2003, the original four ministers received the first annual Commitment to Development Award from the Center for Global Development, the preeminent US think tank/lobbying group for development. The award cited them for their 'dedication, vision, and leadership in reducing global poverty and inequality in developing countries, challenging the norms of the development establishment and highlighting the importance of policy coherence'. Nancy Birdsall, CGD's President at the time said in presenting the award: 'These four women define what it means to be pro-development leaders. Through their leadership development policy issues have been placed more squarely on the agenda of political leaders across Europe and North America.'[68] Subsequently, others have praised the U4 contribution to raising the levels of ODA in Germany and the UK but also more broadly in the OECD, to mobilizing support for the achievement of the MDGs and, after challenging the norms of the establishment, introducing new, innovative approaches to aid implementation that put the recipient in the driver's seat and thereby raised the long-term effectiveness of economic assistance. These approaches to aid implementation were codified n the Rome–Paris–Accra agreements for which the U4 also have received kudos (see Chapter 10).

Even as globally there was backtracking on aid effectiveness commitments, and coherence issues were generally ignored, the performance of the U4 countries remained consistently above the average for DAC members as measured by the Commitment to Development Index compiled annually by the CGD since 2003 (see Appendix, Table A-3). Looking at the aid indicator first, (Table A-3a), which is a composite of the volume and quality of aid, the Netherlands, Norway, and the UK have ranked consistently in the top five for each three to four-year sub-period since 2003–5 until 2016–18, while Germany improved its position slightly but was consistently above average. Looking at the second panel (Table A-3b), which takes into account a variety of indicators affecting development including policies on the environment, trade, security, and refugees, it was Germany that made the most impressive improvement over time reaching third position overall in the OECD ahead of the other three, and the Netherlands the greatest deterioration, but all four still ranked in the top quartile of DAC members in 2016–18.

Finally, the above-mentioned Brookings study on fragility also had a ranking of individual donor performance in fragile and stable states using the criteria of aid effectiveness discussed earlier. The results showed that three of the four U4 countries (the Netherlands, Norway and the UK) ranked at the top of the list on both sets of countries, while Germany was somewhere in the middle. Not a bad result for the legacy of the U4.[69]

As we look ahead, it is useful to recall the ODI study mentioned earlier which concludes:

> Part of the political question is: are we looking to buy results, or make deep-rooted changes? Do we wish to help build institutions so that countries can take on development challenges themselves, or do we want to deliver results ourselves? A long-term approach to development questions which interventions make the most sense, even if some, like budget support, have fallen out of favor. Whether through bilateral or multilateral aid, or working through international institutions, a long-term lens changes the terms of the debate on the very idea that aid projects can be planned and implemented with certainty about the outcomes.[70]

The U4 had always had a long-term lens, focused on support for deep rooted changes needed to help build institutions so that countries can take on the challenges themselves. A Dutch MP once told Herfkens that he was baffled that she pushed for these reforms—whose results would never show up during her time in office. I am sure the other three have had similar experiences.

Kemal Dervis, former senior official at the World Bank and later Administrator of the UNDP wrote as early as 2005 about the 'remarkable efforts by the British, Scandinavian, Dutch and German development ministers in support of resource mobilization for poverty reduction since the mid-1990's' and that the Utstein

Group was 'organized around the principle that coherence in wealthy nation's policies such as trade, anticorruption, conflict management and foreign is critical for support of development in poor countries.[71]

Isenman writes:

> The group aimed to be a catalyst, calling on donors to try harder on quantity and quality of aid and to see their role as contribution rather than causality. The group didn't cause revolutionary change, let alone create such permanent change by itself. But it arguably played an important contributory role as a catalyst for progress in quantity and quality within the aid and development community and to varying extents within its members' own countries over about 15 years. That is no small accomplishment.[72]

Key to their success, as acknowledged by many quoted in this volume, has been their willingness to work together. As another African proverb states: 'a single bracelet does not jingle'. Four articulate voices joined in support of poverty eradication made a difference that each alone could never have achieved. Their efforts changed the lives of millions, especially women.

During the last ten years we have witnessed a deterioration of the global community's commitment to development. We can feel nostalgic about the old days at the turn of the century when the world appeared far more committed to cooperation in support of noble causes. But nostalgia can also be harnessed for good. We can explore how the U4 experience can be used to help address the challenges of the future including the achievement of the Sustainable Development Goals.

Notes

1. Larry Summers, 'Weak economy, angry politics', *Washington Post*, 10 October 2016.
2. UN, *Report of the Commission of Experts of the President of the UN General Assembly on the Reform of the International Monetary System* (New York: United Nations, 2009).
3. UN, The Millennium Development Goals Report 2015 (New York: United Nations, 2015).
4. Eveline Herfkens, ODI speech, 1 September, 2015.
5. UN, *Transforming Our World: The 2030 Agenda for Sustainable Development*, A/Res/70/1 (New York: United Nations, 2015).
6. The amounts of ODA to LDCs post 2002 have been significantly affected by large amounts directed to Afghanistan, especially by the USA.
7. Eveline Herfkens, 'Aid Effectiveness: Lessons Learned—and Forgotten [in Dutch], in S. Vermeer, L. Schulpen, and R. Ruben (eds), *Hoe nu Verder* (Arnhem: LM Publishers, 2014).
8. See https://www.ndb.int/.
9. An agreement was reached in 2010 to reallocate some of the IMF quotas away from Europe and in favour of developing country constituencies, but the agreement was held up for six years(!) in the US Congress until it was finally approved in 2016.
10. IDA, 'Addressing Debt Vulnerabilities in IDA Countries: Options for IDA 19' (Washington, DC: IDA, 2019), p. 11.

11. Malpass, interview by Masood Ahmed, 5 November 2019.
12. In earlier periods major donors were reviewed more frequently, i.e. every three to four years.
13. OECD, DAC, *Peer Review United Kingdom* 2001 (Paris: OECD, 2001).
14. OECD, DAC, *Peer Review Netherlands 2001* (Paris: OECD, 2001).
15. OECD, DAC, *Peer Review Netherlands 2006* (Paris: OECD, 2006).
16. OECD, DAC, *Peer Review Germany 2001* (Paris: OECD, 2001).
17. OECD, DAC, *Peer Review Germany 2005* (Paris: OECD, 2006).
18. OECD, DAC, *Peer Review Norway 2005* (Paris: OECD, 2005).
19. OECD, DAC, *Peer Review Germany 2010* (Paris: OECD, 2010), p. 15.
20. OECD, DAC, *Peer Review Germany 2010*, pp. 21, 23.
21. OECD, DAC, *Peer Review Germany 2015* (Paris: OECD, 2015).
22. OECD, DAC, *Peer Review Norway, 2008* (Paris: OECD, 2008), p. 10.
23. OECD, DAC, *Peer Review United Kingdom 2014* (Paris: OECD, 2014), pp. 15–21.
24. OECD, DAC, *Peer Review Netherlands 2017* (Paris: OECD, 2017), pp. 16, 19.
25. This section is adapted in part from Constantine Michalopoulos, *Aid, Trade and Development* (Cham: Palgrave MacMillan, 2017), pp. 287–90, by permission from Springer Nature.
26. T. Abdel-Malek and B. Koenders, 'Progress towards More Effective Aid: What does the Evidence Show?' 4th High Level Conference on Aid Effectiveness, 2011, http//www.% 20Busanhlf4.org.
27. Abdel-Malek and Koenders, 'Progress towards More Effective Aid'.
28. Herfkens, 'Aid Effectiveness', p. 60.
29. James Adams, email, 11 June 2019.
30. UN, 'Mexico High Level Meeting Communique', The Global Partnership for Effective Development Cooperation and the Post 2015-Development Agenda, 16 April 2014.
31. Nancy Birdsall and Homi Kharas, *The Quality of ODA, 3rd edn* (Washington, DC: CGD and Brookings, 2014), p. 3.
32. Global Partnership for Effective Development Collaboration [GPEDC], *Making Development Co-operation More Effective* (Paris and New York: OECD/UNDP, 2016).
33. GPEDC, Making Development Co-operation More Effective.
34. UN, 'Third International Conference on Financing for Development', A/RES/69/313, 2015.
35. 'A Joint Evaluation of Budget Support: Synthesis Report', 1994–2004, Executive Summary, University of Birmingham, Birmingham, May 2006.
36. 'Joint Evaluation of Budget Support', pp. 21–2.
37. IOB Evaluation nr 308, 2008: Het Nederlandse Afrikabeleid 1998–2006, ISBN 978-90-5328-359-2.
38. Oxfam, 'Fast forward: How the European Commission can take the lead in providing high quality aid for education and health', Oxfam International briefing paper no.111, May 2008, available at https://www.oxfam.de/system/files/fast_forward.pdf.
39. Jonathan Beynon and Andra Dusu, *Budget Support and MDG Performance* (Brussels: European Commission Directorate-General for ACP, 2010).
40. Apparently, the meaning of 'fungible' is not easily translated in Germanic languages.
41. Craig Walters and Brendan Whitty, *The Politics and Results Agenda in DFID*, 1997–2017, ODI Report (London: ODI, 2017), p. 9.
42. Hilde F. Johnson, comment, 21 July 2019.

43. ACET, 'Mobilizing and Managing External Finance for Inclusive Growth: Synthesis Report', December 2018 (Accra: ACET, 2018).

44. Paul Isenman and Alexander Shakow, 'Donor Schizophrenia and Aid Effectiveness: The Role of Global Funds', IDS Practice Paper 2010–01, IDS University of Sussex, 2010, p. 10.

45. Isenman and Shakow, 'Donor Schizophrenia and Aid Effectiveness', p. 11.

46. Isenman and Shakow, 'Donor Schizophrenia and Aid Effectiveness', p. 12.

47. Isenman and Shakow, 'Donor Schizophrenia and Aid Effectiveness', pp. 7–9.

48. Ian Mitchell and Caitlin McKee, 'How do you Measure Aid Quality and Who Ranks Highest?' 15 November (Washington, DC: CGD 2018).

49. M. M. Kavanagh and L. Chen, 'Governance and Health Aid from the Global Fund: Effects Beyond Fighting Disease', *Annals of Global Health*, 85(1) (2019), pp. 69, 1–9.

50. Mitchell and McKee, 'How do you Measure Aid Quality and Who Ranks Highest?', p. 6.

51. Heidemarie Wieczorek-Zeul, email, 2 August 2019.

52. Hilde F. Johnson, email, 17 August 2019.

53. Paul Isenman, email, 31 May 2019.

54. Walters and Whitty, The Politics and Results Agenda in DFID, 1997–2017, p. 11.

55. Hilde F. Johnson, comment, 21 July 2019.

56. Clare Short, comment, 7 August 2019.

57. Pablo Yanguas, *Why we Lie about Aid: Development and the Messy Politics of Aid* (London: ZED Books, 2018), p. 48.

58. Yanguas, Why we Lie about Aid, p. 68.

59. World Bank, *Africa Health Forum*, 2013; siteresources.worldbank.org, 15 June 2019.

60. https://www.cgdev.org/section/events, 13 June 2019.

61. Dan Honig, *Navigation by Judgement* (New York: Oxford University Press, 2018), p. 114.

62. Honig, *Navigation by Judgement*, p. 115.

63. https://www.cgdev.org/section/events, 13 June 2019.

64. OECD, DAC, 'Principles for Good International Engagement in Fragile States and Situations', April (Paris: OECD, 2007).

65. Laurence Chandy, Brian Seidel, and Christine Zhang, *Aid Effectiveness in Fragile States*, Brooke Shear Series No. 5 (Washington, DC: Brookings, 2016).

66. G20, 'Making the Financial System Work for All', Report of the G20 Eminent Persons Group on Global Financial Governance, p. 16.

67. EU Commission, 'The New European Consensus on Development' (Brussels: EU, 2017).

68. CGD press release, 'Quartet of Female Ministers Win Inaugural Commitment to Development Award', 28 April (Washington, DC: CGD, 2003).

69. Chandy et al., Aid Effectiveness in Fragile States, p. 26. Sweden, the Netherlands, and the UK are the top three for stable countries while Denmark, Canada, and Sweden are at the top for fragile states. The USA and France are at the bottom for fragile states, while the US and GAVI perform least well for stable ones.

70. Walters and Whitty, *The Politics and Results Agenda in DFID, 1997–2017*, p. 11.

71. Kemal Dervis, *A Better Globalization*, Washington DC: Center for Global Development, 2005, p. 87.

72. Paul Isenman, email, 1 June 2019.

12

The Future

Introduction

The other day I heard somebody say: 'Do not look back too much. You may stumble.' Good advice for a writer of history. At the same time, I have always kept in mind another warning which I read in a museum on the *stasi* in Leipzig; 'Warning! History can lead to insight and may cause increased awareness.' And so it does.

Much has changed since the Utstein Four burst onto the international scene twenty years ago: a resurgent nationalism and xenophobia are undermining efforts to address global problems; China's meteoric growth is challenging US economic supremacy; India, Brazil, and South Africa, all complex societies with many unresolved domestic issues, are playing an increasingly important role in world forums. Europe is partly mired in the Brexit mess amidst growing polarization. And a revanchist Russia is seeking to recover part of the former Soviet Union's influence by virtue of its vast territory and nuclear arsenal. It is natural for many to feel gloomy about global trends.

Yet, the world today in many respects is a better place than it was twenty years ago: the share of the global population living in absolute poverty is about 10 per cent, the lowest in human history; people live longer than they did twenty years ago; they are better nourished, live healthier lives, and are better educated; and their total number is likely to stabilize, as population growth is slowing.

Many challenges remain: while global inequality has declined, within country inequality has increased; women still fare worse than men in practically all aspects of the human condition; and climate change is inexorably marching on, threatening the very existence of humankind. Still, 'A peaceful earth inhabited by about 10 billion people without anyone suffering poverty is not a wild fantasy. It is feasible. That is what the UN Sustainable Development Goals (SDGs) are about.'[1]

Among the many things the U4 were credited with was their contribution to the achievement of the Millennium Development Goals (see Chapter 7). Are there any lessons from the U4 experience of twenty years ago that can be useful in addressing the challenges humanity faces in achieving the SDGs? In many conversations the U4 have tended to belittle their contribution. I have heard them say, using a football example: 'the environment we faced was very supportive: it was as easy as scoring goals in an empty net'. I think otherwise. This chapter will discuss the lessons we can draw from the U4 experience to address the SDG challenges of the future.

The Sustainable Development Goals (SDGs)

Agreed by 170 heads of state in September 2015, the SDGs have been character-ized as inspirational, transformative, holistic, ambitious, and universal. They range from the reiteration of themes present in the MDGs, such as the eradication of poverty by 2030 (Goal 1), to reduction in inequality within and between countries (Goal 10), as well as extend to new areas such as climate change (Goal 13), and promoting peaceful and inclusive societies for sustainable development (Goal 16). They are far more explicit and ambitious in promoting gender equality and the empowerment of women and girls (Goal 5).[2]

The seventeen goals are accompanied by 169 targets to be met mostly by 2030 but a few even earlier. Some of these targets are quantifiable and very precise: for example, target 3.1 is 'to reduce by 2030 the global maternal mortality rate to less than 70 per 100,000'; others are very general and non-quantifiable, for example target 8.9 calls for 'devising and implementing policies by 2030 to promote sustainable tourism that creates jobs and promotes local culture and products' (see Box 12.1).

The MDGs were derived from the UN conferences of the 1980s which drew together global experience in international development and were confirmed in the Millennium Declaration. They were relatively few and mostly quantifi-able. The SDGs were negotiated through a lengthy UN inter-governmental process coupled with extended consultations, both thematic and regional, with various stakeholders in the most inclusive process the UN has ever put in place. They resulted in the inclusion of a very large and diverse set of targets and indicators of different scope and priority. While some are concrete and quantifiable, many are not; making monitoring progress in their achievement problematic.

In addition to establishing these goals and targets, it was agreed to monitor progress through a review and reporting mechanism. The High Level Policy Forum (HLPF) is to meet annually and, at a higher level, every four years to review progress in achieving them. Unlike the MDGs which explicitly focused on progress made by developing countries and, separately, though less precisely, on developed country commitments to help these countries do so, the SDGs are commitments by all countries. Thus, all countries were invited to conduct and submit a Voluntary National Review (VNR) of progress in achieving the SDGs. Overall, between 2016 and 2019, 142 VNRs have been presented at the annual UN High Level Political Forum. Among the G20, OECD, and other countries with populations greater than 100 million, all have submitted or will submit a VNR by 2020—with the exception of the United States.[3]

Despite the common guidelines prepared by the UN to inform the preparation of VNRs, the scope and breadth of these voluntary reviews vary greatly. Some countries present a review covering all (or most) of the seventeen SDGs, whereas

Box 12.1. The Sustainable Development Goals

- Goal 1. End poverty in all its forms everywhere.
- Goal 2. End hunger, achieve food security and improved nutrition, and promote sustainable agriculture.
- Goal 3. Ensure healthy lives and promote well-being for all at all ages.
- Goal 4. Ensure inclusive and equitable quality education and promote lifelong learning opportunities for all.
- Goal 5. Achieve gender equality and empower all women and girls.
- Goal 6. Ensure availability and sustainable management of water and sanitation for all.
- Goal 7. Ensure access to affordable, reliable, sustainable, and modern energy for all.
- Goal 8. Promote sustained, inclusive, and sustainable economic growth, full and productive employment, and decent work for all.
- Goal 9. Build resilient infrastructure, promote inclusive and sustainable industrialization, and foster innovation.
- Goal 10. Reduce inequality within and among countries.
- Goal 11. Make cities and human settlements inclusive, safe, resilient, and sustainable.
- Goal 12. Ensure sustainable consumption and production patterns.
- Goal 13. Take urgent action to combat climate change and its impacts.
- Goal 14. Conserve and sustainably use the oceans, seas, and marine resources for sustainable development.
- Goal 15. Protect, restore, and promote sustainable use of terrestrial ecosystems, sustainably manage forests, combat desertification, halt and reverse land degradation, and halt biodiversity loss.
- Goal 16. Promote peaceful and inclusive societies for sustainable development, provide access to justice for all, and build effective, accountable, and inclusive institutions at all levels.
- Goal 17. Strengthen the means of implementation and revitalize the global partnership for sustainable development.

others focus on a few. In some cases the reports have been prepared through inclusive consultation processes, while in others they have been prepared by governments with the support of international organizations. As a result, the reports' effectiveness and impact vary considerably, especially as the programmes presented and showcased are not evaluated systematically.[4]

The SDGs are being promoted by many UN and non-UN entities. Herfkens, in a 2018 meeting with UN heads of agencies in Geneva, was amazed to find out how committed and supportive of the SDGs the agencies were compared to her experience with the MDGs fifteen years earlier.[5] A UN SDG action campaign committee has been established (successor to the UN Millennium campaign) with the mandate to raise awareness of the SDGs globally while scaling up, broadening, and sustaining a global action movement in support of the goals. The campaign has a very ambitious mandate but is grossly underfunded. Though several countries have national campaigns, compared with the MDGs far fewer resources are being devoted to SDG promotion globally.

Progress in achieving the SDGs has been compiled annually in reports by the Bertelsmann Foundation and by the Sustainable Development Solutions Network (SDSN); the reports are very detailed and show country by country progress in meeting the SDGs. Because many of the targets are not quantifiable, progress is shown by four qualitative indicators: 'SDG Achievement', 'Challenges Remain', 'Significant Challenges Remain', 'Major Challenges Remain'. Their latest report makes for sombre reading. Some of their main conclusions are:

- 'Eradicating extreme poverty remains a global challenge with half of the world's nations not on track for achieving SDG 1 (No Poverty).
- Trends on climate (SDG 13) and biodiversity (SDG 14 and SDG 15) are alarming. On average, countries obtain their worst scores on SDG 13 (Climate Action), SDG 14 (Life below Water) and SDG 15 (Life on Land).
- While one-third of food is wasted, 800 million people remain undernourished, 2 billion are deficient in micronutrients, and hunger and obesity are on the rise.
- Human rights and freedom of speech are in danger in numerous countries.'[6]

Similar conclusions are presented in the UN report prepared for the September 2019 UN General Assembly meeting, which was supposed to review progress on their achievement.[7]

Given these developments, and the current international environment, it is hard to see how many of these goals can be achieved without radical changes in the approach and policy implementation. What are the main issues with the SDGs and what lessons does the U4 experience offer in addressing them?

One of the SDGs innovations, the need to deliver at home, may actually mitigate against their achievement. The emphasis on what are predominantly national issues means that developed countries tend to emphasize domestic goals and targets, which they aim to address in any case, rather than global ones. As a result, Goal 17, which has to do with helping developing countries achieve their goals through more ODA or improved access to developed country markets, is receiving hardly any attention. Developed countries do not need the SDGs to address issues about which their citizens are already concerned which relate to their poverty or gender equality, or for that matter climate change and freedom of speech. Indeed, the SDGs may give cover for increased inward-looking practices and a domestic focus in OECD countries.

In the meantime, there is strong evidence that many developing countries cannot achieve their goals without assistance from developed countries. A recent IMF study concluded that

> delivering on the SDG agenda will require additional spending in 2030 of US$500 billion for low-income developing countries and US$2.1 trillion for emerging market economies. There is a sharp contrast between the two groups. For emerging market economies, the average additional spending required represents about 4 percentage points of GDP. This is a considerable challenge, but in most cases these economies can rely on their own resources to achieve these SDGs. The challenge is much greater for low-income developing countries. Here, the average additional spending represents 15 percentage points of GDP. Developing countries themselves own the responsibility for achieving the SDGs, especially through reforms to foster sustainable and inclusive growth that will in turn generate the tax revenue needed. Raising more domestic revenue is an essential component of this strategy. Increasing the tax-to-GDP ratio by 5 percentage points of GDP in the next decade is an ambitious but reasonable target in many countries. But in addition to domestic resources, the scale of the additional spending needs in low-income developing countries (LIDCs) requires support from all stakeholders—including the private sector, donors, philanthropists, and international financial institutions. Delivering on official development assistance targets can help in closing development gaps in many LIDCs.[8]

The SDGs deal with the responsibilities of developed countries with respect to ODA rather lightly. Target 17.2 calls for developed countries to implement their commitments—whatever they are—with respect to the overall 0.7 per cent ODA/GNI target and the sub-target of 0.15–0.20 per cent ODA/GNI to the LDCs. They are silent on the needs of the broader group of low-income developing countries or the fact that, as the IMF paper suggests, so-called 'emerging economies' can address the SDG investment needs with their own resources.

The SDGs as well as the above-mentioned IMF study are furthermore totally silent on approaches to improve the effectiveness of aid or the substantive monitoring of donor practices which has effectively stopped, as discussed in Chapter 11. Donors have frequently reverted to practices proven ineffective in the 1990s. Moreover, some ODA today is actually used to 'provide incentives' to authoritarian regimes, including not-so-poor Turkey or failed states like Libya, to curb migration and return refugees to their home countries. Reintroducing substantive monitoring of aid practices is essential to future efforts to increase aid effectiveness even as aid is admittedly of relevance to a smaller group of developing countries.

Moreover, public awareness of these issues is critical in pushing government to be accountable for their global commitments. If citizens, or parliamentarians in most OECD countries, want to find out how their country is doing on providing aid, they have easy access only to the country's ODA/GNI ratio, which obviously gives little information on what their country actually does to help poor countries with programmable aid. Thus, a UK citizen can be proud of the UK achieving the 0.7 ODA/GNI target—without any understanding of how in fact 'real' aid has been diminished. Similarly, a German citizen may become aware that Germany is close to achieving the promised 0.7 per cent ODA/GNI target—without realizing that a large part of this budget is spent on caring for refugees who live in Germany.

The presence of many very important goals, some of which require transformative changes such as, for example, change of diets to ensure sustainable consumption, or the change in the mode of transport to promote energy savings, means that the SDGs can only be achieved when efforts by governments are complemented by the engagement of other stakeholders, such as the private sector, philanthropists, academia, and civil society. These actors were more involved in the process of defining the SDGs and are also more engaged in their implementation than was the case with the MDGs. But when so many actors are involved accountability for action is diffuse and uncertain. The greater involvement of the private sector—which considers it to be to its advantage to invest in activities that explicitly promote SDG achievement—is a positive step not present in earlier times. But, when too many actors are responsible, nobody is accountable.

The presence of so many goals, many of which are not quantifiable or on which information is not readily available, makes it more difficult to rally public opinion, or for that matter government action, around a few key clearly understood, simply stated objectives. Indeed, there are synergies among many of the SDGs. The above-mentioned Bertelsmann report attempted to organize implementation of the seventeen SDGs along the following 'transformations': (1) education, gender, and inequality; (2) health, wellbeing, and demography; (3) energy decarbonization and sustainable industry; (4) sustainable food, land, water, oceans; (5) sustainable cities and communities; and (6) digital revolution for sustainable development. The transformations respect strong interdependencies across the SDGs and can be operationalized by well-defined parts of governments in collaboration with civil society, business, and other stakeholders.[9]

Marina Ponti, director of the UN SDG action campaign, suggested in an interview that there is some preliminary thinking among those involved in SDG advocacy to try to prioritize the seventeen SDGs and focus on three main issues: inequality, gender, and climate change.[10]

I believe that moving in this direction would be a great improvement over the present situation and an improvement over the complex packaging of the

Bertelsmann report mentioned above. By focusing on these three areas in addition to the fundamental goal of eradicating poverty it would be possible to develop a campaign based on available information, which can then be used to increase awareness, leading to government policy commitment and, ultimately, action to move forward. It is critical, however, that the goal on ridding the world of extreme poverty (SDG 1) in combination with addressing inequality remains most prominent.

Information, for example, regarding inequality in income is available which permits the measurement of inequality both between and within national sub-groups. Similarly, for non-income indicators of inequality with respect to the education and health goals, the 2010 UN Human Development Report introduced a new approach by adjusting existing indicators to create the 'Inequality-Adjusted Human Development Index', discounting each component's average value according to its degree of inequality and permitting country performance to be monitored over time. And there are many ways of measuring progress in addressing climate change or gender issues.

All these improvements will fail to make a difference in the absence of political leadership. Both Ponti and the Bertelsmann/SDSN Report identify this as the number one problem holding back SDG achievement. According to the latter (p. x):

> High-level political commitment to the SDGs is falling short of historic promises. Our in-depth analyses show that many have not taken the critical steps to implement the SDGs. Out of 43 countries surveyed on SDG implementation efforts, including all G20 countries and countries with a population greater than 100 million, 33 countries have endorsed the SDGs in official statements since January 1st, 2018. Yet in only 18 of them do central budget documents mention the SDGs. This gap between rhetoric and action must be closed.

Leaving aside the disastrous role the USA is currently playing on global issues ranging from trade to climate change, Europe's role has also been disappointing: the Commission's White Paper on the Future of Europe mentions the SDGs only when praising achievements of EU diplomacy; there is no consideration of whether implementing the SDGs might have a bearing on Europe's own future.[11]

Although the universal and integrated scope of the SDGs implies that they have to be addressed with actions that go well beyond development aid or environmental protection, these two issues are still important as well as neglected. Current ODA levels to low-income countries are much less than what these countries need to achieve the SDGs. And of course, nobody talks anymore about the need to modify the Common Agricultural Policy to benefit developing countries. Similarly, on the environment, the emission of greenhouse gases would have to be reduced twice as fast if the self-set Nationally Determined Contribution (NDC) target under the Paris Climate Agreement (which is part of the SDGs, as defined by the 2030 Agenda) is achieved. And it is not just the European Commission: only three member states, including Germany, are setting sustainable development goals into their legislation.

An independent commission sponsored by the Social Democrats in the European Parliament concluded that at 'European level, the Commission has not yet even started to address the full extent of the institutional changes called for nor have the other institutions. The EU's main governance process, the European Semester, remains by and large untouched three years after the agreement on the SDGs.'[12]

The EU Council 'Conclusions' at its meeting of 9 April 2019 contains a strong endorsement of the SDGs: 'The Council underlines the urgent need for accelerating the implementation of the 2030 Agenda both globally and internally, as an overarching priority of the EU, for the benefit of its citizens and for upholding its credibility within Europe and globally.'[13] The 'Conclusions' say all the right things including about policy coherence for development and the need for financial flows to developing countries, but are short on specifics: for example 'Official Development Assistance' does not appear in the text. Instead we have to be content with 'sustainable finance'. And it remains to be seen to what extent the Council's 'Conclusions' actually translate in members' national policies, or the work of the Commission.

In 2018 the G20 commissioned a report on 'Making the Financial System Work for All'[14] by a group of eminent persons. Recall in this connection the fact that, although the MDGs derived from the UN Conferences of the 1990s, the specific MDG targets were put together in the end with the UN working together with the World Bank and the IMF. Remarkably, the above 2018 report on the future of the financial system does not mention the SDGs even once. According to sources close to the authorship of the report, the SDGs were not mentioned in order to make the report palatable to the USA.

Fundamentally, by being primarily aspirational, the SDGs do not address the problem of how to strengthen developed country commitment to help address global issues. Except for concerns about climate change, developed country commitment to address global issues, such as global poverty, is less than in the early 2000s. It can only be improved through the kind of political leadership provided at that time by the U4 ministers and other leaders at the global level.

In addition, it is necessary for citizens to hold governments and political leaders accountable. In democracies, politicians tend to act more forcefully when they think they can win votes with their actions. But for citizens to demand action it is vital that they are aware of their government commitments, which in turn requires NGOs, parliamentarians, business leaders, and other citizens' organizations to mobilize public opinion in support of the goals. At present, this is happening only with respect to climate change. But that is promising. It shows that mobilization around global issues is still possible and perhaps can be taken further. People far beyond the UN corridors and bureaucracy need to become aware and excited about these goals, much like the MDGs which unleashed the largest anti-poverty movement in human history to hold governments to account for the promises they made.

The High Level Policy Forum in September 2019 issued a 'Political Declaration' in which the participants in the SDG Summit emphasized 'That eradicating poverty in all its forms and dimensions, including extreme poverty is the greatest global challenge and an indispensable requirement for sustainable development'; and recognized 'the need to accelerate action on all levels and all stakeholders'. To this end they committed to:

- Leaving no one behind
- Mobilizing adequate and well-directed financing
- Enhancing national implementation
- Strengthening institutions for more integrated solutions
- Bolstering local action to accelerate implementation
- Reducing disaster risk and building resilience
- Solving challenges through international cooperation and enhancing the global partnership
- Harnessing science technology and innovation with a greater focus on digital transformation for sustainable development
- Investing in data and statistics for the Sustainable Development Goals
- Strengthening the High Level Forum.[15]

The 'Declaration' says all the right things, especially in highlighting the emphasis on eradicating poverty. But it contains no special recognition of the responsibilities of developed countries to assist low-income countries to achieve the goals; and there are no developed country commitments in that regard. There is a vague request that 'everybody, governments, the private sector and all stakeholders need to increase the level of ambition in domestic public and private resource mobilization...and deliver on commitments to international development cooperation'.

In the past many UN resolutions faced the problem of a gap between rhetoric and action. The commitments under the High Level Policy Forum are so vague that it is difficult to even identify a potential gap. Recall in this connection Chapter 7 where it was pointed out that this was precisely the pattern in many decades of UN resolutions before it was broken with the MDGs, or I should say before the U4 helped break it. It is clear that despite the commitments made at the SDG Summit, the world on its current path is not properly mobilized and will not likely achieve the SDGs.

'For the first time since a new development agenda was adopted in 2015 to make the world a better place for everyone, government leaders assembled at the

United Nations in late September (2019) to take stock of progress. The verdict of this summit was not good. The 17 Sustainable Development Goals (SDGs), were on life support in the eyes of many experts in and around the high-level UN sessions. Some goals were in danger of reversing earlier gains.'[16]

Against this dismal panorama, a new report was prepared for the gathering of government officials on the SDGs during the UN General Assembly session in late September 2019, with a proposed new approach. The report, titled 'The Future Is Now: Science for Achieving Sustainable Development', recommends focusing on the six target groupings mentioned above that could create synergies and result in fundamental transformation. They named four 'levers' that could be used to spur action: governance, economy and finance, individual and collective action, and science and technology.[17]

It is unclear whether the report's specific recommendations for 'bundling' can be used in actual policy formulation. But the report highlights again the need for target grouping and prioritization if progress is to be achieved. At the same time the report's calls for action do not highlight the developed country responsibility to assist developing countries in meeting the transformational challenges they face. Instead, there is a very general call for action:

> Multilateral organizations, governments and public authorities should explicitly adopt the SDGs as a guiding framework for their programming, planning and budgetary procedures. To accelerate the implementation of the 2030 Agenda, they should devote special attention to directing resources including finances, official development assistance at levels that meet international commitments, and technologies to the six entry points applying knowledge to the interlinkages across Goals and targets contributing to the realization of co-benefits and resolving trade-offs.[18]

Lessons from the U4 Experience

Today the international environment for achieving the SDGs is obviously less supportive than in the early 2000s. But the leadership provided by the U4 also played a role in achieving the MDG results. It was not simply pushing the ball into an empty net.

Perhaps the first lesson to be drawn from that experience is that one should not be looking at statements by individual country leaders, heads of state, and government as indications of political leadership regarding the SDGs or anything else. It is only when these statements are based on the hard work of their ministers and their staff (who are imbued with a commitment to the goals and policies that address global poverty and other challenges faced by humanity which are then reflected in budgets and parliamentary approvals) that things actually happen.

Second, ministers must be willing to promote global objectives, even when these at times conflict with narrowly defined short-term national interests; and they must have sufficient standing in their own government to develop consensus for specific actions. Ministerial rank helps in dealing with bureaucracies.

Third, it is critical that the effort be collective. The U4 were most effective when they spoke with one voice. It is hard to determine the minimum number of countries necessary for international action. Sometime two or three may suffice. But the group should have enough international standing that others will listen. In case of the U4, it was a major asset that the four included two G8 countries and two countries with a long tradition of credibility in the area of international solidarity.

Fourth, the collective effort by the U4 was not enough by itself. Consensus for international action was expanded by the four ministers developing networks of like-minded countries both among their OECD colleagues and with developing countries. It was then extended through their active participation in the IFIs and the UN and collaboration with their leaders. Indeed, the collaboration of the World Bank, the IMF, and the UN was critical in the achievement of the MDGs. The link between PRSPs and the MDGs was essential in making real progress at the country level.

Fifth, collaboration is unglamorous and requires hard work and submersion of individual egos. But it is absolutely critical to meet the challenges posed in achieving the SDGs.

Sixth, the role of civil society is pivotal to promote awareness and create political constituencies for good development policies. At the time, the U4 understood that for their large national NGO communities, promoting global poverty eradication was essential to maintain and deepen the pro-development constituency and public opinion. This provided them with the political space to prevent national interests driving development policy.

The question is: can this experience be put to good use in order to change the current path which is not likely to lead to the achievement of the SDGs?

The Next Steps

Looking ahead, the UN is planning a 75th anniversary celebration in 2020. It may present another opportunity for world leaders to energize all stakeholders around the achievement of the SDGs and by taking steps to promote collaboration between the UN and the IFIs. Davidse, the Dutch Executive Director at the World Bank notes that, again, World Bank programme implementation appears to be more effective when the partner country has plans linked to the achievement of the SDGs. The World Bank has a new leader, as does the IMF, and there is a new European Commission.

Christine Lagarde will be missed as her commitment to the SGDs was very strong. She wrote:

> The United Nations' Sustainable Development Goals embody the contours of the world we want and need: fairer, free of poverty and deprivation, a world that respects natural limits. The SDGs are the antidote to the loss of trust in institutions of all kinds and the loss of faith in global co-operation. To achieve these goals by 2030 we must place emphasis on inclusion—both in terms of income inequality and gender equity. This should be a priority for 2019 and beyond.[19]

Still, the new leadership in both Washington institutions and in Brussels offers a great opportunity for establishing a new synergy between them and the UN, with a focus on how best to achieve the SDGs.

Putting nostalgia to good use means looking back in history and trying to distil the essence of what promotes change. Just like twenty years ago, there is an urgent need for a new 'conspiracy of implementation', through another group of 'drivers' mobilizing international support around a collective agenda for change. Focusing efforts on a few key SDGs and making sure the most critical global institutions work together will be fundamental to delivering change. Similarly, making sure leaders in developing countries are at the centre of the mobilization, linking global efforts to implementation at the country level, is essential for success. This implies a robust commitment that can stand against self-interest and an eye for the technical details that often impede progress. Furthermore, the notion of mutual accountability will be even more important and would strengthen the credibility of this new 'conspiracy'. Maybe this time, the drivers would come from a group of leaders in both OECD countries and developing countries? This would be in the spirit of the SDGs.

The role of U4 leadership in promoting change that helped achieve the MDGs around the turn of the last century is uncontestable. But it is impossible to predict the new leaders who would promote future change and when and where they might emerge.

In retrospect, 2019, exactly twenty years from the Utstein meeting, may prove to have been a pivotal year, as progressive forces may have finally put a stop to the onslaught of nationalism, protectionism, and xenophobia. 2020 will see a new UK, definitely negotiating an exit from the EU, and the possibility of a new US administration more interested in maintaining the global institutions it has helped build and more supportive of the SDGs, as well as new leadership in the main multilateral institutions.

One reason for these possibilities materializing is the most recent mobilization around SDG 13 and the emergence of young voices such as the Swedish teenager, Greta Thunberg. The massive demonstrations in support of action on climate change in September 2019 were reminiscent of the massive 'stand-up' demonstrations in support of the MDGs in 2006–9. Indeed, the ability to confront political leaders courageously and directly has proven to bring about change, not only in public opinion, but also in the discussions behind closed doors among decision-makers. This was also the experience of the U4 twenty years ago.

In this setting it is possible that new political leaders may emerge next year or the year after, or the year after that. It may be that these new leaders were impressed by a visit of the U4 to their village or school twenty years ago, when they were young, and now have become ministers in their countries. When they do, they would benefit from looking at the U4 experience with the MDGs as they decide to work together to achieve the SDGs. In this connection, they should develop their own 'conspiracy of implementation' and pay close attention to developed country actions to support the efforts of poor developing countries to eradicate extreme poverty. Given the limited progress that their elders have made so far, probably it will not be possible to achieve the SDGs by 2030. However, as sometimes attributed to C. S. Lewis: 'You can't go back and change the beginning, but you can start where you are and change the ending.' It would certainly be worth trying.

Notes

1. 'Development Achievements', *D&C*, 45(9–10) (2018).
2. United Nations, *Transforming Our World: The 2030 Agenda for Sustainable Development*, A/Res/70/1 (New York: United Nations, 2015).
3. J. Sachs, G. Schmidt-Traub, C. Kroll, G. Lafortune, and G. Fuller, *Sustainable Development Report 2019* (New York: Bertelsmann Stiftung and Sustainable Development Solutions Network, 2019).
4. Sachs et al., *Sustainable Development Report* 2019, p. 4.
5. Eveline Herfkens, email, 2 September 2019.
6. Sachs et al., *Sustainable Development Report 2019*, p. 5.
7. UN, *The Sustainable Development Goals Report 2019* (New York: UN, 2019).
8. Gaspar Vitor, David Amaglobeli, Mercedes Garcia-Escribano, Delphine Prady, and Mauricio Soto, 'Fiscal Policy and Development: Human, Social, and Physical Investment for the SDGs', IMF Staff Discussion Note SDN/19/3 (Washington, DC: IMF, 2019).
9. Sachs et al. Sustainable Development Report.
10. Marina Ponti, interview by C. Michalopoulos and E. Herfkens, 11 July 2019, transcript.
11. European Commission, *White Paper on the Future of Europe* (Brussels: European Commission, 2017).
12. Independent Commission for Sustainable Equality, 'Executive Summary', Parliamentary Group of the Progressive Alliance of Socialists and Democrats, 2017.
13. EU Council Conclusions, 9 April 2019 (Brussels: EU, 2019).
14. G20, 'Making the Financial System Work for All', Report of the G20 Eminent Persons Group on Global Financial Governance, 3 October 2018. The G20 is a group of twenty developing and OECD countries that meet annually to discuss global financial issues.

15. UN General Assembly, 'Political Declaration of the SDG Summit', Final Agreed Text, 2 July (New York: UN, 2019).
16. IPS, 'Salvaging the MDGs: New Thinking to Spur Action Takes Shape', 11 October 2019, available at http://www.ipsnews.net/2019/10.
17. UN, *The Future is Now: Science for Achieving Sustainable Development*, Global Sustainable Development Report 2019 (New York: UN, 2019).
18. UN, *The Future is Now*, p. 33.
19. Christine Lagarde, 'Towards a Legacy for Inclusion', *The Economist*, 'The World in 2019', https://te.tbr.fun/towards-a-legacy-of-inclusion/.

Appendix

Table A-1. ODA relative to GNI (1993–2017)

Country	1993–1997	1998–2002	2003–2007	2015–2017
Germany	0.317%	0.267%	0. 329%	0.627%
Netherlands	0.802%	0.812%	0.792%	0.667%
Norway	0.919%	0.843%	0.914%	1.053%
United Kingdom	0.288%	0.291%	0.409%	0.700%
U4 Average*	0.482%	0.447%	0.508%	0.697%
United States	0.122%	0.108%	0.108%	0.179%
Total DAC	0.258%	0.220%	0.276%	0.310%

*Weighted by volume

Source: OECD (2018), net ODA. doi: 10.1787/33346549-en (accessed 21 November 2018)

Table A-2. Distribution of allocable bilateral ODA by developing country income group 1993–2016

Donor Country	Recipients	1993–1997	1998–2002	2003–2007	2015–2016
Germany	LDCs	30%	30%	25%	23%
	Other lower and lower-middle income	39%	33%	40%	39%
	Higher-middle income and higher income	32%	37%	35%	38%
	Total	100%	100%	100%	100%
Netherlands	LDCs	41%	43%	51%	61%
	Other lower and lower-middle income	26%	32%	32%	16%
	Higher-middle income and higher income	33%	24%	17%	23%
	Total	100%	100%	100%	100%
Norway	LDCs	57%	51%	56%	49%
	Other lower and lower-middle income	25%	23%	24%	27%
	Higher-middle income and higher income	19%	27%	20%	24%
	Total	100%	100%	100%	100%
United Kingdom	LDCs	43%	45%	40%	51%
	Other lower and lower-middle income	37%	33%	47%	34%
	Higher-middle income and higher income	20%	22%	13%	14%
	Total	100%	100%	100%	100%
United States	LDCs	27%	25%	31%	53%
	Other lower and lower-middle income	36%	50%	21%	29%
	Higher-middle income and higher income	36%	25%	48%	18%
	Total	100%	100%	100%	100%
Total DAC	LDCs	31%	32%	34%	45%
	Other lower and lower-middle income	39%	41%	32%	34%
	Higher-middle income and higher income	31%	28%	34%	21%
	Total	100%	100%	100%	100%

Source: OECD (2018), distribution of net ODA. doi: 10.1787/2334182b-en (accessed 24 November 2018)

Table A-3a. Average country rank: commitment to development index aid

Country	2003–2005	2006–2010	2011–2015	2016–2018
Germany	12.3	11.4	12.8	11.7
Netherlands	5.3	5.2	6.2	5.7
Norway	7.3	7.2	5.4	5.7
United Kingdom	4.0	4.0	4.0	4.7
France	16.0	16.2	12.4	13.0
United States	21.0	21.6	20.2	23.7
Japan	8.3	7.8	10.8	13.0

Source: Center for Global Development (accessed 21 November 2018)

Table A-3b. Average country rank: commitment to development index total

Country	2003–2005	2006–2010	2010–2015	2016–2018
Germany	14.0	12.8	10.6	5.3
Netherlands	2.0	3.8	6.6	7.3
Norway	10.7	8.2	7.8	9.3
United Kingdom	4.7	8.2	6.2	6.0

Source: Center for Global Development (accessed 21 November 2018)

Bibliography

Abdel-Malek, T. and Bert Koenders, 'Progress towards More Effective Aid: What Does the Evidence Show?', 4th High Level Conference on Aid Effectiveness, 2011, http//www. Busanhlf4.org.

ACET, 'Mobilizing and Managing External Finance for Inclusive Growth: Synthesis Report', Accra: ACET, 2018.

Adams, James, Interview with Eveline Herfkens and C. Michalopoulos, 7 May 2018, transcript.

Africa/OECD Ministerial Consultation, 'Big Table I', Addis Ababa, 19–20 November 2000.

Africa/OECD Ministerial Consultation, 'Big Table II', Amsterdam, 14–16 October 2001.

Africa/OECD Ministerial Consultation, 'Big Table III', Addis Ababa, 17 January 2003.

The African, 'EU Ministers Hail Warioba Report', 12 April 2000.

The African, 'EU Ministers Urge Donors to Support Poor Countries', 13 April 2000.

The African, 'Ministerial Declaration on more Effective Working', 17 April, 2000.

Agriculture against Poverty, 'The Norwegian Government's Action Plan for Agricultural Development', 2004, https://www.regjeringen.no/globalassets/upload/kilde/ud/pla/2004/0001/ddd/pdfv/210700-landbruk.pdf.

Ahmed, Masood, Memorandum to the IMF Managing Director, 17 July 2000, IMF Archives.

Ahmed, Masood, Memorandum to the IMF Managing Director, 16 July 2002, IMF Archives.

Al Jazeera, 'Wolfowitz to Resign from World Bank', 18 May 2007.

Amoako, K. Y., *Know the Beginning Well*, Trenton, NJ: Africa World Press, (forthcoming).

Annan, Kofi, Letter to Eveline Herfkens, 18 August 1999, Netherlands Archives, dossier 3.12.

Atwood, J. Brian and Richard Manning, 'DAC High level Forums on Aid Effectiveness', in a volume on the history of the DAC, ed. R. Carey (forthcoming).

Berg, Elliot (coordinator), *Rethinking Technical Cooperation*, New York: UNDP and Development Alternatives Inc. 1993, cited in Helleiner et al. (1995), Development Co-operation Issues *Between Tanzania and Its Aid Donors*, Report of the Group of Independent Advisors, 1995, http://www.tzdpg.or.tz.

Berteling, Jan, *Relations between the World Bank and UN Bodies*, The Hague: Ministerie an Buitenlandse Zaken, 1999.

Beynon, Jonathan and Andra Dusu, *Budget Support and MDG Performance*, Brussels: European Commission Directorate-General for ACP, 2010.

Birdsall, Nancy and Homi Kharas, *The Quality of ODA*, 3rd edn, Washington, DC: CGD and Brookings Institution Press, 2014.

Brown, Gordon and Clare Short, Letter to James Wolfensohn and Michel Camdessus, 18 February 1999, UK DfID Archives.

Brown, Gordon and Clare Short, Letter to Horst Köhler and James Wolfensohn, 7 July 2000, UK DfID Archives.

Camdessus, Michel, Letter to Gordon Brown and Clare Short, 10 March 1999, IMF Archives.

Carbone, Mauricio, *The Politics of Foreign Aid*, New York: Routledge, 2007.

CGD press release, 'Quartet of Female Ministers Win Inaugural Commitment to Development Award', Washington, DC: CGD, 2003.

Chandy, Laurence, Brian Seidel, and Christine Zhang, *Aid Effectiveness in Fragile States*, Brooke Shear Series No. 5, Washington, DC: Brookings Institution Press, 2016.

Chibber, Ajay, 'Overview', in *Reform and Growth*, ed. Ajay Chibber, R. Kyle Peters, and Barbara J. Yale, New Brunswick, NJ and London: Transaction Publishers, 2006.

Christian Democratic Party, *Counter White Paper: A South-Policy Based on Solidarity, Major Interventions in Norwegian Development Policies* (1995–6).

Clinton, Hillary, keynote speech: 'Education for All' conference, Amsterdam, 9 February 1999.

Commission on Legal Empowerment of the Poor, https://en.wikipedia.org/wiki/Commission_on_Legal_Empowerment_of_the_Poor.

Cornia, Giovanni, A., Richard Jolly, and Frances Stewart, *Adjustment with a Human Face*, 2 vols, Oxford: Clarendon Press, 1987.

Daily News, 'EU Ministers Advise on Promoting Education', 12 April 2000.

Davidse, Koen, Interview by C. Michalopoulos and E. Herfkens, 5 January 2019, transcript.

Dervis, Kemal, *A Better Globalization*, Washington DC: Center for Global Development, 2005.

'Development Achievements', *D&C*, 45(9–10), 2018.

Development Today, "The Nordic Plus Group Launches Ambitious Goals for Harmonization" 4, 2004.

Doran, Peter 'WSSD: An Assessment for the International Institute for Sustainable Development' (processed), 3 October 2002.

The Economist, 'Help in the right places', 21 March 2002.

EITI, https://eiti.org/.

Elliot, Victoria, 'The Poverty Reduction Strategy Initiative', in *Reform and Growth*, ed. Ajay Chibber, R. Kyle Peters, and Barbara J. Yale, New Brunswick, NJ and London: Transaction Publishers, 2006.

EU Commission, *The New European Consensus on Development*, Brussels: EU Commission, 2017.

EU Commission, *White Paper on the Future of Europe*, Brussels: EU Commission, 2017.

EU General Council, Presidency, 'Conclusions' European Council, Laaken 14–15 December 2001.

EU General Council, Presidency 'Conclusions' Barcelona European Council 15–16 March 2002 (Brussels: EU, 2002).

EU General Council, 'Conclusions', 9 April, Brussels: EU, 2019.

Financial Times, 'US pledges higher overseas aid', 15 March 2002.

Financial Times, 'High hopes in Monterrey', 18 March 2002.

Financial Times, 'US wakes from 20-year slumber in development field', 25 March 2002.

Financieel Dagblad, 'Industrialized countries in conflict about tied aid to developing countries', 23 June 2000.

Frankfurter Allgemeine, 'Handeln fur die Armen', 25 March 2002.

G8, Africa Personal Representatives, 'Joint Progress Report on the G8 Africa Partnership', Bonn/Berlin: Federal Ministry for Economic Cooperation and Development, 2007.

G8, 'Joint Progress Report on the G8–Africa Partnership', Bonn/Berlin, Federal Ministry for Economic Cooperation and Development, 2008.

G8 Summit, 2009, 'Chair Summary', https://ec.europa.eu/economy_finance/publications/pages/publication15572_en.pdf.

G20, 'Making the Financial System Work for All', Report of the G20 Eminent Persons Group on Global Financial Governance, 3 October 2018.

Gaspar, Vitor, David Amaglobeli, Mercedes Garcia-Escribano, Delphine Prady, and Mauricio Soto, 'Fiscal Policy and Development: Human, Social, and Physical Investment for the SDGs', IMF Staff Discussion Note SDN/19/3, Washington, DC: IMF, 2019.

German Government Coalition Agreement/Koalitionsvereinbarung zwischen der Socialdemocratischen Partei Deutchlands unde Budnis/90 Die Grunen Bonn, October 1998, http://www.spd.de/fileadmin/documente.

Ghani, Ashraf and Clare Lockhart, *Fixing Failed States*, Oxford and New York: Oxford University Press, 2008.

Global Partnership for Effective Development Collaboration, *Making Development Co-operation more Effective*, Paris and New York: OECD/UNDP, 2016.

The Guardian, 'Tanzania can fight anti-graft war effectively', 11 April 2000.

Helleiner, Gerry K., Tony Killick, Nguyuru Lipumba, Benno J. Ndulu, and Knud Eric Svendsen, '*Development Co-operation Issues Between Tanzania and Its Aid Donors*', Report of the Group of Independent Advisors, 1995, http://www.tzdpg.or.tz.

Herfkens, Eveline, 'Aid Works: Let's Prove it', *Journal of African Economies*, 8(4), 1999, 481–6.

Herfkens, Eveline, 'Macedonia: A key to regional stability needs more aid' *IHT*, 30 April 1999.

Herfkens, Eveline, Letter to Dutch Parliament, 16 July 1999, Netherlands Ministry of Foreign Affairs Archives.

Herfkens, Eveline, Letter to Parliament, 27 October 1999, Netherlands Ministry of Foreign Affairs Archives.

Herfkens, Eveline, Letter to Kofi Annan, 29 November 1999, Netherlands Ministry of Foreign Affairs Archives, dossier 3.12.

Herfkens, Eveline, Letter to James Wolfensohn, 9 February 2000, Netherlands Ministry of Foreign Affairs Archives, dossier 2.10.

Herfkens, Eveline, Letter to Mark-Malloch Brown, 20 February 2000, Netherlands Ministry of Foreign Affairs Archives, dossier 3.10.

Herfkens, Eveline, Speech to the UNDP, 28 February 2000.

Herfkens, Eveline, Speech UN Security Council, New York, 30 November 2000.

Herfkens, Eveline, Speech at Leiden University, 8 March 2001.

Herfkens, Eveline, 'TRIPS and Public Health: Opportunities for Doha', *Bridges*, 12 October 2001.

Herfkens, Eveline, Letter to Dutch Parliament, 6 March 2003, Netherlands, Ministry of Foreign Affairs Archives.

Herfkens, Eveline, Speech at Finance for Development Conference, Monterrey, 22 March 2002.

Herfkens, Eveline, 'A breakthrough on aid in Monterrey', *The Earth Times Monthly*, May, 2002.

Herfkens, Eveline, *Africa and Development Cooperation*, Zimbabwe: ACBF Development Memoirs Series, 2004.

Herfkens, Eveline, Speech, Conference on Financing the MDGs, EU Parliament, Brussels, 15 April 2004.

Herfkens, Eveline, 'The successes and challenges in mobilizing support for the Millennium Development Goals', *UN Chronicle*, 45(1), 2006.

Herfkens, Eveline, Speech to G8 Parliamentarians, Berlin, 30 May 2007.

Herfkens, Eveline, Speech, National School of Government/International Women's Leadership Conference, London, 4 March 2010.

Herfkens, Eveline, 'Aid Effectiveness: Lessons Learned— and Forgotten [in Dutch], in *Hoe nu Verder*, ed. S. Vermer, L. Schulpen, and R. Ruben, Arnhem: LM Publishers, 2014.

Herfkens, Eveline, Speech for ODI, 2015.

Herman, B, 'The Politics of Inclusion in the Monterrey Process', DESA Working Paper #23, ST/ESA/WP/23, New York: UN, 2006.

Honig, Dan, *Navigation by Judgement*, New York: Oxford University Press, 2018.

Hulme, David, 'The Millennium Development Goals (MDGs): A Short History of the World's Biggest Promise', Brook World Poverty Institute, BWPI Working Paper 100, Manchester: University of Manchester, 2009.

IHT, 'If we are serious, we do something about poverty, 10 August 1999.

IHT, 'It's time for the EU barriers to fall', 10 October 2000.

IHT, 'The rich countries will have to do better', 21 March 2002.

IHT, 'The Monterrey consensus', 25 March 2002.

IMF, Archives: https://www.imf.org/en/About/Archives

World Bank/IMF, Development Committee, "The Initiative for Heavily Indebted Poor Countries", (Washington DC: IMF, 1998).

IMF, 'Corruption: Costs and Mitigation Strategies', Staff Discussion Note, Washington, DC: IMF, 2016.

IMF, Debt Relief Trust Fund Accounts, 2017, https://www.imf.org/external/SelectedDecisions/Description.aspx?decision=14649-(10/64).

IMF/IDA, Operational issues paper of December 1999, Washington, DC: IMF, 1999.

Independent Commission for Sustainable Equality, 'Executive Summary', Parliamentary Group of the Progressive Alliance of Socialists and Democrats, 2017.

Interpress Service, IPS, 9 September 2003.

IOB Evaluation nr 308, 2008: Het Nederlandse Afrikabeleid 1998–2006, ISBN 978-90-5328-359-2.

Ireton, Barrie, *Britain's International Development Policies: A History of DFID and Overseas Aid*, Basingstoke: Palgrave Macmillan, 2013.

Isenman, Paul, Interview by C. Michalopoulos and E. Herfkens, 2 May 2018, transcript.

Isenman, Paul and Alexander Shakow 'Donor Schizophrenia and Aid Effectiveness: The Role of Global Funds', IDS Practice Paper 2010-01, IDS, University of Sussex, 2010.

Johnson, Hilde F., Speech at ODI, 19 February 1998.

Johnson, Hilde F., Statement to Parliament on development cooperation, 5 May 1998, Norway, Parliamentary Archives.

Johnson, Hilde F., Speech, Washington, DC, 20 February 2002.

Johnson, Hilde, F., Opening statement at 'Education for All' conference, Amsterdam, 10 April 2002.

Johnson, Hilde, F., Statement to Parliament on development cooperation, 30 April 2002, Norway, Parliamentary Archives.

Johnson, Hilde F., Speech, 'Education: A Weapon against Poverty', Nordic Solidarity Conference on Education and Development Cooperation, 3–4 June 2002.

Johnson, Hilde F., *Waging Peace in Sudan*, Eastbourne: Sussex Academic Press, 2011.

'A Joint Evaluation of Budget Support: Synthesis Report, 1994–2004, Executive Summary, University of Birmingham, Birmingham, May 2006.

Köhler, Horst, Letter to Heidemarie Wieczorek-Zeul, 16 May 2002, IMF Archives.

Köhler, Horst, Interview by Eveline Herfkens, 20 February 2019, transcript.

Köhler, Horst and James Wolfensohn, Letter to Claire Short, 23 March 2001, IMF Archives.

Köhler, Horst and James Wolfensohn, Letter to Gordon Brown and Clare Short, 13 December 2001, IMF Archives.

Krueger, Anne O., 'A New Approach to Sovereign Debt Restructuring', Washington, DC: IMF, April 2002.

Laborde, D., 'Looking for a Meaningful Duty Free Quota Free Market Access Initiative in the Doha Development Agenda', ICTSD, Issue Paper 4, Geneva: ICTSD, 2008.

Lagarde, Christine, 'Towards a Legacy for Inclusion', *The Economist*, 'The World in 2019', December 2018.

Lancaster, Carol, 'The World Bank in Africa', in *The World Bank: Its First Half Century*, vol. II, ed. D. Kapur, J. P. Lewis, and R. Webb, Washington, DC: Brookings Institution Press, 1997.

Lancaster, Carol, *George Bush's Foreign Aid: Transformation or Chaos?* Washington, DC: CGD, 2008.

The Lancet, 'The Devastating Impact of Trump's Gag Rule', 393(10189), 15 June 2019.

Manning, Richard, *Using Indicators to Encourage Development*, DIIS Report 2009–11, Copenhagen: Danish Institute of International Studies, 2009.

Manuel, Trevor, Speech at 'Financing for Development' conference, Doha, 30 November 2008.

Martinez-Diaz, Leonardo and Ngaire Woods, eds, *Networks of Influence*, New York: Oxford University Press, 2009.

Michalopoulos, Constantine, *Emerging Powers in the WTO*, Basingstoke: Palgrave Macmillan, 2014.

Michalopoulos, Constantine, *Aid, Trade and Development*, Cham: Palgrave, 2017.

Mitchell, Ian and Caitlin McKee, 'How do you Measure Aid Quality and Who Ranks Highest?', Washington, DC: CGD, 2018.

Le Monde, 'A Monterrey, les Etas s'engagent a minima sur l'aide au developpement', 25 March 2002.

Ndulu, Benno, Interview by Eveline Herfkens, 21 November 2018, transcript.

Nekkers, J. A. and P. A. M. Malcontent, eds, *Fifty Years of Dutch Development Co-Operation 1949–1999*, The Hague: Jdu Publishers, 1999.

Netherlands Government Coalition Agreement, The Hague: Tweede Kamer de Staten-General Kabinetsformatie 1998, Tweede Kamer vergaderjaar 1997–1998 26o24 nr.10.

Netherlands Ministry of Foreign Affairs Archives: https://archives.eui.eu/en/fonds/mfa?item=NL&id=245

Netherlands Ministry of Foreign Affairs, , Archives, Tanzania dossier 1.5.

Netherlands Ministry of Foreign Affairs, 'Adrian Wood mission report', 7 February 2001, Archives, dossier 13.

New Statesman 8 May 2006.

New York Times, 'Wolfowitz resigns ending long fight at world bank', 18 May 2007.

Norway, Ministry of Foreign Affairs, 'A Conspiracy of Implementation', follow-up of the Utstein Meeting, 8 May 2000, Norway, Archives of Royal Ministry of Foreign Affairs.

NRC, 'Conspiracy of Dissatisfied Quartet', 27 July 1999.

NRC, 'Stop belastingvoordeel voor investeerders Derde Wereld', 19 March 2002.

OECD, *Shaping the 21st Century*, Paris: OECD, 1996.

OECD, *DAC Journal*, 3(4), Paris: OECD, 2002.

OECD, *Harmonization of Donor Practices for Effective Aid Delivery*, DAC Guidelines and References Series, Paris: OECD, 2003.

OECD, *DAC in Dates*, Paris: OECD, 2006.

OECD, *The OECD at Fifty: Development Co-Operation, Past, Present and Future*, Paris: OECD, 2011.

OECD, DAC, 'Development Cooperation Chairman's Report', Paris: OECD, 2009.

OECD, DAC, *Peer Review Germany 2001*, Paris: OECD, 2001.

OECD, DAC, *Peer Review Netherlands 2001*, Paris: OECD, 2001.

OECD, DAC, *Peer Review United Kingdom 2001*, Paris: OECD, 2001.

OECD, DAC, *Peer Review Germany 2005*, Paris: OECD, 2006.

OECD, DAC, *Peer Review Norway 2005*, Paris: OECD, 2005.

OECD, DAC, *Peer Review Netherlands 2006*, Paris: OECD, 2006.

OECD, DAC, *Peer Review Norway 2008*, Paris: OECD, 2008.

OECD, DAC, *Peer Review Germany 2010*, Paris: OECD, 2010.

OECD, DAC, *Peer Review United Kingdom 2014*, Paris: OECD, 2014.

OECD, DAC, *Peer Review Germany 2015*, Paris: OECD, 2015.

OECD, DAC, *Peer Review Netherlands 2017*, Paris: OECD, 2017.

OECD, DAC, *Development Co-operation 2018*, Paris: OECD, 2018.

OECD, DAC, *Principles for Good International Engagement in Fragile States and Situations*, Paris: OECD, 2007.

Orbie, Jan and Simon Lightfoot, 'Development: Shallow Europeanization?, in *Foreign Policies of EU Member States*, ed. Amelia Hadfield, Ian Manners, and Richard G. Whitman, London and New York: Routledge, 2017.

Otsuki, T., J. Wilson, and M. Sewadah, 'What Price Precaution? Europe's Harmonization of Aflatoxin Regulations and African Groundnut Exports', *European Review of Agricultural Economics*, 28(3), 2001, 263–84.

Oxfam, 'Fast forward: How the European Commission can take the lead in providing high quality aid for education and health', Oxfam International briefing paper no.111, 2008, https://www.oxfam.de/system/files/fast_forward.pdf.

Ponti, Marina, Interview by C. Michalopoulos and E. Herfkens, 11 July 2019, transcript.

Reuters, Eric Onstad Interview-Trade Barriers block Africa growth-Dutch Minister 12 October 2001.

Richelle, Koos, Interview with Eveline Herfkens, 28 August 2018, transcript.

Sachs, J., G. Schmidt-Traub, C. Kroll, G. Lafortune, and G. Fuller, *Sustainable Development Report 2019*, New York: Bertelsmann Stiftung and Sustainable Development Solutions Network (SDSN), 2019.

Sandefur, Justin, 'Tanzania Outlaws Fact Checking, Seeks World Bank Aid to Create New Facts', CGD, 28 September, 2018.

Shakow, Alexander, Interview by C. Michalopoulos and E. Herfkens, 12 March 2018, transcript.

Short, Clare, Speech, UNCTAD Conference, Geneva, 2 March 1999.

Short, Clare, statement to Parliamentary Committee, 23 May 2000, UK DFID Archives.

Short, Clare, Speech, Nottingham, 23 November 1999, UK DFID Archives.

Short, Clare, Speech to Adam Smith Institute, 3 December 1999.

Short, Clare, EFA speech, Paris, 30 October 2001.

Short, Clare, Letter to Sher Bahadur Deuba, prime minister of Nepal (on behalf of Utstein: Johnson, Karlsson, Wieczorek-Zeul), 14 September 2002, UK DfID Archives.

Short, Clare, *An Honourable Deception?* London: Free Press, 2004.

Short, Clare, 'The dangers of a broken multilateral system in a divided world' speech, University of Bath, 23 February 2006.

Short, Clare, 'More aid and less justice will not make poverty history', speech, Oxted, 20 February 2008.

Smith, Dan, 'Towards a Strategic Framework for Peacebuilding: Getting their Act Together', Evaluation Report 1/2004, Oslo: Royal Norwegian Ministry of Foreign Affairs.

Summers, L. 'Weak economy, angry politics', *Washington Post*, 10 October 2016.

The Times, London, 20 February 2002.

Trouw, 'Jumping over one's shadow', 24 July 1999.

UK DfID, Archive: https://webarchive.nationalarchives.gov.uk/+/http://www.dfid.gov.uk/.

UK DfID, 'Eliminating World Poverty: A Challenge for the 21st Century', White Paper on International Development, 1997.

UK DfID, 'Eliminating World Poverty: Making Globalization Work for the Poor', White Paper, London: DfID, 2000.

UK DfID, 'Follow-up Matrix to 3rd Utstein Ministerial Meeting in Birmingham' (processed), 14 June 2002.

UK DfID, 'Sierra Leone, Strategy', UK DfID Archives, 2002.

UN, *Progress Report on Cooperation between the UN and the Bretton Woods Institutions* (processed), New York: UN, 1999.

UN, *Delivering as One*, Report of the Secretary General's High Level Panel, New York: UN, 2006.

UN, *The Doha Declaration on Financing for Development*, New York: UN, 2009.

UN, Report of the Commission of Experts of the President of the UN General Assembly on the Reform of the International Monetary System, New York: UN, 2009.

UN, 'Mexico High Level Meeting Communique', The Global Partnership for Effective Development Cooperation and the Post-2015 Development Agenda, New York: UN, 2014.

UN, *The Millennium Development Goals Report 2015*, New York: UN, 2015.

UN, 'Third International Conference on Financing for Development', A/RES/69/313, New York: UN, 2015, https://news.un.org.en/story/2003/10/84092-un-chief-executives-board-begin-its-fall-2003-session-tomorrow.

UN, *Transforming Our World: The 2030 Agenda for Sustainable Development*, A/Res/70/1, New York: UN, 2015.

UN, *The Future is Now: Science for Achieving Sustainable Development*, Global Sustainable Development Report 2019, New York: UN, 2019.

UN Economic Commission for Africa, 'Big Table', Special Session, Washington DC, 28 October 2003.

UN General Assembly, 'Political Declaration of the SDG Summit', Final Agreed Text, 2 July 2019, New York: UN, 2019.

UN Security Council, resolutions: S/RES/1820 (2008), 19 June 2008; S/RES/1882 (2009), 4 August 2009; S/RES/1888 (2009), 30 September 2009; S/RES/1960 (2010), 16 December 2010.

UN/World Bank, *Partnership Framework Agreement for Crisis and Post-Situations*', New York: UN, 2008.

UN, WSSD, *Plan of Implementation*, A/Conf.119.20, 4 September 2012.

Utstein Ministerial, 'Minutes', The Hague, 2000.

Utstein Ministerial, 'Minutes', Birmingham, 2001.

Utstein Ministerial, 'Minutes', Wiesbaden, 2002.

Utstein Ministerial, 'Minutes', Dubai, 2003.

Utstein, Stavern Meeting, 21–2 June 2018, transcript.

Volkskrant, 'The fight against poverty demands action from rich countries now' 9 November 2001.

Walters, Craig and Brendan Whitty, *The Politics and Results Agenda in DFID*, 1997–2017, ODI Report, London: ODI, 2017.

Wieczorek-Zeul, Heidemarie, Speech, 'Finance for Development' conference, Monterrey, 22 March 2002.

Wieczorek-Zeul, Heidemarie, Letter to Utstein (Johnson, Short, Van Ardenne, Karlsson), 13 January 2003.

Wieczorek-Zeul, Heidemarie, 'An Important Step Forward', *D-C*, December 2005.

Wieczorek-Zeul, Heidemarie, Speech, '1957–2007: The European Union and the Advancement of Women: Women Building the Future of Europe', Brussels, 8 March 2007, Committee on Women's Rights and Gender Equality of the European Parliament.

Wieczorek-Zeul, Heidemarie, *Welt Bewegen*, Berlin: Vorwärts Buch, 2007.

Wieczorek-Zeul, Heidemarie, Notes for meeting with Trevor Manuel, 25 May 2008.

Wieczorek-Zeul, Heidemarie, Speech, 'Financing for Development' conference, Doha, 29 November 2008.

Wieczorek-Zeul, Heidemarie, *Gerechtigkeit und Frieden sind Geschwister*, Marburg: Schuren, 2018.

World Bank *Global Economic Prospects, 2002*, Washington DC: World Bank, 2002.

World Bank, *Are We on Track to Achieve the Millennium Development Goals?* ABCDE Conference, ed. Francois Bourgignon, Boris Plescovic, and Andre Sapir, Washington, DC and New York: World Bank and Oxford University Press, 2005.

World Bank, 'Report of the Ad Hoc Group', 11 April 2007, downloaded from *The Wall Street Journal*, 18 May 2007.

World Bank, 'Report of the Ad Hoc Group' (R2007-0089), 14 May 2007, downloaded from *The Wall Street Journal*, 18 May 2007.

World Bank, *The Growth Report*, Washington, DC: World Bank, 2008.

World Bank, 'World Bank Gender Strategy', *World Development Report*, Washington, DC: World Bank, 2012.

World Bank, 'Africa Health Forum 2013', https://www.worldbank.org/en/events/2013/04/18/africa-health-forum-2013-finance-and-capacity-for-results.

World Bank/IMF, Development Committee, communique, 28 April, Washington, DC: World Bank/IMF, 1999.

World Bank/IMF, Development Committee, communique, 18 November, Washington, DC: World Bank/IMF, 2001.

World Bank/IMF, Development Committee, communique, 28 September, Washington, DC: World Bank/IMF, 2002.

The Wall Street Journal, 'Wolfowitz', 18 May 2007.

Yanguas, Pablo, *Why we Lie about Aid: Development and the Messy Politics of Aid*, London: ZED Books, 2018.

Zalm, Gerrit, Interview by E. Herfkens, 29 August 2018, transcript.

Die Zeit, 'Four women for one alelluja', 17 April 2002.

Index